BECOMING A
BAR MITZVAH

A Treasury of Stories

BECOMING A
BAR MITZVAH

A Treasury of Stories

Arnine Cumsky Weiss

**With a Foreword by
Rabbi David Geffen, Ph.D.**

Scranton: The University of Scranton Press

Library of Congress Cataloging-in-Publication Data

Weiss, Arnine Cumsky.
    Bar mitzvah / by Arnine Cumsky Weiss ; with an introduction by David
Geffen
        p. cm.
    ISBN 1-58966-064-1
        1. Bar mitzvah—Anecdotes. 2. Jewish teenagers—United States—
Biography—Anecdotes. 3. Jewish teenagers—Religious life—
United States—Anecdotes. I. Title.

BM707.W45 2002
296.4'424--dc21   2002018404

Distribution:

The University of Scranton Press
445 Madison Avenue
Scranton PA 18510
Phone: 570-941-3081
Fax: 570-941-8804

This book is lovingly dedicated to the men in my life:

My father—*Manny Cumsky*, of blessed memory
Who provided the structure;

My husband—*Jeff*,
Who provided the support;

And my sons—*Matt and Ben*,
Who added the color.

CONTENTS

FOREWORD

BAR MITZVAH
by Rabbi David Geffen, Ph.D.

Professor Robert Gordis, the noted Bible scholar and thinker, was a leading pulpit rabbi for over half a century. He once asked, "Why is the Bar Mitzvah of a 13-year-old boy such a celebration? When a young man gets married, he leaves his home so that he and his wife can establish their own home. That child will never return to live with his parents again. How wonderful that after a boy celebrates his Bar Mitzvah," Gordin emphasized, "he continues to live with his parents. Together they interact as he grows into manhood and Jewish maturity. What joy and happiness they derive from having their son with them. Truly a Bar Mitzvah, even more than a wedding, should be celebrated and enjoyed to the fullest."

The origin of the age of 13 as a time for a Bar Mitzvah is found in the *Ethics of the Fathers* listing of the stages of life. In chapter 5:21 the text states that "13 is the age for observing the mitzvot (commandments)." Although the term *Bar Mitzvah* occurs several times in the Talmud, it only refers to one who is obligated to observe the commandments of Judaism. The Talmud does emphasize that a boy under the age of 13 who could appreciate the meaning of certain ritual acts could be called to the Torah, could wear *tefillin,* and could fast on Yom Kippur.

The first Bar Mitzvah ceremony occurred sometime after the year 1400. The essentials of this ritual were praying with *tefillin* for the first time and having an *aliyah,* being called to the Reading of the Law. Among East European Ashkenazi Jewry, a boy was usually called to the Torah on the first Monday or Thursday after his 13th birthday (according to the Hebrew date), when he would recite the Torah blessings and perhaps chant some verses from that week's Torah reading. In Western Europe, however, a 13-year-old would be called to the reading at Sabbath morning services. In addition to reciting the Torah blessings, the boy would chant "a portion of the Law," the *Maftir aliyah*, and the Haftorah reading from the Prophets. This is now the prevailing custom throughout the world. In addition, after the son had completed the second Torah blessing, his father would recite a special formula, beginning *Barukh She-Petarani*—"Blessed are Thou, O Lord, Who has freed me from this responsibility," designating the boy's new status of religious responsibility.

In both the Ashkenazi and Sephardi communities, the Bar Mitzvah ceremony came to include a discourse or talk (*derashah*) by the 13-year-old. This demonstrated his understanding of the rabbinic commentaries, and, in some cases, he expounded points in Talmudic law. Today's Bar Mitzvah talks can deal with an entire range of subjects.

Additional practices were gradually adopted, some religious and others of a social nature. Once the boy had mastered the notes of the Torah reading, he might chant not only the particular section for his *aliyah*, but the entire weekly reading (*parasha*) as well. Boys were trained as prayer leaders and, while some conducted the Sabbath eve (*Kabbalat Shabbat*) service on Friday night, others might lead the entire Sabbath morning service.

There used to be a Bar Mitzvah repast for family and friends, served after the weekday morning service or at the "third meal" (*se'udah shelishit*), eaten after the Sabbath afternoon *Mincha* service. Later, this was expanded into a *Kiddush* for all present at the Sabbath morning service, which was followed by a family dinner. Nowadays, the Bar Mitzvah reception or dinner often becomes a lavish event, with the Bar Mitzvah boy receiving gifts from his parents, relatives, and other guests.

At the Bar Mitzvah service itself, the boy is showered with candy following the conclusion of his Haftorah. This practice originated among Sephardic Jews and congregations in Israel and is now practiced in Orthodox, Conservative, and Reform synagogues. In modern times, it has become customary for the rabbi to address a Bar Mitzvah boy after the Torah is returned to the Ark. A special *Mi Sheberakh* prayer is recited for the young man.

In the twentieth century, the Bar Mitzvah ceremony has acquired extra importance as an occasion for a young person to affirm his Jewish heritage. All streams of American Jewry utilize the Bar Mitzvah as leverage for persuading families to join a synagogue and enroll their child either in an afternoon Hebrew school or in a Jewish day school. Many synagogues require five years of religious education prior to Bar Mitzvah, and according to the regulations of Britain's United Synagogue (Orthodox), no Bar Mitzvah boy may read *Maftir* unless he has passed an examination in Hebrew and Jewish knowledge.

In Israel, secular kibbutzim introduced various nonreligious types of Bar Mitzvah ceremony. Since 1967, many boys—from Israel and abroad—celebrate their Bar Mitzvah at the Western Wall in Jerusalem, where they read from the Law on a Monday or Thursday morning. Some hold collective or individual ceremonies in the ruins of the ancient synagogue at Masada, at the excavations of ancient synagogues in Israel, and even on a boat on the Sea of Galilee.

A new development relating to this ritual is to be found via men over age 13, having a Bar Mitzvah after studying for a specific period of time. This practice began in the United States in the 1970s, when rabbis and cantors trained men who had missed out on a Bar Mitzvah because of the Depression. In addition, for older men there has been the development of celebrating the 50th, 60th, and 75th anniversary of their Bar Mitzvah.

In the last few decades of the twentieth century a *tzedakah-mitzvah* element has been added to many a Bar Mitzvah celebration. This first began via the "twinning with a Jewish boy in the then Soviet Union." At a Bar Mitzvah in the United States, the picture of the Soviet boy was placed on an empty chair at the front of the synagogue. The next *tzedakah*-mitzvah step was the Bar Mitzvah boy purchasing a number of trees in a Jewish National Fund forest in Israel. For every gift the boy received, his thank you included a tree certificate. Most recently, a Bar Mitzvah's gift money has been designated for Jewish community agencies. At many Bar Mitzvah celebrations today there are no flowers, but instead a brightly decorated basket of canned goods and nonperishable foods on each table. These are given to individuals after the celebration itself.

The ceremony of Bar Mitzvah is one of the most popular in Judaism because young people are still in a formative period of their lives and individuals are searching for another way to reemphasize their Jewish identity. With the proper training and right emphasis, the Bar Mitzvah can be a lifelong experience inspiring the individual to enhance his own Jewish soul and spirit.

ACKNOWLEDGMENTS

I would like to thank all of the contributors and their families for their generosity of spirit in sharing their stories with me. From the initial contact, through the interview, to the final draft of each story, each participant has given me a tremendous amount of time. Their time has not only been given during our communications, but also in digging-up long forgotten speeches, finding photographs, and researching any details that would enhance the story. And in telling their stories, they have shared intimate details of very personal experiences. During many interviews, I found my eyes welling-up with tears, and in some cases I cried right along with the interviewees. Many of the families were also marvelous sources of referral for additional stories. Carol Yunker is a one-woman font of abundant useful information. She also provided a great turkey stuffing recipe! There was no mass advertising that yielded a wealth of responses. The stories were found like precious gems, one at a time. I would also like to thank Paula David, John Pransky, Michael Kretman, Martin Kessel, and Pinchas Gutter for allowing me to include their stories told in their own words. The stories are all very powerful.

My sincere gratitude goes to Rabbi David Geffen. I started this project by bouncing some ideas off Rabbi Geffen, and he remained, throughout the process, a valued sounding board. He shared his expertise by writing the introduction to this book and allowed me to read and write about his wonderful family in one of the chapters. I want to thank Father Richard W. Rousseau, S.J. and Patricia Mecadon at the University of Scranton Press who took a chance and made working with them such a pleasure.

Many people were a source of referral, information, support, and encouragement. Many thanks to Julene Gilbert; Julie

Blumenfeld; Burnsie Gruber; Eldridge Street Synagogue; Carole Gersten; Gene Tashoff; David Fink; Rabbi Friedman; John Corkill; Devorah Turin; Cindy Shapiro; Meyer Weill; Ruth Seligman; Victor Goretsky; Brauna Fortgang; Kathleen Goldberg; Cheryl Magen; Chaim Katz; Dr. Judy Davis; Joanne Jackoswski; Rabbi Alan Klein; Dolores Gruber; Daniel Levenson; Lisa Richards; Rabbi Label Itkin; Rabbi Dovid Saks; Brian Schiff; Ted Silary; Susan Gottesman; Sheila Carluccio; Tovah Weiss; Janice Cutler; Harriet Block; Ray and Pauline Lederman; Jessica Ames; Stacy Chakin; Rabbi Chaim Tatel; Ziporah Marans and *AMIT Women*; Gina Thackara from the *Scranton Times*; Dr. Marilyn Daniels; Jerry Weinberger, Esq.; Faye Brand; Phyllis Block; Fran and Richard Grossman; Steven Schloss at the *Jewish Week*; Rabbi Susan Elwell; and Karen Klemens for transcribing one of the stories.

Special thanks to Naomi Eisenberger from ZIV Tzedakah Fund for her kindness and willingness to share many of the wonderful stories. And even though I never met him, many thanks to Danny Siegel for inspiring so many of the young people. Deep gratitude to Dr. Yale and Marilyn Bobrin and Kristin and Carl Curtis, whom I met as part of the Leukemia Team in Training. Preparing for and participating in the Dublin marathon led to my meeting these wonderful people, and I hope we will remain lifelong friends. Sincere appreciation to Dr. Hector Diaz, Ruth Gerrity, and Mike O'Malley, who listened patiently to me prattle on every Thursday at the Scranton State School for the Deaf as we waited for the next student. And a big hug to my mother, Helen Cumsky, who kept looking for and found a few stories and has been doing lots of pre-publication press at Meals on Wheels and 550 Clay Avenue.

Extra special thanks to Barbara Graham, who went out of her way to advertise and solicit stories, whether it was on her Temple Chat or in her temple. She also read many of the stories and offered her encouragement. With much love to my children, who listened to each new story whether they wanted to or not and graciously tolerated my distraction. With an extra special nod to Matt, who served as the inspiration for both books.

To my sister Yolana and brother-in-law Roy, I thank you for your joi de vivre, your excitement, and your enthusiasm. You have shared every step of the way with me and served as cheerleaders, baby-sitters, chief cooks, bottle washers, and best friends.

My final thank you is devoted to my husband, Jeff. He has served above and beyond the job description—he read, edited, re-read, repeatedly and graciously offered tech support, and solicited stories, all the while offering support, laughter, encouragement, and love. *Baruch Hashem*, I am blessed.

INTRODUCTION

My oldest son survived cancer. This little tidbit of information has come to define me in a way that nothing else does, as in "I'm a married mother of three, work as a freelance sign language interpreter, and my oldest son, who is now only 16, has survived cancer."

With every other aspect of my life, I worked at it, strived for it, and yet this last role, the mother of a survivor, was assigned to me without my consent. We—yes, "we," the five of us— endured three years of chemotherapy, two bouts of hair loss, and a daunting uncertainty that if we didn't know where this disease came from in the first place, how do we know it won't come back?

Yet we have triumphed, emerging as a tighter unit, grateful to medical science and our doctors who worked in partnership with Hashem.

For my first child and the first boy on my side of the family to become a Bar Mitzvah, *dayenu*, this would have been enough to elicit tremendous excitement and enthusiasm. However, compounded with the fact that this young man was a "survivor," the Bar Mitzvah became a community event, with standing room only in the synagogue. In addition, since I am a sign language interpreter, the entire service was interpreted into American Sign Language, making it accessible to my deaf friends and colleagues. For the most part, it was the first time that this community had witnessed an interpreted ceremony.

Stepping back and observing the situation as an outsider, I recognized that we had something rather unique happening here. This was a beautiful, spiritual ritual for a young man who, in the process of "becoming a man," had demonstrated more moxie than most men ever do. I thought, "Well, if we have something special, I'm sure that other people have also had special circumstances regarding becoming a Bar Mitzvah."

After contemplating this idea for several months, I met Mr. John Pransky, who at age 83 was about to celebrate his second Bar Mitzvah. Because long ago the life expectancy was much shorter than today, according to tradition, when you reach age 70, it is like experiencing a rebirth; therefore, 13 years later, a man may choose to have a second Bar Mitzvah celebration.

Meeting Mr. Pransky was for me *bashert*, and I realized it was now time to pursue, interview, and record people who have had interesting, unusual, inspirational, and/or humorous stories related to their Bar Mitzvahs and to compile them into two books (there is a separate Bat Mitzvah book).

The process started with a small ad in five local Jewish newspapers, asking people to share their stories with me. Anticipating that I would be bombarded, I set parameters to weed out the kinds of stories I did not want—glitzy, expensive, and extravagant parties. Rather, my focus was on remarkable people and special situations.

My worries about rejecting stories that did not fit my criteria were for naught. Five ads in five newspapers yielded one phone call and one story. However, it was a great story about a young man, who on the morning of his Bar Mitzvah discovered that due to a clerical mix-up, he had learned the wrong *parasha* for the week. He had to make a decision about whether to chant the "wrong" *parasha* that he had spent months studying and perfecting or to recite the appropriate *parasha* for that week. He had 20 minutes to prepare. I loved the story, and having just one person respond to my ad gave me the confidence I needed to pursue the book. Someone took me seriously! I was going to take that and run with it.

Now, I needed to find stories. A friend of mine, Barbara Graham, a Temple president, put an ad on her Temple Chat. I put my own ad on the Jewish Announce List and responded to other ads with queries for stories. I mentioned to anyone who would tolerate my exuberance that I was working on a book. My family and friends turned out to be a great source of referrals. And, as I started finding stories, the very generous contributors would then refer me to other stories. The scope of the book expanded with each new addition. What started out as a book of "nice" stories has grown to incorporate our history, our tenacity, and our diversity.

In the process of interviewing, I found myself heartened and humbled at the length to which people have traveled to ensure that their children experience the same "rite of passage" that is the right of every Jewish child. I am thrilled by the depth of meaning that is held for this act of "becoming a man or woman." I am inspired that in this material world, many young people still strive to keep the "mitzvah" in the process of "coming of age." And I recognize that depending on the level of observance, becoming a Bar or Bat Mitzvah is most often the cord that connects one to one's Judaism.

For me, this has been the ultimate "when life gives you lemons . . . make lemonade" story. I had no control over a silent killer that threatened to take my boy, but we have all chosen to take back that control in our own way. Matthew, age 16, is a tall, strong young man who has channeled his energies into school, sports, and acting. And I am further enchanted with God's blessings and the miracle of life.

1

THE UNDEFEATED

Stephen Bernstein, Ph.D.—January 25, 1947

The title of this story, "The Undefeated," is from the book with the same name by Abraham Hyman, published by Gefen Publishers. This story was written with the benefit of interviews with Dr. Stephen Bernstein, Mrs. Sophy Bernstein, and Rabbi Herbert A. Friedman. Mrs. Bernstein's written account of the Bar Mitzvah was used as a resource, and the final address is from Rabbi Philip Bernstein's speech delivered at his son's Bar Mitzvah.

Photo courtesy of Rabbi Herbert A. Friedman

V.E. Day . . . V.J. Day . . . The war was over! Victory! Victory? War-torn Europe was left in shambles, with refugees scrambling (or walking, limping, or being carried) to get home. But not everyone experienced a warm homecoming and a sweet reunion. A huge population had no place to go. There were 250,000 Jewish refugees without a country who wanted them, let alone a home. Their former homes had been illegally confiscated and their families brutally decimated. Those who actually made their way back to their

1

erstwhile towns and villages were greeted by the same neighbors who had either sold them out or turned a blind eye to their deportation and who now resented their survival and impending return. Homeless and without proper documents, Jewish refugees who had already endured starvation, humiliation, and unspeakable horrors found themselves "displaced." While others celebrated the end of the war with confetti, tickertape parades, and stolen kisses from exuberant GI's, ragged and weary survivors were still trying to survive.

Without an alternative, with no place to call home, 250,000 displaced persons (DPs) found their way to camps overseen by the U.S. Army on German soil. The camps were supposed to be a kind of "holding tank" while plans were made for the relocation of the refugees. Unfortunately, with many countries refusing an "en masse" entry, this temporary reprieve evolved into a three-year ordeal.

The army, unprepared to deal with civilian matters, was forced into establishing a separate branch under sector G5 to ameliorate the situation. With so many unknowns and uncertainties, the army needed the counsel and the guidance of someone who understood this population. The army found its mentor in Rabbi Philip Bernstein, a well-respected, knowledgeable, and diplomatic leader in the Jewish community. Rabbi Bernstein, promoted to the rank of major general, became the adviser on Jewish affairs to the commanding generals of the European theater.

Bernstein, his family, and Rabbi Herbert A. Friedman and his wife were installed in Bad Homburg, a small town twenty-five miles outside of Frankfurt. The house belonged to a former Wermacht general who was imprisoned for Nazi war crimes. The house came not only furnished, but also complete with the general's former staff. Frau Bender, the cook, subtly demonstrated her disdain for the new occupants. The war may have been over, but loyalties run deep. She would steal, sell, or give away the provisions from the Army PX and replace them with an inferior substitute. Since the house became more like "headquarters," the Frau had ample opportunity to humiliate her new employers. Over drinks and cigars, while Bernstein was diplomatically explaining the needs of the DPs to the commanding generals, Bender would serve food in which she had neglected to add all of the necessary ingredients.

The work of Bernstein and the other Jewish chaplain knew no day or night, nor was it confined by some predetermined job description. Overcrowded trains bursting with refugees arrived often at the camps. On one occasion the travelers took one look at the surrounding barbed wire and armed guards and refused to disembark. With the memories of other trains and other destinations still too fresh, they were unwilling to exchange one form of bondage for another. The chaplains boarded the trains. By relying on a reserve of psychological and clerical tools, coupled with common sense and deep compassion, they averted a crisis and emptied the train

These chaplains were modern-day warriors . . . Maccabees. In the Chanukah story, Judah Maccabee led a small band of renegades against a powerful army that would not let them live and worship as Jews. These chaplains, too, fought for a place—specifically, *Eretz Yisroel*, the land of Israel—where the DPs would finally have a home. The British government that controlled Palestine had set a quota of 1,500 new immigrants per month. At that rate it would take almost fourteen years to empty the camps! The rabbis implored President Truman, Great Britain's Prime Minister Bevin, and even the Pope to change immigration policies. Although Truman was sympathetic and intervened on the behalf of the DPs, Bevin wouldn't budge and the quota remained intact. Therefore, the only emigration taking place was on a limited legal level or wielded by the underground activities of the Haganah.

In addition to their globe-trotting expeditions, these rabbis continued their day-to-day offerings of comfort, support, and encouragement. When that relentless, inevitable question arose, "When, Rabbi, when?" they answered gently, but honestly. Ministering to survivors who had witnessed, firsthand, unimaginable nightmares required a special tact and finesse. And yet the spirit of the people in the camps was heartening and inspiring. Instead of broken spirits, evidenced by fragile psyches and diminished faith, there was a determination to start over and rebuild, even on tenuous ground. A rash of weddings was spurred on by brief courtships, and in spite of sparse quarters and limited privacy, a record number of babies was born in the camps. Diapers were hung on makeshift lines, and the crying of infants was a welcome sound to those who had lost so much.

However, resources were limited, and baby clothes were difficult to get from the Army PX. Therefore, Sophie Bernstein, the rabbi's wife, enlisted her mother-in-law and her sewing circle back in Rochester, New York, to sew layettes for the newborns. Lovingly tied with blue and pink ribbons, these packages subtly symbolized the connection, concern, and support of the larger Jewish community.

Marriages, *Bris Milot*, and the inevitable funerals kept the Jewish chaplains quite busy. However, there was, as of yet, one Jewish ritual that had not taken place—a Bar Mitzvah. The Bar Mitzvah, the rite of becoming a man and being counted as a member of the adult Jewish community, had not taken place in Germany since 1940. The synagogues had been defaced or destroyed, the schools emptied and defiled, and ultimately the people deported and destroyed.

Stephen Bernstein was supposed to become a Bar Mitzvah amidst adoring family and friends in a community where his parents were well respected and he was well loved. However, when his father was dispatched to Germany, all of his plans to have the ceremony in familiar surroundings were dispatched, too. During a freezing cold winter, among still hostile, though defeated, enemies, Stephen embarked on the task of learning a new Bar Mitzvah *parasha*. While his father was engaged in more global affairs, the responsibility of his reeducation fell on Atty. Abe Hyman and Rabbi Herbert A. Friedman, Bernstein's hand-picked aide. While Hyman regularly visited the DP camps, he would take Stephen with him, and they would study the lessons in the jeep. On one of these trips, Hyman shared a story that disclosed to young Stephen the vindictive nature of the townspeople. U.S. Army personnel tended to drive their jeeps without windshields. Belligerent members of the beaten Nazi party, who were anti-American, would tie taut, almost invisible, wires across the road. At high speeds, these traps were capable of beheading an unsuspecting driver.

When Hyman took Stephen out, their vehicles always had a windshield.

While Stephen did his part in preparation for his Bar Mitzvah, his parents attended to their own myriad of details; not the least of these was finding a place to hold such a large gathering. Although the great synagogue still stood in Frankfurt, the Nazis had succeeded in reducing its former grandeur to rubble. His parents' search led them to a large auditorium on the fourth floor of a building that had formerly been a school for adult Jewish education. Although the beauty of the stained glass windows had been marred with painted black circles in order to conceal a Star of David, the room remained intact. The rest of the building was used as a makeshift hospital for German war prisoners, wearing the same striped pajamas that they had ruthlessly inflicted on their former captives.

Getting the food was the next hurdle to overcome. Unfortunately, no phone calls could be made to the caterer. The army commissary was the only source of food, and rationing was strictly enforced. Repeated correspondence, always in quadruplicate, finally yielded the necessary supplies, which proved to be only raw materials. These had to be taken to a baker, who, for a pound of coffee, tea, and cocoa, turned them into edible and attractive foodstuffs. On the Friday before the Bar Mitzvah, Sophie and Phil Bernstein bounced around in both the front and the back of an Army jeep, while balancing 300 pink frosted cupcakes on their laps. They arrived at their destination only one cupcake short. After an eighteen-mile journey in which he did his best to minimize the jolts and jostling, the driver was rewarded with one of the treats—quite a delicacy, in an era marked by rationing and shortages.

In order to enhance this significant and historic celebration, the guest list was extensive and impressive. General Joseph T. McNarney, the commanding general in the European theater; his staff, other U.S. generals; the Jewish chaplains; and a few hundred surviving Jews from this community of Frankfurt comprised the invited guests.

On the morning of January 25, 1947, this moving assembly made its way up four flights of stairs under the scrutiny of hospitalized prisoners and the watchful eyes of MPs posted strategically for protection. The stark and barren room had been transformed under the loving hands of the invited DPs, grateful for all of Rabbi Bernstein's efforts. A *bimah* and an ark had been unearthed, erected, and draped in velvet. In lieu of flowers, which were impossible to get, palms adorned the room, infusing it with life.

Chanting the Torah for the first time is frightening at best, but with the top brass from the U.S. military watching intently from the first row, the Bar Mitzvah boy was indeed more nervous than most. It was understandable, though, for this day was filled with expectations. Stephen Bernstein, at the age of 13, carried the weight of millions lost. Optimistically, he and his Bar Mitzvah symbolized the hope, faith, and future of a people who were down, but not out. The undefeated. A people who, in the midst of their enemies, screamed out loud, "WE'RE STILL HERE!" Stephen's recitation was moving and beautifully tender. He sang for all of those who never would and reopened the way for those to come. Upon completion of his Haftorah, Stephen's father, Rabbi Philip Bernstein, addressed the gathering, but more specifically his son:

> This must be, also, a very extraordinary and heart-stirring event for many of the Jews who are here this morning. The very fact that no Bar Mitzvah has been held in Frankfurt since 1940, the very fact that since liberation there was not a single Jewish boy in this once great city of Frankfurt who reached the age of 13, tells more forcefully than I could dare put into words what happened to the Jewish children. . . .
>
> Yes, we are surrounded by memories today, by tragic memories of a greatness that was and is no more, and of a people who are no longer among the living.
>
> But that is of the past. The very fact that we are gathered here to worship this morning is a source of hope for the future. On every side you see the wages of the terrible sin which was committed by the mighty and the wicked. . . .
>
> The oppressor may triumph for a moment. He may enjoy for a short time the rewards of gangsterism, but his house is built on sand. It cannot stand against the wrath of the Lord. It cannot withstand the irresistible moral laws of

history. But, Israel survives. This very Bar Mitzvah in these very extraordinary circumstances demonstrates the indestructibility of our people and our faith. *Am Yisrael Chai.*

It is this heritage which we formally transmit to you today, Stephen. When I place my hands upon your head in benediction, I will be the humble instrument through which will flow the stream of history and memories of the great and good in Israel, the ideals and aspirations of our people, the strength and the lift of our faith. It is something of which you may be proud. But, it is also something which places upon you a solemn responsibility to be worthy of its precepts, to be loyal to its ideals, and to express them in a life of service.

So, be the Lord with you as I will let you go.

2

A WEALTHY MAN

Justin Deutsch—April 29, 1994

Justin is a full-time student at Wikes University and is majoring in Sociology. He also teaches guitar, performs, and is a certified luthier.

Photo by Jim Nicolais

T he typical Bar Mitzvah photo: the prepubescent short kid with a bad haircut, dwarfed by the looming Torah in his arms, smiling outwardly, as if it's not too heavy, but reeling inwardly because at the most awkward point in his life, with his voice betraying him in squeaks and whistles; his skin, a turncoat; and his body, a total Benedict Arnold, he has to stand in front of several hundred of his closest friends and relatives and sing and chant in a language that is not his native tongue and address the whole crowd with profound words that he is not sure he really understands. You know that picture.

Well, if a picture is worth a thousand words, than one look at Justin Deutsch's Bar Mitzvah photo tells you that his story is anything but typical. The photo shows Justin, with his brother Jonathan; father, Henri; and mother, Marilyn, all quite tall in contrast, lined up at urinals assuming uh . . . ur . . . the position, having wrapped "Comic Relief" T-shirts around their midsections for all to read. If a picture is worth a thousand words, then this snapshot speaks volumes.

Between the ages of 12 and 14, Jewish kids who live in even moderately populated Jewish communities tend to spend their weekends going from one Bar or Bat Mitzvah party to the next. A different theme, a change in menu, and maybe even the bands and DJs vary from week to week, but the kids are pretty much treated to a cookie-cutter party that varies only when they insert the name . . . "and now, let's welcome the _____." It can be tiresome for even the biggest party animal, but it is torture for a kid who, in spite of being well-liked, hates these artificial social gatherings. Even before he reached the Bar Mitzvah season, Justin and his best friend, Aaron Miller, found themselves outside or in the game room at JCC mixers and dances. So, as he got older and these parties commenced without interruption, he found himself in a quagmire of trying to be respectful to his friends and classmates and yet dreading each time he faced the party crowd, knowing, even at the age of 13, that this was not his scene.

When it came time to plan Justin's Bar Mitzvah, he stated flat out that he didn't want a party. He didn't want to go, so why subject other people to something he didn't even want to attend. He also felt that it was a complete waste of money to make a party for him. When Justin was in middle school and his mother gave him spending money for a field trip to Boston, Justin and Aaron found themselves distributing their newly acquired wealth between the homeless men and women on the street. He would not abide by his family wasting money on a frivolous party.

So the family brainstormed several times to decide what they could do instead to celebrate Justin's Bar Mitzvah. They decided that they would take the money they would have spent on a party and donate it to two worthwhile charities. The first was Comic Relief. Comic Relief was chosen because 100 percent of all funds raised are donated to homeless people. There are no deductions for administrative fees. In addition to supporting a worthy cause, this family thrives on humor. Justin's first full sentence was "May the Schwartz be with you!" When Justin sent his donation to Comic Relief, the organization acknowledged his gift with a little blurb in its newsletter, along with the Bar Mitzvah photo of Justin and company proudly promoting the cause with the "Comic Relief" logo draped over their hindquarters.

The second gift went to *Achusat Sara* Children's Home outside of Tel Aviv in Israel. This residence serves as a combination orphanage and child-welfare center. Some of the children in this co-ed residential center have lost their parents, others have been abused and neglected, and several are children of immigrants who have not yet found their way. The children enter this homey environment and learn to feel part of a family. The staff adapts the program to fit the particular needs of the youngsters, with attention to academic, social, emotional, and spiritual needs. For many of the children, this is their first exposure to Judaism. In their course of study, the 12- to 13-year-olds prepare en masse for the one community Bar and Bat Mitzvah celebration that is held once a year. So, instead of spending the money on his own party, Justin sponsored the Bar and Bat Mitzvah party of thirty-seven other children.

His gift went quite a long way. A communal dinner was prepared by ladies in the town, and the families of the children were invited, as well as local townsfolk. The gift enabled the school to purchase all of the raw materials—flour, sugar, chickens, and potatoes—and turn them into a sumptuous feast, enough to feed the 160 invited guests. Every child received a new set of clothes, working from the underwear and socks outward. Whereas the boys were attired in their new shirts and pants, the girls were a variation on a theme. Fabric was purchased, one pattern, and the handy seamstresses whipped up jumpers, skirts, dresses, and smocks, all in the same blue and white material. They looked like the Von Trapp family after Maria had cut up the curtains and outfitted her charges with play clothes.

After the meal, Justin shyly presented each child with a backpack filled with books and other fun school supplies. In spite of the language barrier, they could understand each others' smiles. It was quite emotional to see a Bar Mitzvah boy who chose not to celebrate with a party of his own, but rather to provide the means for thirty-plus kids to have that opportunity. Justin was accompanied on this trip by his mother, maternal grandmother, and paternal grandfather. Not to deduct anything from his gift, his grandfather paid for the family to attend the celebration at *Achusat Sara.*

His gifts, in lieu of a party, in no way precluded Justin from preparing for his own Bar Mitzvah ceremony. He dutifully joined his temple's Bar and Bat Mitzvah class and went somewhat begrudgingly several times a week. An otherwise good student, he struggled with the Hebrew. Maybe it was the group setting, his shyness, or the presentation, but whatever the cause, he just wasn't getting it.

On one of his daily visits to the Deutsch house, Aaron Miller said to Justin, "I can't believe you still don't have the tune, yet. I can teach it to you in ten minutes!" The two went upstairs to Justin's room and, true to Aaron's word, emerged ten minutes later with Justin chanting like a pro. Maybe it was the peer-tutoring approach or the one-on-one instruction, but something clicked. Spurred on by this success, Justin transferred to individual Bar Mitzvah lessons. Now, instead of griping about his Bar Mitzvah preparation, Justin went to his new teacher, Emily Trunzo—a supportive, soft-spoken woman—quite willingly.

The rabbi of the temple had heard about Justin's difficulties in the class and expected him to only do the barest minimum for the Friday evening service. The rabbi went to the Thursday evening "dress rehearsal" to prepare himself for how much he would have to do the next night. Not only the rabbi, but Marilyn and Henri Deutsch watched open-mouthed as Justin surprisingly ripped through the *entire* service. Marilyn was more taken with her son's stage presence than with the words he recited.

He looked so comfortable, so sure of himself. He looked, well—like a man!

The dress rehearsal was not a "one-hit" wonder, and Justin repeated his stellar performance in front of the congregation the next night. In light of his altruistic actions, his speech was very appropriate:

> It says in my Torah portion: You shall live in booths for seven days, to remember that God made the Israelites live in booths when He brought them out of the land of Egypt. The purpose of the booths is to make us realize how the less fortunate live.
>
> When we remember how we used to live in poverty, we realize why we believe in *tzedakah*. *Tzedakah* is the Hebrew word for "justice." Charity is when you feel so bad for someone that you give to a person, or a group who can help that person. From what I know, justice is making things fair and equal, not just giving out of guilt and sorrow. That is why I chose to give to two helpful organizations—so that I can help to make the world more just. I am not giving charity, but *tzedakah*.

Justin's *tzedakah* did not begin or end with his Bar Mitzvah. He has became an active volunteer in the St. Francis Soup Kitchen, as well as at Habitat for Humanity, and now, in addition to his money, gives his time and energy. Justin, now a 6′4″ college student, is still quiet, unassuming, and a little shy. He wasn't looking for accolades, attention, or any type of recognition. He just wanted to make things a little more "just." A famous rabbi once stated that the wealth of a man is measured not in his bank account, but in how much he gives away. At the age of 13, Justin Deutsch became not only a man, but a wealthy one.

3

THE HARVEST

David Levitt—November 26, 1994

David is a student at the University of Florida in Gainesville. In May 2000, Tampa Bay Harvest calculated that 1,000,000 pounds of school food had gone to the hungry since the first donation in November 1994.

Photo by Ray Bassett with Maddock Photographers

Food—Glorious Food! Its significance in the Jewish religion far surpasses simple life sustenance. It defines, identifies, separates, and governs us. Many of the 613 commandments focus on what we can and cannot eat. The historical relevance of holidays is often unknown or disregarded, but Grandma Miriam's matzoh ball soup, Aunt Ruth's latkes, and Cousin Esther's hamentaschen are assigned almost sacred status.

Our most basic tenets are set in examples related to what our forefathers (and mothers) ate and drank. Eve gave Adam the forbidden fruit, prompting their eviction from the Garden. Abraham fed the "strangers," angels in disguise, teaching us *Hasnaches Orchim*, kindness to strangers. When Rivka kindly offered water to the servant Eliezer and his camels, he knew that she was the "girl" to marry Abraham's son Isaac. And Esov sold his birthright to his brother, Yaacov, for a bowl of soup.

Israel is the land of *milk and honey*, we *break bread, reap* in joy, sit beneath the *fig* tree, and ply our love with flagons and *apples*. God commanded the Jewish people to be "fruitful and multiply." Even our endearments encompass edibles such as "cookie," "pumpkin," "peanut," "honey," and, of course, my little "knish"!

It is no wonder, then, when David Levitt was deciding on a Bar Mitzvah project, he chose something involving food. When David was preparing to become a Bar Mitzvah, he was told that meant that he was supposed to assume responsibility in the Jewish community by doing something helpful. His mother, Sandy, felt that the process should involve more than a recitation and a party. She felt that "becoming a man" meant demonstrating our responsibility to each other. Doesn't it say, "If I am only for myself, what am I?"

Their inspiration came in the Sunday paper. An article in *Parade* magazine highlighted the work of a businessman from Louisville, Kentucky, named Stan Curtis who founded Harvest USA, a national organization responsible for delivering donated and leftover food to soup kitchens and shelters. After a few phone calls, Sandy found out that not only was there a branch office in their area, Tampa Bay Harvest, it was one of the largest ones in the country. David started volunteering and in the process "volunteered" his mom and dad. He was willing to provide the manpower to do the "shlepping," but since he was only 11, his parents had to drive.

On his very first day of middle school, David Levitt introduced himself to the principal and asked if the school could donate the leftover food from the school's cafeteria to homeless shelters. The response, typically bureaucratic, included

". . . there are insurance issues . . . health issues . . . I don't have the authority. . . . and I'll look into it."

Not one to take "no" for an answer, David wrote to and personally visited every member of the School Board of Pinellas County, including the superintendent. The board invited him to make a presentation at its upcoming school board meeting. On his 12th birthday, with his mom and dad, grandmother and grandfather, and the rabbi in tow, David addressed the school board. He proposed that leftover food from not only his school, but the entire district, over 100 schools, be donated to soup kitchens and homeless shelters. The proposal was passed unanimously! Having no idea of the magnitude of what just transpired, David walked out smiling and said, "Ok, what's next?"

Several months later, when no action had taken place, David called Mary Dowdell, director of Tampa Bay Harvest, to find out what was wrong. She told him that there was a hitch. The Health Department required that the food be transported in airtight containers. Tampa Bay Harvest has a mission "to feed"; there is no budget and all of their work involves donated food and volunteer help. The school board had no budget to purchase any containers, either.

They had come this far. David was not about to let a few containers get in his way. He and his mom went to the local Publix supermarket and jotted down names and addresses of every plastic manufacturer. They launched a two-person letter-writing campaign, soliciting plastic bags and containers. After several rejections, they received a $100 gift certificate from Publix and a brief message from Glad © products: "Your shipment is on its way." That afternoon a truck arrived with eight cases of bags in various sizes. David called Mary Dowdell and said, "I have the bags, let's go!"

This prompted another trip to the school board. On November 12, 1994, two days after his 13th birthday and two weeks before his Bar Mitzvah, the project was given the green light and ten schools—including Osceola Middle School, which David attended—started donating their leftover food to shelters. What a Bar Mitzvah present! He saw his dream come into reality. David continued to do his volunteering on weekends, but since the actual transporting of the food from school took place during the weekdays, other volunteers from Tampa Bay Harvest actually picked it up.

On David's Bar Mitzvah invitation, the family asked guests to bring canned goods that would be donated to Tampa Bay Harvest. They collected and donated 500 pounds of food. David's most special gift came from Mindy Linn, his former baby-sitter. She was working her way through college and sent him a note with regrets that due to limited funds, she couldn't buy him a present. Instead, she was volunteering at a soup kitchen, in David's name, as her gift to him.

Making a speech at your Bar Mitzvah can be the most difficult part of the ceremony. But since David had already become a spokesperson for Tampa Bay Harvest, addressing the assembled guests in their temple was a breeze. He stood in his multicolored tallis, in honor of his *parasha* about Joseph and his multicolored coat, and shared the following:

> (Like Joseph in my *parasha*), last year I met a "stranger in the field" that changed my life. That stranger is not a person. . . . it is a charitable, nonprofit organization called Tampa Bay Harvest whose mission is to feed the hungry without a budget to do so. Through Tampa Bay Harvest I have learned that a kid can make a difference, and that adults will take time to listen to a kid. I've learned a lot about the hungry and homeless and how easily *any* person can get into such a situation. And probably the most important thing I learned is how good it makes you feel when you are doing something that helps others. I know my experience with Tampa Bay Harvest has made me a better person. May I always champion causes such as this as long as I am able.

After the Bar Mitzvah, someone took his name to Jeb Bush, son of George and brother of George W., who was running for governor of Florida. Jeb was writing a book called *Profiles in Character* about foundations to the family's future impacting the future of Florida. He was highlighting stories of people who have made a difference. David Levitt is the youngest person to appear in the book, showing that even a kid at the age of 11, if determined enough, can make things better. As a result of this story, a member of the Bush campaign called David and invited him and his family to the debate between Jeb and Lawton Chiles. When it came time for closing remarks, David's mouth dropped open as Bush told the audience that ". . . David Levitt asked the 'why not' question. When it's a good idea, why don't we try it? Why don't we keep persisting until it happens? He kept asking that question for two years. And then it happened." Jeb told the audience that he, as governor, would like to emulate that same "why not" attitude in order to make things happen.

When the Bar Mitzvah was over, David could have "kicked back" and just focused on his music and the theater, two extracurricular activities that he loves. It's funny. While adults were singing his praises, a couple of mean-spirited kids didn't like all of this attention showered on David. They would scream nasty, ugly, anti-Semitic names at him and went as far as knocking his trumpet off his bike and roughing him up. He was just determined to continue his volunteer work, at any cost. The program started with only 10 schools and quickly grew to include almost 110 schools that donated their leftover food to hungry people. That equals hundreds of thousands of pounds of food.

During an interview on an oldies radio station, the disc jockey suggested to David that since he had been so successful countywide, why not "shoot" for a program that was "state-wide." It took only this little spark to propel David and his mother to call congressman and senators, looking for a sponsor to launch a bill.

State Representative Dennis Jones sponsored a bill to encourage food providers such as restaurants, hospitals, caterers, and so on, to donate their excess food to homeless shelters and soup kitchens. The bill passed through the House, but did not make it through the Senate, due to lack of connection and sponsorship. Undaunted, they were willing to try again the following year. This time, Senator Charlie Crist was more than just a sponsor. He and his people took the very simple bill and inflated it, adding provisions and making it more sophisticated. The bill really amended the "Good Samaritan" law, covering transporters of food and encouraging food suppliers to feed the hungry simply by donating their leftover food.

Through this ongoing relationship with Crist, David had the opportunity to become a page in the Senate during his spring break in 1998. As exciting as it was just being in the Senate, David figured that his main responsibilities would be to deliver messages and bring coffee. It was a very surprised David who found out that during the week he was a page, Crist was pushing to have the bill brought to the floor for a vote. Now, with his hopes raised, David started to feel disappointed as the week drew to a close and torte reform was monopolizing the floor. True to his word, Senator Crist stood up and begged the speaker's pardon for the interruption. He said that the young man who had spearheaded a bill that he was sponsoring was in the Senate and he wondered if they could temporarily table the issue at hand and address this other bill. Since there were no objections, Crist turned to 16-year-old David and asked him if he wanted to say anything. Unprepared, David took the floor and explained the bill "off the cuff." He was greeted with applause upon completion and was there to witness his pro-posed bill pass with a unanimous vote! He also made history. This was the first time in Florida that a person, other than a senator, had spoken from the Senate floor. Not bad for 16.

Two weeks later, David was called to the front office of the car wash where he worked. He entered the office, racking his brain about what he might have done wrong. He was greeted instead by television cameras, as someone handed him the telephone. On the other end was Governor Lawton Chiles, who called to let David know that he had just signed SB (Senate Bill) 466 CS (Committee Substitute) for HB (House Bill) 105 into law!

David appeared on national television, including *Oprah Winfrey* and *The Montel Williams Show*. His story has appeared in books and magazines. And he has been honored locally, statewide, and nationally. He has received the Giraffe award for "sticking his neck out" and the very prestigious Prudential award, which he won while still in middle school. One of his most glorious moments came when, as a recipient of the presidential "Point of Light" award, he went to Washington, D.C., and was presented his award by the First Lady in the Old

Executive Office Building. As his name was called out, he went up to receive the Tiffany-made award. He flashed a broad smile at Hillary Clinton as he extended his hand and said, "What do you do with the White House leftovers?"

4

JUSTICE

Alan M. Dershowitz—September 8, 1951

Alan M. Dershowitz is the Felix Frankfurter Profesor of Law at Harvard Law School. A graduate of Brooklyn College and Yale Law School, Dershowitz joined Harvard Law School at age 25 after clerking for Judges David Bazelon and Arthur Goldberg. He is the author of a dozen fiction and non-fiction works. More than a million of his books have been sold worldwide.

Rabbis are experts in finding some connection, no matter how remote, between the weekly *parasha* and the life of the Bar Mitzvah boy. However, it was not a stretch when Rabbi Samuel K. Mirsky told the congregation how appropriate this *parasha*, *Shoftim* (Judges), from the Book of Deuteronomy, was for a young boy who had aspirations of becoming a lawyer. The *parasha* deals with the lofty ideas of justice and leadership.

In his thickly accented but quiet voice, Rabbi Mirsky began his weekly sermon, *"Tzedek, Tzedek, Tirdof* ('Justice, Justice, shall thou pursue'). Why does the Torah use the word *tzedek* twice?"

He proceeded to offer several interpretations; however, the favorite one for the Bar Mitzvah boy was that one *tzedek* stands for the "means of justice" and one stands for the "ends of justice." Without the means, you can't be sure of the end. Process is important.

After the rabbi's sermon, the Bar Mitzvah boy, Alan Dershowitz, addressed the congregation. His speech, a well-guarded secret, had only been shared with his Uncle Joe Fuchs, his Bar Mitzvah teacher. Fiercely independent, this young man wanted to present his own thoughts, uninfluenced by anyone. In a loud, clear, confident voice, Dershowitz delivered his somewhat provocative ideas, contrasting his *parasha* with the fact that there was still injustice in the world.

For the boy who would become a man for whom public oration was a way of life, davening, *layning*, and speaking in front of the very large congregation was undaunting. He was comfortable and confident; however, he was not completely without concern. First of all, he had bad allergies, and at the height of hay fever season, he was afraid he would sneeze on the *bimah*. Second, one week before the Bar Mitzvah, he developed a boil on his upper right arm. Every time he bent his arm to shake hands, he was painfully reminded of the boil's existence. And finally, he worried that if he made even the most minute mistake in the *trup*, not even in the words, he would have half of the congregation yelling, "No, no, no!"

In an effort to avoid the cacophony of corrections, he decided that he just wouldn't make any mistakes. This wisecracking, joke-telling, lousy student chanted the entire *parasha* and Haftorah perfectly.

His parents were extremely proud, which was important, because in those days Dershowitz was a major source of consternation to his family. His family had education and the pursuit of excellence as strong family values, and Alan proved a disappointment, with his less-than-stellar school performance. In addition, he was always getting suspended. People thought his mother worked at the school because she was there so often!

He followed the rules of his Orthodox family, but he did it without feeling. He kept kosher and *layed* his *tefillin* daily, but it was not meaningful to him. His life centered around basketball, baseball, and the Dodgers. His grandmother would chide him in Yiddish, "*Shtoos, Shtoos*" (nonsense), "*Narishkeit*" (childishness), about his interest in and enthusiasm for sports. While his family thought he should be studying Talmud and emulating Torah scholars, he was looking up to Duke Snyder, Peewee Reese, and especially Jackie Robinson, because this man was someone who had broken in—someone who was the first.

The summer before the Bar Mitzvah, a huge fight broke out between Alan and his parents. He wanted to go to camp, as he always did. Knowing his poor academic track record, his parents felt that he should stay home and use the additional time to prepare for his Bar Mitzvah. A compromise was reached. After promising to study his *parasha* every day, with the commitment that his head counselor would check on his progress, he was permitted to go to camp, returning only days before the big event. In addition to his regular camp gear, he packed his *Tikkun*, so he could keep his promise.

While back in Brooklyn, he was regarded as the "worst scholar," whereas, at Camp Lebanon, in Somerville, New Jersey, he was voted the "best athlete." With all-around natural talent, he excelled in basketball, baseball, track, swimming, and volleyball. One of the counselors that summer was Bernie Schwartz, who would make his mark later as Tony Curtis.

Since both his Ringel and Dershowitz grandparents were founders of the Young Israel movement in Williamsburg, it was fitting that Alan's Bar Mitzvah took place in the Young Israel of Boro Park. Life was oriented around the *shul*. His mother served as president of the sisterhood, while his father did his stint as president of the men's club. Even Cub Scouts and Boy Scouts meetings were held in the synagogue.

The family hosted a *Kiddush* downstairs for the entire congregation. Then the invited guests assembled across the street for lunch. Young Israel has no catering hall, so the neighboring *shul*, Beth El, was kind enough to share its resources. Harry Dershowitz, Alan's father, had a small store on Broadway that sold men's underwear and work clothes. The family had a modest income, but hosted a beautifully catered luncheon for their son, who was the first grandchild on both sides of the family to become a Bar Mitzvah.

There is an old joke about a Jewish man who is stranded on a desert island. He feels compelled to build two *shuls*. One *shul* that he will attend and the other one that he wouldn't go near! Like the old joke, Dershowitz and his friends (with whom he is still close, to this day) all attended different Orthodox synagogues. In addition to Young Israel and Beth El, there was Shomrei Emunah (affectionately called "show me your money") and the Sephardisha *shul* (which probably had a name, but is immortally remembered in this way).

In those days, a really big monetary gift for a Bar Mitzvah was *chai*, $18. Most boys considered themselves fortunate to receive $5 or $10. When friends gathered that Saturday night at the Dershowitz home for an informal gathering, younger brother Nathan served as the "bag man," enthusiastically collecting the proffered gifts.

Because Dershowitz attended a school that was forty-five minutes away from his home, he coveted only one gift, a new bicycle. His aunts and uncles chipped in together and proudly presented him with a new blue Schwinn. On October 5, less than one month later, the bike was stolen on a Friday afternoon in front of Herman Gersky's house. The chain with the lock was obviously no deterrent to a determined thief. The family didn't have the resources to replace it; the best his relatives could come up with was a makeshift bike assembled from used bike parts. While most of his friends enjoyed their new bikes, Dershowitz experienced the double insult of having experienced the ephemeral pleasure of the blue Schwinn, while now suffering the indignity of a cruddy, rickety Frankenstein of a replacement.

That special day culminated with the evening get-together. In spite of an academic record marred by detentions, suspensions, and poor grades, Dershowitz, in his new brown suit, showed everyone what he was made of. The first grandchild on both the Ringel and Dershowitz sides, named proudly for his great-grandfather Avraham Mordechai Ringel, and the descendent of a long line of rabbis, demonstrated his gutsy "right stuff" in a way that would become his trademark. The morning began with *"Tzedek, Tzedek, Tirdof,"* imprinting a motto that would last a lifetime.

5

DOWN BUT NOT OUT

Scott Goldman—Fall, 1974

This story was in part inspired by a speech delivered by Bruce Mansdorf at his son Nick's Bar Mitzvah.

Everyone had a wonderful time at Scott Goldman's Bar Mitzvah party—that is, everyone but the Bar Mitzvah boy. He wasn't there. Saddled with 103° fever, he stayed home while his parents, brother, friends, and relatives enjoyed themselves at his celebration. Yet he received his best gift that night. Though he was stuck at home, alone and disappointed, his best friend, Gary Kornfeld, came over and hung out with him instead of going to the party. He wasn't very lively due to his elevated temperature, but Scott still recognized the sacrifice and appreciated the company.

It had all started that morning. This was his Bar Mitzvah day. He attributed those funny feelings in his stomach to nerves and awaited his turn in the service. After all, he had something to prove. He had sort of fired his Bar Mitzvah teacher. Well, maybe not fired, but after the first few lessons, he refused to study with this assigned teacher. On their first meeting, Mr. S. took it upon himself to change Scott's Hebrew name. Even though Scott had attended Temple Israel religious school for years as "Yoshiya," Mr. S. said, "Wrong, your name is Yissacher." He was controlling, bucolic, and ineffective. Rather than meeting in person, his idea of "quality time" was to call a student and demand that they sing their *parasha* on the phone. Living in a house with an older brother who would later use this exchange as fodder for merciless ridicule, Scott finally refused to participate in these remote lessons. He decided he'd rather suffer the consequences of practicing alone, instead of subjecting himself to abuse on both ends of the telephone. Duly armed with the printed copy and a tape with the tune, he relied on his own natural musical ability to learn his Haftorah.

Standing in front of the congregation and "feeling the music in his blood," he chanted from the *bimah*. When he completed the *bracha* after the Haftorah, he felt so proud that he had studied independently and pulled this off. Even though he was very shy and didn't often have a forum in which to shine, his Bar Mitzvah gave him the opportunity to show that he could sing—and sing well. He almost immediately felt the weight of this responsibility lift and replaced it quickly with a new sense of self-respect. All of these feelings, however, would disappear in a matter of minutes.

The Bar Mitzvah boy thought that Rabbi Simon Schupp was the epitome of what a rabbi should be. He was part showman, part spiritual leader; his speeches were packed with emotion. Today's topic itself was highly charged—the *Akedah*, when God tested Abraham's faith and ordered him to sacrifice his cherished and long-awaited son Isaac. The rabbi faced the Bar Mitzvah boy on the *bimah* and started his oration. In the parasha, Abraham is called three times, and each time his response is *"Hineni"*—"Here I Am." He doesn't retort, "What?" or "What!" or even a more civil "What do You want?" in response to being summoned. Instead, he strongly demonstrates his willingness to serve, by replying each time in the ready, "Here I Am"— *"Hineni."*

While the rabbi expounded on the first call to Abraham, Scott wondered if he was just in awe of standing so close to the rabbi, but he felt himself sway and grabbed the side of the lectern. With Abraham's second call to action, Scott started to perspire. And in his dramatic voice Rabbi Shupp described Abraham yelling out *"Hineni"* for the third time—boom! The Bar Mitzvah boy, along with the lovely flowers, went down with a crash.

It is up to debate who arrived on the *bimah* first. Aunt Marion and Aunt Henrietta, with their smelling salts raised for the charge, shuffled competitively down the aisle. Luckily, Dr. Steve Rosenthal, the pediatrician, raced toward the front, and was able to revive the prostrate young man. Somewhat befuddled and dazed, but fortified with a butterscotch candy someone had shoved in his mouth, the embarrassed "man of the hour" was led away to a more private place to recuperate. In this back room, the doctor realized that it was not a simple case of nerves gone awry; this kid was sick. Despite the fever and the humiliation of passing out in front of the whole congregation, Scott rallied himself and asked to go back and finish the service. Seeing how important it was to him, the doctor discharged his patient to the sanctuary. Scott completed his celebratory rite, much to everyone's amazement.

After a barrage of congratulatory hugs and handshakes, interspersed with good-natured teasing about his first "exit" from the *bimah*, the Bar Mitzvah boy was whisked away to the confines of his home. Disappointed about doing all of the work and not having any of the fun, he was cheered up by the loyalty of his friend.

Not long after the Bar Mitzvah and feeling much better, Scott joined his friends in a little mischief. They "borrowed" Mr. Goldman's car. His dad decided to fit the punishment to the crime. If Scott wanted to drive so much, he could fill that need by parking cars in the family-owned parking lot. Except for a respite during college and a four-year departure to California, Scott has been in that parking lot ever since. But on those premises, in addition to parking cars, he does magical, musical things. Transcending the reality of his tiny office, Scott, wearing cut-offs and a T-shirt, dreams his dreams and is making them happen. From the cramped space in the middle of the lot he has written music and lyrics, produced several records, sold the rights to major labels, managed a local performer, and become the agent for bands up and down the East Coast. The music that was always in his soul—demonstrated so poignantly at his first solo performance, his Bar Mitzvah—keeps his vision clear and his goals established.

On a more private stage, he sings nightly to his two young sons. When they are old enough, he'll share the tale of his Bar Mitzvah. He'll tell them that he went down, but he might not mention that when he could've stayed hidden, he chose instead to go back to the *bimah*, face the congregation, and finish the job. It's odd that although he missed most of the rabbi's speech that day, somehow the message got through. When his clients, patrons, family, and, most especially, his boys call for him, he doesn't say, "I'm busy"; "Not, now"; or "Don't bother me"; but rather, "Here I am" (*Hineni*).

6

SECOND TIME AROUND

John Pransky—August 8, 1998
(written by John Pransky)

At age 87, John Pransky was recently honored with an award for being a Mason and a Schriner for sixty years. Married to Baila for over fifty years and the proud father of Glenn and Daniel (and their familes), Pransky is a devoted family man who continues the other joy in his life—singing.

S habbat shalom! What a glorious occasion this is for me to have my dear family and friends here to share this very special *simcha.* In days of old, when man's lifespan was 3 score and 10—that is, 70 years—the learned rabbis declared that at this point man should start counting his years again, starting from year 1 and upon arriving at 13 he may celebrate a second Bar Mitzvah. For me, this is a great gift because my

29

first Bar Mitzvah was saddened by my father's sudden death shortly before.

At a first Bar Mitzvah a young man will relate his future ambitions and goals. At this, my second Bar Mitzvah, I have the privilege of sharing with you where my goals and experiences have taken me, so permit me to reminisce a bit.

I was blessed with a wonderful immediate and extended family. My parents practiced and taught us a proud sense of Judaism. As a matter of fact, I inherited from my father and his five brothers a keen love for *hazzanous*—that is, cantorial singing and music. At family gatherings we would always sing together as a choir our favorite cantorial selections. I was very fortunate in having a most extraordinary dedicated Hebrew teacher and scholar, Mr. Barnet Cohen, in Winthrop, Massachusetts, where I was raised. He instilled in me a love for the Hebrew language and Torah study. He taught me *nusach*, which are the prayer melodies, some of which I used today. At age 11, I was a member of the synagogue choir and then at the age of 14 I occasionally performed as a cantor in a small nearby New England community. I have been singing in choirs wherever I have lived, to this very day here at Temple Israel.

My mother played a vital role in encouraging me to further my Jewish studies and involvement. But one of her greatest achievements was introducing me to Baila, who happily has been my wife for 46 years.

As for my education and work, I graduated high school in 1934 and immediately entered Northeastern Law School, attending at night and working in the family business during the day. I received my Bachelor of Law degree and passed the Bar exam four years later. Then I continued my routine of work and school, earning my Master of Law in 1940. I decided to continue in the family sewing machinery business, rather than practice law, as I found it to be more exciting and rewarding. Thanks to Uncle Sam, I had a change of careers, a result of my joining the Army in 1943. After basic training, I joined the American Division, Judge Advocate Section, making the best practical use of my legal background, and served in the South Pacific and Japan. I was much involved in conducting the Sabbath and holiday services there—of course, weather and battle conditions permitting. Because we were so far away from our families, these services provided us with some of our few fond reminders of home. My military experience was very rewarding because of the many lasting friendships that were developed and the unusual experiences I encountered that I've related to my children and now to my grandchildren.

Upon my discharge from the Army in 1946, I returned to Boston and resumed my involvement in the family business, joining up with my older brother Abe. The pretty girl to whom my mother introduced me became my inspiration and life-long partner in 1952. We were then blessed with two wonderful sons, Glenn and Daniel, who have enriched our lives in many ways.

In 1960, while on business in Atlanta, I met Morris Speizman, who enticed me to visit him in Charlotte. The vitality, beauty, and favorable business potential greatly impressed me to the degree that I felt this would be a fine place to establish a business and raise a family. My challenge was selling my young wife on the idea of moving our family to a city she had never visited. When I presented the idea to her, to my pleasure, Baila was as enthusiastic as I. Just a few months later we found ourselves happily settled here in this beautiful city. We immediately became active members of Temple Israel, both of us joining the choir and participating in many other temple activities.

The religious community here has always been a focal point of many of our family's involvements. Some of our closest friendships were developed right here at temple. Both of our sons were Bar Mitzvah'd here and were deeply involved in all temple and youth activities until leaving for college. And now it is my pleasure to celebrate my second Bar Mitzvah here at Temple Israel with you.

Among the numerous activities in which our sons participated, Camp Ramah was one of the most rewarding and memorable. It was our sons' enriching Judaic experience there that inspired us to establish the Pransky Family Ramah Scholarship Fund. This enables deserving youngsters in our religious school to attend Ramah and enjoy the rich cultural and religious environment that greatly benefited our sons.

Over the years, we have been blessed with lovely additions to our family. Glenn's wife, Terry, and our two precious grandchildren, Jackie and Lena. And Daniel's wife, Sandy, who is expecting our third grandchild in November.

Thirty-seven years ago I made the wise decision to move my family to Charlotte and establish Piedmont Sewing Supply. My company's success is greatly attributed to my dedicated employees and loyal customers, friends, who all helped make everything possible.

I have recently retired and sold the business to a capable young man, who will continue the name and traditions that I established. Now, I will have the pleasure of working for charitable organizations, trying to perfect my game of golf, if that is possible, undertaking new traveling adventures, spending more time with family and friends, and, of course, occasionally being involved with Piedmont Sewing. I also look forward to spending more time with the Shriner's Chanters Group, of which I have been a proud member since 1965. I sincerely appreciate their joining us here today. We will be singing for you at the end of the services.

Baila and I want to thank all of you for joining us in this special Bar Mitzvah celebration. Our sincere thanks to Rabbi Ezring and Cantor Roochvarg and the temple personnel for their gracious assistance. To my devoted sons, Glenn and Daniel, and their wives, Terry and Sandy, we are grateful for your assistance and devotion. Most of all, I want to thank my *aishis chayil*, my woman of valor, Baila, for being my guiding light in making this celebration such a joyous and memorable *simcha*.

Again, thanks to all of you for joining us. I want to wish you all a hearty Shabbat Shalom.

7

A JOYOUS BAR MITZVAH

Brian Daniel David—July 12, 1999
(written by Paula David)

Brian David is an easy-going young man who enjoys playing his guitar and spending time with his friends, his brother, and four sisters. He is active in Special Olympics sports and is proud of his part-time job at Starbucks. He still attends Camp Ramah in Canada every summer where he now works in the dining room, setting up and clearing tables. Brian continues to learn and grow, thriving on his ability to daven, sing, and participate in the Ramah community where he first "became a man".

Brian is 22, has Down's Syndrome and is pretty deaf, none of which keeps him from being active, a singer, a dancer, and the pivotal person in our family. This is his seventh year at Camp Ramah, Canada, where he was one of the original "Tikveh" campers . . . the camp's first foray into special needs and putting into action the conviction that Judaism belongs to all Jews. There are five boys and seven girls in the program, and they are either integrated into regular

33

senior camper programs or have their own special classes and activities, where appropriate. They have developed signs (a combination of American Sign Language and creative expression) for the daily services, and the rest of the camp members thought it was so cool, they now all use sign language while davening.

I was the skeptical one early on. Brian's English was less than articulate, his Hebrew nonexistent, and no one could love him or care for him the way his doting family could. The first year he learned what camp was, and from then on, he owned it! You can't imagine the feeling that we, his family, have each Visitor's Day as Brian schleps us around camp, showing off his *mishpacha*, and even more so when other kids come up to meet us just because we are his parents. Kids of all ages went out of their way to high-five him or just give him a hug in passing. Brian, who was always the recipient of strange stares and nudges in synagogues (he was oblivious, his sibs were not!), took to daily davening like a little yeshiva *bocher*, put on his *tefillin*, wrapped himself in his tallis and had a rapturous look on his face. None of this occured when he turned 13. At that time, Brian wasn't part of a welcoming, inclusive community and didn't understand the concept of prayer, so we didn't need a Bar Mitzvah. Apparently, turning 13, you become a man anyway. Since Brian didn't know any better, and his grandparents didn't take him that seriously, we didn't worry about it. Now that he had a community and an amazing understanding, we decided to do it, at camp, where he was loved and respected and there was much reason to celebrate.

I can't tell you the pride, joy, and gratitude we all felt. The entire camp sang and signed a *Shechianu*, Brian did the *brachot* for the Torah reading and was so thrilled, he almost burst. In-between very serious davening, he blew kisses to his fans; raised his *tefillin*-wrapped arms in a girl-powered, two-fingered salute; shook hands; and accepted congratulations in two languages. He helped his siblings set up the Torah and do their *aliyahs*, assuming they wouldn't know how because they weren't campers. He couldn't do the *parasha*, but an incredible young woman (with Downs) from Cleveland could, and did! Afterward, when I thanked her, she explained that it was her honor to do it for Brian, as she knew that Brian was thinking it. The camp members held their breath while he did his solos and cheered in one voice when he succeeded. Never was a service quite like this. We sat in the makeshift *shul*—the largest building in camp—with some kids on the floor, some in bleachers, and some just inching up to the *bimah* so they could help Brian if he needed it. Following the service, everyone started to dance. Brian was lifted up in a chair, received hundreds of handmade cards, and, with his face bursting in a grin, just kept saying, *"Todah Rabah."*

We stayed for breakfast with the kids, and they kept coming up to wish us *Mazel Tov* and vie for the privilege of being one of Brian's "best" friends—another lesson in which "family" grows not only through bloodlines, but through being nurtured. For a few hours Brian's birth-family felt the meaning of true inclusiveness, and when we left him there with his camp-family, we knew that it was possible for him to be not just a man, but a mensch in his own community. The most beautiful part is that he already knew it!

Our family has not yet been able to process exactly how thrilled we are with Brian's Bar Mitzvah, the genuine love and enthusiasm from the entire camp, the support and caring from the staff, and the generally wonderful time we had. I haven't quite found the words yet, and that in itself is remarkable! However, the glow in Brian's eyes and the joy in his face continue to light our hearts and our house.

We have always loved Brian and been proud of his accomplishments. Yet we, his family, never had the imagination, the skills, and the courage to push him in new directions that Ramah seems to have done just by existing. He arrived home from camp and immediately set the table, wolfed down his supper, and followed with *Birchat Hamazon* (the blessing after the meal). As he pulled various papers and craft projects out of his duffle bags, he serenaded us with appropriate Hebrew prayers, songs, and words that had been part of his camp life. In spite of his deafness and speech problems, we were able to recognize the tunes and the words he meant. We put on the audiotape Ramah had made in '97, and Brian clapped his hands and shouted, "Shayna . . . last year . . . next year

Shayna's back." He proceeded to sing along with the entire tape, showing more enthusiasm and accurate pronunciation than the Spice Girls and Peter, Paul, and Mary combined.

This is from the child who we thought would never have the capacity to understand what goes on in *shul*, never mind have a sense of Jewish identity. This is now the child who inspires his four siblings to accompany him to services and learn his camp songs so that they can all sing together. This is the child who gathers *kippot* for family dinners and makes sure everyone has a *siddur* in front of his or her plate. This is the child who wraps himself up in his *tallit* and *tefillin* and quietly davens when he is sad. This is the child who, on the eve of his homecoming, after jumping on his bed, greeting his cats, and checking out his videos and the fridge is now packing to return for the next summer.

Our family has never really enjoyed or felt connected to a synagogue, mainly because of the reception (or lack thereof) that Brian received. Camp Ramah has given Brian a magical sense of belonging that we were unable to provide and are thrilled to see. Only his family, which has lived with him twenty-four hours a day, can appreciate what challenges and rewards Brian's counselors face. His efforts at communication demand total concentration and a diligent imagination. His hygiene requires monitoring, and his determination to achieve is matched by his occasional determination to do exactly as he pleases. He can be demanding, annoying, and moody. He can also be joyful, enthusiastic, and loving with every fiber of his being. Obviously, his counselors dealt with both extremes of behavior, but the enthusiasm and rapport they shared with Brian indicate to us that they understood his frustrations and took pleasure in his accomplishments, affection, and usually sunny nature.

Brian has always been our family barometer about who "special people" are. He knows immediately when a person is accepting, kind, and honest. Most of us don't have that gift and get caught up in the myriad traps that false faces can set. We have all learned much about the value of intellect versus the value of a good soul. Although we still value learning, academic achievement, and intellect, Brian has forced us to redefine our definitions of success.

In the past several summers we've seen both the general campers and the staff respond to Brian and, more important, have seen his response to them. This has been one of the joyful highlights of our parenting years. This past summer on July 12, at his Bar Mitzvah, we saw him flanked by his counselors; the entire camp stood behind him and beside him. Our friends and cousins who attended couldn't believe the love and acceptance they witnessed—not just with Brian, but with all the Tikvah campers. We've seen Brian's face shine at camp before, but this time we saw a glow radiating from so many faces, it lit up the whole room.

His counselor, Michael, spoke of how Brian would wake him in the morning . . . with his big hug and gentle pressure to get moving! Those special moments have always been one of our family's cherished secrets, and much to our delight . . . the secret is out. We're not the only ones who understand that a disability isn't necessarily a handicap. The counselors and the rest of the camp have shown us a world that can indeed be a better place, one that will recognize and respect Brian for who he is and let him know he belongs. Our prayers and energies to ensure that our son find a place to stand on his own and be recognized for himself have already been answered.

8

A DIXIE BAR MITZVAH

Rabbi David Geffen, Ph.D.—November 11, 1951

Rabbi David Geffen, Ph.D., is the spiritual leader of Temple Israel in Scranton, Pennsylvania.

Photo by Robert Ventre

David Geffen learned some of his most valuable lessons in the synagogue, and they had nothing to do with the service. In the '40s and '50s, the Deep South was segregated. Schools were completely separate. Black people sat in the back of the buses and trolleys and couldn't drink water, swim, or eat in the same place as white people. The black soldiers who were sent to southern boot camps prior to being shipped overseas during World War II could not walk into a coffee shop and get a sandwich. It didn't matter that they wore the uniform of the United States Army or that they were on their way to defend and die for this country. They were black, and they could pick up their food around back in the kitchen.

The first place that David witnessed integration before it was mandated by law was the synagogue—his grandfather's synagogue. The nannies, maids, and butlers who helped to raise the Jewish children of the South were invited to celebrate the Bar Mitzvahs. When they came into the synagogue, the men sat with the men and the women sat with the women. If you came late, you sat in the back, regardless of race.

In his grandfather's *shul*, Shearith Israel—known as "The Little *Shul*"—young David learned about equality and freedom. He had studied about Moses leading the Jewish people out of slavery in Egypt. He had read about the Emancipation Proclamation. But in his day-to-day life in Atlanta, Georgia, in the '40s and '50s, he saw that although slavery was over, inequality was not. There were signs over drinking fountains that said "Whites Only." At public pools, that same sign was hung in a prominent place. And yet in the most holy place he knew, blacks and whites sat together. There were no segregation laws here. The law in this place was contained in the huge scrolls behind the velvet curtains. And the law was enforced by a gentle man who led by example. He did not sit separated from his congregation "on high" on the *bimah*. He sat in the first seat next to the Eastern Wall, next to his son and grandson. He didn't preach about "equal status," he lived it.

Rabbi Tobias Geffen was the spiritual leader and then the Rabbi Emeritus at Shearith Israel for sixty years. He was the first Orthodox rabbi to take up permanent residence in the Deep South. His life was the epitome of service and tolerance of differences. He championed the cause of Orthodox women who, after they had a civil divorce, needed to procure a *get* from their ex-husbands in order to marry again. In one case, he tracked down the offending husband in jail in Oklahoma and went personally with two witnesses and a scribe to obtain the proper papers and signatures. Not only was he available to his congregants, his name became legendary throughout the

South as someone who would answer queries on a wide range of issues and would assist wherever he could.

During the Depression, a young Jewish man from Philadelphia hitchhiked down South looking for work. He made the mistake of getting into the wrong vehicle—a getaway car from a recent robbery. This young man was apprehended with the criminals, tried, convicted, and sentenced to the famous chain gangs in Georgia's Reidsville Prison. He wrote to Rabbi Geffen, simply asking for matzah and a *Haggadah* for Passover. The rabbi quickly packed up what was requested, along with some Passover food prepared by his wife, and sent it off. It was several weeks before he received a response. The prisoner explained that he had just been released from solitary confinement for refusing to work on Passover and had only now been given the package. He went on to compare the package to "manna from the heavens." The rabbi, along with his son Samuel, a lawyer, looked into this case. Through hard work, correspondence, and many contacts right up to the governor's office, they were able to secure the prisoner's release, but not before this innocent man had spent over a year in jail.

Rabbi Geffen had eight children. When he first arrived in Atlanta in 1910 from Lithuania, there was no Hebrew school, so he educated both his sons and his daughters. As they grew older and married, the only one to remain in Atlanta was their son Louis, an attorney, with his wife, Anna, and their son David. Out of the eighteen grandchildren, David was the only one who not only saw his grandparents often, but studied with his grandfather every day after school. David had originally been enrolled in the synagogue's Hebrew school. When he reached the age of 11, his father was not happy with his progress and decided that David would be better served if he studied with his grandfather, who had a wonderful way of teaching.

It was also time to start preparing David for his Bar Mitzvah. Rabbi Geffen studied the Torah portion with Rashi (commentary) every day with his grandson. David's father, Louis, took on the pleasurable role of teaching his son the Haftorah and how to daven. They also decided that David should deliver two speeches on the special day—one in Hebrew and one in

English. The Hebrew one was written by Rabbi Geffen, and all of the boys in the family recited it. The English speech was written by David's parents, and all he had to do was memorize it.

The best part of the Bar Mitzvah was the cousins. They all came! This occasion was also just one of two times that David was on the *bimah* with his grandfather. (The second time occurred when he received the Jewish Boy Scout *Ner Tamid* award, presented by his grandfather.) David breezed through the preparations for his Bar Mitzvah. His whole life revolved around Judaism, so he felt no real pressure and no fear. This was just another milestone. When it came time for the speeches, David spoke first. He flew through the Hebrew. Then for the English speech, he blanked out, had to adlib the whole thing, and afterward couldn't tell you what he had said. Since there were so many dignitaries from the family in the congregation that day, many of them were asked to say a few words. His grandfather spoke next in Yiddish; both uncles, who were rabbis, spoke in English; his grandfather's brother, a cantor from Savannah, spoke in Hebrew; and then the younger rabbi in the congregation made the last speech in English.

The atmosphere in a southern synagogue is different because of the language—both the English and the Yiddish are sometimes spoken with a drawl. The melodies are a combination of Lithuanian *nusach* (tunes) and Young Israel musical teachings. *Adon Olam,* the last song of the service, is sung to the tune of "Dixie," and the Confederate flag was displayed until the 1960s. While up North, bagels and lox are common fare, two typical foods served during a southern Bar Mitzvah meal are succotash and okra. Another custom was the carved ornaments that adorned the Bar Mitzvah cake. And, of course, everyone drank Coca Cola. Rabbi Geffen not only gave the first legitimate *hechsher* (stamp of approval) deeming Coke kosher for Passover and everyday use, he also suggested what ingredients to substitute for the previously used nonkosher ones back in 1935. Being a man of his word, Rabbi Geffen never revealed the secret of the special formula.

There was a long-standing relationship between Emory University and the Geffen family. Emory had a tradition of classes being held on Saturdays. After World War I, Rabbi Geffen went to talk to the administrator of the school, Bishop Candler, and asked for a special exemption on behalf of his son and another young Jewish boy. He asked that they be allowed to attend the university without being punished for refusing to violate the Sabbath. They walked to school, so there was no problem there, and it was arranged that they did not have to take notes or tests on Saturdays. Between 1919 and 1935, six Geffen children attended Emory. They received eight degrees, the most of any one family in the history of the school. David was the only one of the next generation to attend Emory. Because he lived at home, he continued to study with his grandfather every day until he graduated from college.

David followed in his grandfather's footsteps and became a rabbi. At his graduation/ordination from the Jewish Theologi-cal Seminary of America, one of the guest speakers was Rabbi Tobias Geffen. There was some dissension among the Ameri-can Orthodox leaders that an Orthodox rabbi would partici-pate in an ordination at a Conservative school. At the age of 95, Rabbi Geffen paid no heed to such unproductive criticism.

Rabbi David Geffen, after receiving his Ph.D., in addition to his *smicha* (rabbinical degree), served as a chaplain in the army during the "gearing up stage" for the Vietnam War. He went on to serve as spiritual leader in a congregation in Wilmington, Delaware, for the next seven years. And then, as in his Bar Mitzvah *parasha, Lech Lecha,* when God told Abraham to "Go to a land that I will show you," Rabbi David, his wife, Rita, and their three children moved to Israel. He wrote for the World Zionist Organization Press Syndicate and the *Jerusalem Post.* As a pulpit rabbi, his sermons were heard by the members of his congregation. As a writer, his work was read all over the world.

In Israel he conceived the idea of writing the "American Heritage *Haggadah.*" It is a fusion of American history and the Passover story, a traditional *Haggadah,* complemented with photos, cartoons, letters, and drawings from America's histori-cal observance of the holiday—Americana Judaica. It's a unique compilation that brings the holiday to life. During the seders, we not only read about but are also supposed to feel as if we were taken out of bondage and given our freedom. It is no wonder that David Geffen wrote a *Haggadah*, because the lessons of freedom and equality were learned firsthand from a gentle, kind, and tolerant man who lived to be 99 years old and who taught by example. David Geffen learned about equality by being treated equally and witnessing others experience the same respect. In a time when civil laws did not protect the unalienable rights of all men, David Geffen was reared by a man who followed a different set of rules.

9

CHILDREN OF CHERNOBYL

May 4, 1999

Technical information was provided by Victor Goretsky, a former radiation inspector and liquidator at Chernobyl. Information on Children of Chernobyl was provided by Devorah Cohen and Sarah Junik.

During the Holocaust, Jewish parents who had some idea of the fate that awaited them as they prepared for deportation pleaded and begged with friends and neighbors to take their children. As heartbreaking as it was to wrench themselves away from their children, they opted for separation since it was a matter of survival. There are still Jewish parents today who find themselves in the same position of pleading for someone to take their children.

In March 1986, abnormal levels of radioactive isotopes were detected at the Chernobyl Nuclear Power Plant. This abnormality was reported to the proper authorities. For his trouble, the inspector making the report was fired and the information was concealed. On April 26, 1986, the number 4 reactor at the power plant exploded, shooting flames into the sky that could be seen miles away. Most of the neighboring communities could see the inferno, but had no idea of its implications. The authorities chose to keep the effects of contamination a secret in the beginning, all the while packing up and moving their own families as far away as they could go. May Day, May 1st, was a lively holiday in the former Soviet Union, and all of the townsfolk came out to either participate in the parades or watch the festivities. Proud fathers danced around with their toddlers held high above the crowd, on their shoulders. Street vendors sold food and trinkets. And all the while, the people were being contaminated by an invisible killer, radiation.

This was the worst nuclear disaster in history, yet Chernobyl is not a household name. Even fifty years after the event, the name "Hiroshima" still invokes horror. Yet Chernobyl is yesterday's news, and the name brings only a brief flicker of recognition, if any. But not so for the residents of the surrounding areas—Chernobyl is a household name. The people are sick, dying, and scared. The air, water, and soil are all contaminated, and it will be decades, if ever, before the environment will be free from contamination. The sarcophagus that was used to cap the damaged reactor is cracked and continues to leak harmful pollutants.

Chernobyl in the Ukraine is near the larger city of Kiev and the border of Belarus. The city of Pripyat, which was built at the same time as the reactors, adjacent to the power plant, became a ghost town. The children of the surrounding communities almost immediately started developing symptoms. They reported leg cramps, vomiting, hair loss, and blindness. Their desperate parents, seeking medical attention, found only brick walls. At the children's hospital in Kiev, the equipment was antiquated, the staff shorthanded, and the medications insufficient. Then the cancers started. Hundreds and thousands of children were diagnosed with thyroid cancer and leukemia. The rate of thyroid cancer was 200 times the normal incidence. Babies were being born in record numbers with birth defects. And there was very little help. In the rural communities surrounding the power plant, some of the people still traveled by horse and buggy. Yet no matter how they traveled, there was nowhere to go for help.

The former Soviet Union has a long history of torturous anti-Semitism. In the late 1700s the Russian government forced the Jews from all over Russia to move to the Jewish Pale of Settlement, thus creating a ghetto near Kiev. The Russians didn't want Jews in their midst, so they herded Jews into a secluded area. Having all the Jews in one place made the repeated pogroms and attacks convenient and more frequent. In the late 1880s and 1890s, pogroms were so prevalent that they prompted one of the largest mass immigrations of Jews from Russia into the United States. If you lay a map of the contaminated area over a map of the former Pale of Settlement, you will find they are one and the same. At the time of the explosion, more than 500,000 Jews lived in that area. And tens of thousands of Jewish children have been affected by radioactive fallout.

For years, the parents' cries went unheeded. Then in 1990, the Lubavitcher Rebbe, Rabbi Menachem Mendel Schneerson, instructed the Chabad Youth Organization in Israel to create the Children of Chernobyl Project. The children were evacuated from their homeland and transported to Israel. The first priority was to provide the best medical care—to get the children healthy. However, the staff members at CCOC (Chabad's Children of Chernobyl) knew that they were not just dealing with an illness, they were taking care of a child. Some of the children were frightened to be away from their parents for the first time. Imagine a first-time sleep-away camp experience. Compound that with a strange language, different customs, and unfamiliar people. But the program functions not only to aid in the wellness of the children, but also to promote their overall well-being. The staff acts like surrogate parents, tucking the children in at night, taking care of bruised knees, and providing lots of hugs. The children stay at CCOC from one to three years, with the ultimate goal being to reunite the children with their families.

There is a strong educational component to the program, both secular and religious. Some of the children arrive with some Jewish background, while others know little about their heritage. It was illegal to practice Judaism under communism, so even though times have changed, there was no place to learn back home. CCOC has separate campuses for the boys and the girls.

And every year, a Bar Mitzvah ceremony is held for the boys who turn 13. Each boy has a chance to celebrate around the time of his own birthday, and then a huge communal celebration is given for all of them. The big event happens on the holiday of L'ag Bomer, which is a traditional time for outings and fun activities. Most of the boys prepare for this day; however, two of the eighteen for this year's celebration arrived just two weeks before the group Bar Mitzvah. There was an excited caravan to the *Kotel* (the Western Wall in Jerusalem), where all of the boys put on *tefillin* and read from the Torah. Then they were taken to a hotel in Jerusalem for a festive buffet, dancing, music, and entertainment. No Jewish event would be complete without speeches, and there were plenty of them. Several of the boys and their teachers addressed the crowd, and then Mrs. Sonia Borchefsky, one of the parents who has been reunited with her son, got up and said a few words.

> Those of you who have not been to Kiev or other places where these boys come from cannot imagine what a dream come true this is. It is even more than we ever dreamed of. That our boys would one day be safe and healthy and enjoying a Jewish celebration like this with so many people who care about them—it's more than a dream come true. It's a miracle.

In September 2000, CCOC welcomed its 2,000th child. Over 1,400 children and their families have been reunited in Israel. The Chabad's Children of Chernobyl project is the only one in the world to permanently evacuate Chernobyl's victims. In addition, it sends medical personnel into Kiev to train the local doctors and nurses in how to treat the deadly diseases that are the effect of radioactive contamination. All of this work comes at a price and is supported only by personal donations. The Bar Mitzvah ceremonies are paid for by patrons, who often are celebrating the same ritual with their own children. When CCOC first started in 1990, the organization was grateful to get the first few children out safely. Since then, over 50 airlifts have been made from the contaminated areas. Once the goal of 2,000 was reached, a new and higher one immediately replaced it. The goal is now to evacuate 3,000 children and then in turn to reunite them with their families.

Chernobyl was a senseless, manmade, preventable disaster. At the International Conference: One Decade After Chernobyl, held in Vienna, Austria, "April 26, 1986" is listed as the most serious accident in the history of the nuclear industry. "Approximately 200,000 liquidators worked in the region of Chernobyl during the period of 1986–1987, when the exposures were the most significant. In total, some 600,000–800,000 persons took part in the clean-up activities to 'liquidate' the consequences of the Chernobyl accident."* In addition to the thousands of illnesses and deaths, "there are significant non-radiation-related health disorders and symptoms, such as anxiety, depression, and various psychosomatic disorders attributable to mental stress among the population of the region."* On December 15, 2000, almost a decade and a half after the disaster, the final reactor was shut down. It took just the flick of a switch, but the memory, as well as the physical and psychological effects, will linger for an undetermined length of time.

When Jews were forced to live in the ghetto of the Pale of Settlement, in spite of the poverty almost every Jewish boy and girl could read and write. Kept secluded and cloistered, the culture of the community thrived and a social welfare system

---

*"International Conference: One Decade After Chernobyl," Summing Up the Consequences of the Accident, Vienna, Austria, April 8–12, 1996, Highlights of Conclusions and Recommendations, pages 1, 5.

was created. With outside influences constantly trying to eradicate and annihilate the Jewish people, we have made an art form out of survival. Faced with a modern enemy, this time an invisible one, a Jewish agency has risen to the occasion to get our children out. Now, when anguished parents make their plea for help, someone is listening.

To contact the Children of Chernobyl:

Chabad's Children of Chernobyl
535 Fifth Avenue, Suite 301
New York, NY 10017
Tel: 212-681-7800; 888-883-1800
Fax: 212-681-9330
Email: onebyone@ccoc.net
www.ccoc.net

10

HEAR O' ISRAEL

Michael Kretman—July 24, 1999
(written by Michael Kretman)

Michael Kretman is working on a Master of Science degree in Jewish Studies at Spertus College in Chicago. He has applied to ALEPH, the Jewish Renewal movements program, for ordination as a Jewish Chaplain. He continues to teach Hebrew in the Temple Hebrew and Sunday School and has a part-time position with Kentucky Refugee Ministries working with immigrants who have HIV/AIDS.

Photo by Charles Lipschutz Photography

"Shema Yisrael, Adonai Eloheinu, Adonai Echad!"

The first time I saw those words, those beautiful Hebrew words, I was 16 or 17 years old. There they were! In an article on Judaism in a *Time* or *Newsweek* magazine, a picture of a Bar Mitzvah boy, all of 13 years old, wearing a yarmulke, wrapped in a prayer shawl, using a *yad* to point to the words in the Torah scroll as he chanted for his Bar Mitzvah.

I probably didn't even know at that point that Hebrew is read from the right to the left. I certainly didn't know the Hebrew letters. But the sound of those words as I read the transliteration reached into my heart, into my soul! I felt an immediate connection to a very personal, loving God.

I memorized those words and repeated them to myself many times every day. I felt a strong connection, a pull toward anything and everything Jewish. Many times in the twenty years since I converted to Judaism, I've read that most Jews by Choice feel they always had a Jewish soul, they just had to find it and to reconnect with it and with the people of Israel. Reading the *Shema* in that magazine led me back to the God of Israel, back to Judaism.

I suppose when you are 16 years old, you can never really visualize yourself as a middle-aged person. Certainly, when I was 16, I never imagined that one day I would be a middle-aged man. I turned 44 years old the day before my Bar Mitzvah. I had converted to Judaism in 1979, at a Conservative *shul*. Six months after converting, I met the person who would become my spouse. But a month after meeting him, I moved to San Francisco, which had been in the planning for months.

While in San Francisco I joined a Reform temple, Sha'ar Zahav, which has an outreach to the gay and lesbian community. At this temple I found my Jewish identity and voice. I was very involved in the *va'ad*. But as life works, I moved back to Louisville eight months later. Deney and I got back together and have been together ever since.

I returned to the Conservative *shul* in Louisville, but had difficulty fitting in. I was returning from a positive gay atmosphere to a very straight, family-oriented congregation. After several years of working at fitting in and having the women there try to "fix me up," I stopped going to *shul*. Being in an interfaith relationship also made it difficult to be "fully" Jewish.

For a long period of time I went to church with my partner, where we were treated as a full and equal couple in the congregation. I even "joined" his church, although I did not believe the doctrine.

In 1990, I was diagnosed with AIDS-related cancer. I felt the pull back to Judaism, but did nothing about it. Then, in 1992, I moved to Washington, D.C., for four months to participate in a clinical drug trial at the National Cancer Institute. While there, I looked at attending the gay/lesbian temple in D.C., but did not. I was afraid that I would not be accepted because I had turned my back on Judaism for many years. I did not know whether one could return to Judaism as a convert because I had turned my back on Judaism.

In 1995, with the help of the Internet, I found that when one converts it is as if one were born Jewish. Once a Jew, always a Jew. That made me feel very good. I began reading and making new contacts, mostly on the Internet. I made an appointment to speak with a rabbi at a local Reform temple. So, I went. She was wonderful—welcoming, friendly, and encouraging. She reiterated what I had learned about returning to Judaism and "once a Jew . . ." Then came the hard part—telling my partner about my desire to leave his church and return to the faith that I had loved since I was about 16 years old. We had several uncomfortable discussions, but he ultimately said, "Belief is a very personal thing. You have to believe what you believe!"

I joined The Temple and slowly got involved. I joined (rejoined) the gay Jewish group in town. My spouse attends services with me, goes to monthly dinners of the gay Jewish group, goes to the temple seder, and supports my return to college to work on my master's degree in Jewish studies.

When I spoke to the rabbi about returning to Judaism, I told her I didn't even have my conversion certificate to "prove" I was Jewish. She didn't care about that, but said I might want to have a Bar Mitzvah to mark my return to Judaism. The thought scared me, and I put it out of my mind.

But then a friend, who is gay and 33 years old, had his Bar Mitzvah at The Temple. He spoke movingly about his lack of Jewish life and education while growing up and the struggles with his coming to terms with being gay as part of his D'var Torah. Many people were crying. At that point, I decided, "If he can do it, I can."

So, I began studying with Rabbi Joe Rooks Rapport, the husband of the first rabbi I spoke with. He is an excellent teacher. We proceeded quickly. My hardest thing was learning the *trup*. I could not grasp the way he taught it. The woman rabbi, Rabbi Gaylia Rooks, volunteered to teach me the *trup*, which helped greatly.

This whole experience of converting to Judaism, choosing to become a Bar Mitzvah, and having the schedule work out so that my Torah portion was the *Shema* is called *bashert* in Yiddish. *Bashert* means "fate" or "destiny." The *Shema* led me to the God of Israel, to Judaism, so it is only good and right that I chanted the *Shema* for my Torah portion.

Moses spoke the words of the *Shema* and *V'ahavta* to his people just before his death. God refused to let him enter into the Land of Israel, so Moses reviewed the laws and commandments of the covenant established between God and the Israelites.

The *Shema* is called the "watch word of our faith." It is a proclamation of our central belief that there is one God, not many, and that God is indivisible. God's dominion is without limit, boundless in space, endless in time. The final word of the *Shema*, *Echad*, means "one, alone, unique." Saying that *Adonai* (God) is unique means that God is totally different from all creatures on earth and, therefore, no creature can be compared to God. God has no physical limitations, no definition! God is not mortal, not limited by human frailties, and not reducible to stone, wood, or metal.

The *Shema* is among the first Hebrew words taught to Jewish children and the last words recited at the time of death. Each time we recite the *Shema*, we re-enter the covenant of ritual and ethical commandments, pledging ourselves to God and to the belief in the ethical monotheism we call Judaism.

The second section of my Torah portion begins with *V'ahavta*, which means, "You shall love." When I think about the words and meaning of this prayer, I wonder why Moses began by saying, "You shall love the Lord your God." Since we understand love to be an emotional feeling, I wonder how the Israelites could be "commanded" to love God. What did Moses mean by "love," and does it mean the same thing today as it did then?

Our society tends to use *love* for everything these days. We love our country and our flag! We love pizza and baseball, and we love certain movies and books. As evidenced by my yarmulke and invitations, you know I love the color purple! We love our cars and our pets. Jews love Torah and Israel! But where does the love of God figure into this equation? How do we know that we love God and that God loves us?

I see God's love for us in the wonderful diversity created of this world—diversity of people, languages, and cultures. Night becomes day. Winter gives way to summer. There are countless species of animals, fish, reptiles, and insects. And foods! Wow, God loves us so much that we even have foods like cheesecake! All those different tastes, textures, colors, and smells.

The world is made up of barren, arid deserts and lush tropical rain forests . . . mountains and valleys . . . oceans, lakes, and rivers! How can anyone not believe there is a God and that God loves us? But what can we give God? How can we show our love for God? Being limited by our human, mortal existence, we can only use earthly parallels in expressing love for God. Loving God means honoring the diversity of God's creation, treating every human being with respect, and acting honestly, justly, and kindly toward everyone. Also, to love God means knowing the joy of generosity. Love leads to giving, to sharing our creativity, our resources, and our wealth with others. Love for God, as with human beings, is an achievement attained throughout a lifetime, not something that occurs in an instant.

I had the awe-inspiring honor of reading from a Torah scroll that had been saved from the Holocaust. Reading from the scroll was incredibly moving for me. I was reminded of the people who had read from this scroll, who were murdered because they were not like the majority of the population, because their beliefs, manner of dress, or traditions were different. This is particularly relevant today because of the increasingly frequent acts of hate we've seen recently. Three synagogues were burned and a gay couple murdered in California. In a Chicago suburb, six Jews were shot! One of those men, Dr. Dean Bell, is my academic adviser at Spertus College. Although he was shot six times, he survived. Now, he must endure months of healing and rehabilitation. But even more painful for him will be the emotional ramifications of being a victim, singled out simply because he is Jewish. In this same murderous rampage, an African-American man and an Asian man were killed. And even closer to us here in Kentucky, we are hearing reports that a soldier at Fort Campbell was beaten to death by other soldiers because he was gay.

All of these incidents indicate a rising climate of hatred and a rejection of God's diversity of creation. But as Jews, we are called repeatedly to re-establish the covenant through the *Shema* and *V'ahavta*, to love God and God's world in all its variety.

11

CHAYEI SARAH

Martin David Kessel, Ph.D.—November 4, 1950
Oxford Hebrew Congregation
Johannesburg, South Africa
(written by Martin Kessel)

Dr. Martin Kessel has a Ph.D. in microbiology (from Hebrew University) and is working in basic research at the National Cancer Institute, NIH. He is also a Professor Emeritus of the Hebrew University of Jerusalem, where he was a faculty member of the Hebrew University-Hadassah Medical School for twenty-five years.

Mine was a very typical Northern Suburbs of Johannesburg Bar Mitzvah, after the fashion at that time. My preparation for the Bar Mitzvah took place over the period of a year, meeting with Cantor Dov Propis at his home approximately once a week. At the age of 12 years old I was blessed with a really beautiful voice that Cantor Propis sought to exploit to the fullest and prepared me to sing my *parasha* and Haftorah with cantorial and operatic flair. I don't really remember the exact *trup*, but do remember on several occasions the embellishments I was encouraged to add to certain of the *trup* notes. I believe that my singing did not disappoint the crowded *shul* on that *Shabbat*—if I think hard, I can conjure up the memory of a hushed congregation listening to the Bar Mitzvah boy of that Shabbat *singing* "like a canary." My parents were naturally very proud of me, and I remember so many people telling me how beautifully I had sung my *Maftir* and Haftorah.

As was the custom at that time, I had a 78 rpm recording made of my Bar Mitzvah, which allowed me also to appreciate that indeed the singing was something special. I in fact remember that at the recording session, we had to do more than one "take" because the recording engineer had not realized how good my voice was and had on the first attempt used inferior recording material that had failed to bring out the full range of my pre-adult voice. One of the great friends of our family was a famous teacher of opera who had come from Russia to live in South Africa and she, too, was very impressed with my voice, but tried to convince me not to over-exert the voice lest it not survive through my adolescence. It, in fact, did not.

Oxford Synagogue in those days was at the heart of the very affluent Jewish community of the Northern Suburbs of Johannesburg, which had by then moved away from the traditionally Jewish areas that were closer to the commercial center of Johannesburg. The Oxford Hebrew congregation was Orthodox—back in the 1950s, Conservatism had not yet appeared as a separate religious movement in South Africa— but certain elements of tradition were very much what one would find in a modern-day Conservative congregation. To be sure, the Orthodox custom of the separation of men and women was enforced, with the ladies occupying seats "upstairs," albeit not behind a *mechitzah*. Dress at synagogue was very formal, and the women especially would use the occasion to show off the latest fashions. I have a strong recollection of a very well-dressed congregation on the day of my Bar Mitzvah.

Following services and *Kiddush* at the synagogue, a formal luncheon was held at our house, where a large marquee had been erected covering the entire front lawn.

What do I remember of the presents I received? The usual surfeit of books that fit very well into our house, which was already well-endowed with shelf upon shelf of books, running the gamut from contemporary fiction to political radicalism. Both of my parents were avid readers—particularly my mother, who did not work and basically led a very leisurely life of golf and playing cards with her wide circle of friends. My father, who was a dentist, was very politically conscious, which was reflected in his library of books and the ever-present *Time* magazine on the night table next to his bed.

I certainly remember receiving a large number of checks as presents, and some of these were very handsome sums from aunts, uncles, and grandparents since on my mother's side I was the oldest grandchild and on my father's side the second oldest. A rather sad memory is of my maternal grandfather, who was too ill to come to the service and the reception—I remember making the special visit to him on that *Shabbat*. He passed away from his illness exactly one week later.

It's hard to believe that all this took place forty-nine years ago, and I certainly look forward to celebrating the 50th anniversary of my Bar Mitzvah next year on *Shabbat Parashat Hayei Sara*—November 25th, 2000.

12

ALL THE WORLD'S A STAGE

Ron Rifkin—November 3, 1951

Rifkin's career has spanned several decades on television and in the movies. He joined the cast of One Day at a Time *as Nick Handris, Bonnie Franklin's love interest. In* The Trials of Rose O'Grady, *Rifkin broke new ground playing the Orthodox Jewish boss of an attorney, played by Sharon Gless. It was the first time on prime time that a Jewish character was not portrayed as a stereotype. His silver screen credits are varied and lengthy, with recent appearances in* L.A. Confidential, The Negotiator, *and* Keeping the Faith. *It is, however, on stage that he feels most at home and has realized most of his critical acclaim. His performance as Isaac Geldhart in* The Substance of Fire, *described as "letter perfect," won him the Drama Desk Award. And in 1998, Rifkin won a Tony Award for his brilliant work in* Cabaret. *Rifkin can be seen weekly on ABC's* Alias.

Abraham Cumsky had no head for business. He much preferred to bury his nose in an ancient Hebrew text and leave less spiritual pursuits to his wife—mainly, the running of the kosher butcher shop that bore their name.

Even with his lack of interest and participation, the butcher shop developed a reputation for selling only the best cuts of meat. If the brisket was tender and the cholent tasty, the beef had been purchased at Cumsky's. Though his skills for commerce were somewhat lacking, he was nonetheless a prolific "producer." He fathered fourteen children.

At the tender age of 16, Abraham married his beloved Frieda while they still lived in Russia. After giving birth to three sons, Frieda left him a widower only eight years later. Single parenthood was not an option in the late nineteenth century for a man with three young sons. Subsequently, Abraham married Frieda's 14-year-old cousin, Rebecca. She was only slightly older than her oldest stepson. Several years later, along with his child bride, three sons, and two new daughters, Abraham Cumsky left Russia for the New World. They entered a port in Philadelphia and eventually settled in the Williamsburg section of Brooklyn.

And the family grew! Even in those days, fourteen children were regarded as not only substantial, but remarkable. One disadvantage of such a large family is that the younger children knew their mother only as an old woman. Their older sisters had to assume the maternal responsibilities of taking them to school and talking to the teachers.

As the children became adults, they left the "nest," but didn't go too far. Many of the siblings married and rented apartments in the same building as their parents. Others moved only a few blocks away. Rebecca and Abraham's brood multiplied exponentially as the next generation was born.*

It was into this multigenerational expanded family that Saul Rifkin was born. Born to Miriam, the thirteenth Cumsky child, and Hy Rifkin, Saul entered a world where the sound of Yiddish wafted above the din of mothers yelling out of windows and children playing on the street. Where the address read "America," but it might have been Eastern Europe, for all of the Old World dress and customs. And where the *Shabbos* settled

---

*The background genealogical information was provided by Yolana Cumsky Stern and Guitelle Cumsky.

over the insulated neighborhood like a magical fog, closing off the "other world" and leaving only the smells of cholent simmering all night, the lights of *Shabbos* candles, and the beautiful music heralding in and escorting out this special day.

Saul Rifkin delighted in his surroundings—his close, abundant family; the *bubbe* and the *zeide* nearby; and the Orthodox lifestyle that influenced his every move. He went to the Torah V'das Yeshiva on Wilson Street and later transferred to the Yeshiva of Central Queens when his family moved to Forest Hills after the birth of his younger brother Arnold. Though separated only by seven years, the brothers were reared in two different worlds. Saul's formative years were cocooned in the midst of aunts, uncles, and cousins, in a comforting cacophony of Yiddish interspersed with shards of broken English. He was schooled in a full-day yeshiva where the classes were presented in a melodious singsong. And he was reared in a *shul* with ornate seats for the rabbi, a blue velvet curtain that covered the silver-adorned *Sefer Torahs*, and a *bimah* in the middle with seats facing on three sides. Arnold, on the other hand, grew up in Forest Hills in a much more assimilated environment, where his Dad's focus turned toward business rather than religion, and he attended a public school with an after-school Talmud Torah program. And they now attended the Queens Jewish Center on 65th Street, which had previously been a fish/butcher shop and held little of the aura of their previous place of worship.

Saul, a bright young man, was accelerated in school and skipped a year. He found himself the valedictorian of his eighth-grade class at the age of 12. With this title came the privilege of writing and then delivering a speech in Hebrew on graduation night. He spent a great deal of time on his speech and with much pride showed it to the principal. Rabbi Charney patently dismissed this young man's ideas, not to mention his hard work. Rather than discuss and revise Saul's speech, he rewrote it and without a second thought expected Saul to pass off this pretense as if the words were his own. Saul couldn't lie. And besides that, the words were boring and pretentious and he could not bring himself to memorize, let alone recite, them. So, he followed the only recourse he felt available to him. Not permitted to deliver his own speech and refusing to present the meaningless prattle of his principal, he stood in front of his classmates, parents, and teachers and spoke in Hebrew doubletalk, isolated words and phrases chained together with inflection and a touch of hand waving for effect. The rabbis were furious. The other students thought it was funny. And most of the parents didn't realize anything was wrong. In a way, this was the first time Saul had turned down a part that he thought wasn't right for him.

In spite of the debacle of the graduation, Saul went on to high school and began to prepare for his Bar Mitzvah. He decided that he wanted to do everything. Since he already knew how to daven, he did not have to prepare for that, but he devoted the better part of a year studying with Mr. Uzilaner, a blind teacher. Saul went to his house three times a week and was always greeted with that "old people's house smell." After a few minutes, he got used to it, but the next time he entered the house, the first thing that hit him was the smell.

For the Bar Mitzvah, in order to accommodate the mostly *Shomer Shabbas* relatives from Williamsburg, Miriam and Hy had to make sleeping arrangements for the extended family. Having arrived before sundown the previous day, everyone walked to the Queens Jewish Center on this chilly November morning. The Bar Mitzvah boy, dressed in his new blue suit, pink shirt, and blue suede shoes, looked cherubic. With his signature sparkly dark brown eyes, characteristic of many of the Cumskys, he was ready for this day. He woke up excited and was not disappointed.

It was a magical day. He loved the music, the ritual, and the singing. Uncle Benny and Uncle Murray, with their sweet voices, joined him and his father on the *bimah*. Saul was so happy, he kept looking up at his mother. He felt as if he was in heaven. It was a great performance, filled with drama and magic, God and history. And family—so much family. The morning was crowned when he was showered with sweetness, pelted by little brown bags that his mother had so lovingly filled with penny candy.

During his early youth Saul had experienced an Old World lifestyle. As he got older, he watched as his parents, uncles, aunts, and eventually his cousins bought into the "American Dream" of going into business and looking for success. It was as if there had been one "pot" when they all started out, and as the sisters or brothers succeeded, they helped each other. They understood business, and that was the aspiration they held for their children. Acceptable exceptions were the coveted professions of law or medicine.

Saul always knew that he would be a performer, but was never sure where that idea/drive/push came from. He had no exposure to theater or the arts. Movies were occasionally shown at home on a rented projector. When he was little, his aunt had a curtain that separated her living area from her sleeping quarters. He would tell his cousins to "announce him," and he would bound out from behind the curtain and deliver some kind of a performance. Saul wasn't athletic, but he was smart and he could sing. His father would bring home records like "Pinchas the Peddler." After listening to them once or twice, Saul had them memorized. His father, Hy, would then drive him over to the in-laws house so he could sing for "the *bubbe* and the *zeide.*"

Saul graduated from NYU in the Bronx and at first made a pretext of majoring in premedical studies. Realizing that this dream of his parents would never come true, he boldly announced that he was going to become an actor. He never faced the rejection of Al Jolson in "The Jazz Singer," but at the same time, his parents were surprised, disappointed, and scared. They weren't hostile, they were worried. Okay, so he wouldn't be a doctor, but where was the accounting degree to "fall back on"? The Rifkins were as supportive as they could be, as their son entered a world that they knew nothing about. Hy was a furrier. He could tell you all about coats. But theater, the stage, drama—this was foreign territory. Then there was the name change! Saul was a perfectly good name, but he told them "Ron," taken from his sister's name, Ronnie Lee, was much more euphonious. Yet at the same time, his family felt great pride that Ron was well educated and spoke English with a flair. It gave Hy great pleasure to hear his son spout off not only in mellifluous English, but also in French.

Except for living room performances in the *bubbe's* house, the Rifkins had never seen their son on stage. It was during summer theater, 1960, in Fishkill, New York, when Hy and Miriam first saw their oldest appear in a production of *The Boyfriend.* Also in that play appeared another young lady from Brooklyn, Barbra Streisand, who even back then demonstrated a drive unparalleled by other members of the cast.

In a moment of romanticizing reverie, Rifkin started "free associating" memories of his childhood at a small party with friends. His central theme was the synagogue. He described the sanctuary with its intricately carved front stage, the blue velvet curtain, the Torahs with their sterling crowns, the central *bimah* with seats facing on three sides, and the women upstairs. His hostess, carried away with the visualization, exclaimed, "That's the Globe Theatre—that's Elizabethan theater! Of course, that's why you became an actor!" There it was—so close, he couldn't see it. He had looked for that elusive spark from his childhood that had propelled him into this exciting, sometimes melancholy, but rewarding career. He had felt it on his Bar Mitzvah—all the beauty, drama, magic, and music of the synagogue. And consciously or not, he has taken all of those qualities and packed them into his performances. It was a Williamsburg *shteble* that spawned a Broadway actor— with the help of a family of fourteen.

13

AN UNEXPECTED BAR MITZVAH

Stanley Smith—Spring, 1981

In spite of the name, Stanley Smith is Jewish. Despite a name that is more generic than Semitic, Stanley tends to dot his conversation with the few words of Yiddish he learned growing up in the East End of London. Being a bit of a wise guy, he relishes the shocked expression of his listeners when they hear mamaloshon *delivered with a Cockney accent out of a man named Smith.*

G rowing up within the sound of Bow Bells, Stanley had a very basic Hebrew education that was abruptly interrupted by the onset of the war. Like most London city kids, he was evacuated briefly to the country. His father was drafted into the army. Stanley's 13th birthday fell during the thick of the war, so there was no question of making a Bar Mitzvah for him. When the war was over, Stan was of age to join the Royal Air Force. His dad, in turn, came home from the British Army. When Stan was in the Air Force, he came home one weekend on leave to attend his brother Arnold's Bar Mitzvah, who was five years his junior. At the time he resigned himself to the fact that life just kept getting in the way and there would be no Bar Mitzvah ceremony for him. He teased that he expected Arnold to share the gifts.

He met and married his wife, Trudy, and they immigrated to the United States. Stanley set up his own trucking business, working out of Freeport, Long Island. They ran rigs up and down the eastern seaboard and as far west as Chicago. He developed a reputation for getting the job done, on time.

One day he got a phone call from someone whom he didn't know and had never heard of, which wasn't unusual in that business. The caller, in heavily accented English, asked if Stanley could pick up two loads of freight in South Carolina. One was to be delivered to New Jersey and the other one to Connecticut. The trucking business is done mostly on trust, so Stanley took down the particulars and dispatched two trucks to do the job. When the drivers returned with signed receipts that the merchandise had been delivered, Stanley called the businessman. He explained that he was going to be in Brooklyn within the next few days and would it be all right if he stopped by to clear up their business matters? The other man agreed, and Stanley found himself that Thursday on 21st Street near Eastern Parkway in Brooklyn.

Now, being in the transportation business, Stanley knew how impossible it was to find parking in Brooklyn. However, cruising down 21st Street, Stanley couldn't believe that there was a parking spot in front of the address he had been given. Looking back on it now, he realized that this visit was *bashert* (meant or fated to happen).

Stanley knocked on the door and was warmly greeted by a bearded Lubavitch rabbi wearing a yarmulke and *tzitzit*. The rabbi confirmed that the visitor was indeed Mr. Smith and, once in possession of the receipts, said he would get the check. He led Stan into his living room, which was decorated all around with photographs of famous rabbis. Not normally paranoid, Stan felt that these righteous men were staring directly at him. The rabbi seated himself across the table from Stan and was about to sign the check, when he casually asked,

"So, how is the trucking business?" Stanley answered, "It's *mishigas* [crazy]." Surprised to hear the Yiddish, the man shot back, "You're Jewish?" When Stan answered in the affirmative, the man quickly asked, "Did you put on *tefillin* this morning?" When Stanley answered that he had never put on *tefillin*, the check vanished off the table, as if a vacuum had sucked it down. The rabbi asked, "What about your Bar Mitzvah?" Stan responded, "Well, as a matter of fact, I was never Bar Mitzvahed. It was a wartime thing and we never got around to doing it."

Without a blink, out came the *siddur*. Out came the *tefillin*. There and then, the rabbi not only showed, but helped, Stanley put on the *tefillin*. In a touching, trusting way, Stanley stretched out his left arm, folded up his sleeve, and watched as this stranger expertly wound the leather strap seven times around his arm, affixing the box with the prayer inside to his upper arm, close to his heart. Next, Stan bent his head, so that the rabbi could bind the *tefillin* around his crown. The rabbi opened the *siddur* and instructed Stan to repeat the Hebrew prayer after him. Upon completion, the rabbi snapped the book shut and said, "Now, you are a Bar Mitzvah. For me, this is a double mitzvah. I helped you to lay *tefillin* and in the process Bar Mitzvahed you. This is the important part . . . the party is nothing."

Incredulous at the swiftness of the whole process, a stunned Stanley asked, "You mean, now I'm Bar Mitzvahed?" As if to confirm the legitimacy of the proceedings, the check reappeared. Stan bid the rabbi a fond farewell. He never heard from the man again.

Stan got in his car and laughed at what he'd had to do to get paid. He thought that the whole thing was a joke. That night he phoned his father and said, "Pop, guess what?" expecting his Dad to share in the joke. Only his father wasn't laughing. His father surprised him with his reply. "You know, Stanley, it was only a couple of days ago I was saying to your mother that the biggest regret I have was that you were not Bar Mitzvahed." Talk about timing. Stanley was surprised that forty years after the fact, he had made his father happy and took away the deepest regret his father ever had. So, in typical fashion, Stan asked, "Can I expect a check?" "I'll send you a pen," was his Dad's response.

Still not taking the whole thing seriously, Stan rang up his sister-in-law, who had a wonderful sense of humor, and he thought he could share the laugh with her. Only she didn't laugh either. "You got Bar Mitzvahed! It's about time. And since you had a Lubavitch rabbi, you were probably more Bar Mitzvahed than anyone else."

Because everyone in his family was offering praise rather than jeers, Stanley himself finally accepted the legitimacy of his Bar Mitzvah at the age of 53. At first, he just couldn't take it in. He thought about how many Bar Mitzvahs he had witnessed in *shul*, when the boy stood up and read from the Torah. But he realized that's just what he did, only he did it in someone's living room. The confirmation of his father and sister-in-law convinced him. Stanley still finds it ironic that he is God-fearing, but irreligious, and that an ultra-Orthodox Lubavitch rabbi performed his Bar Mitzvah ceremony. It was supposed to be a simple business deal. A transaction like thousands he had done before. With the drop of one casual word, a Yiddish expression that he had learned long ago, he changed the outcome of a routine encounter. On the way to pick up a check, Stanley Smith picked up so much more.

14

IT TAKES A VILLAGE

Aaron Nathaniel Weiss—December 26, 1998

An African proverb says, "It takes a village to raise a child." If one looked out from the bimah *at the crowd sharing in Aaron Weiss's Bar Mitzvah, the concept was evident. There sat the infectious disease specialist, the speech therapist, a whole host of teachers, and members of the medical community. These people were all invested in this day, but none so much as Rob and Linda Weiss, Aaron's parents.*

Having successfully adopted their first child, Saul, the Weisses were informed six years later that another little boy was available for them. They brought home Aaron Nathaniel at 2 months. At an appointment with the agency when the baby was 10 months old, they were told that Aaron's biological mother was found to be HIV-positive. She had been randomly tested, and the results made their way back to the agency. It was strongly suggested that Aaron be tested immediately. The first test came back that he was indeed HIV-positive, but the doctors thought that it might be a false positive because babies still retain some of their mothers' antibodies.

Nevertheless, the adoption agency instructed his parents to "give Aaron back," and the doctors would keep him until the inevitable happened. Back in 1986, there were no AIDS "cocktails" or more sophisticated medications. One drug, AZT, might be available, and the maximum lifespan of a child born HIV-positive was five years.

The Weisses couldn't believe their ears. They were being told to "give back" their baby. Aaron was their son, and they were in it for the long haul, as long as that might be. He was retested at 12, 18, and 24 months and with this final test, without question, was diagnosed as HIV-positive, with a compromised immune system. For that's what HIV does—the body is open season for developing infections. In spite of medical and legal problems, though, Aaron was officially adopted at the age of 2.

Being HIV-positive and having full-blown AIDS are not the same thing. When the T cells (one of the blood's white cells) drop below 500, the status changes. At first Aaron's T cell count was high, and everyone was optimistic. And when it dropped, without any "official declaration," his parents knew. At the age of 6, Aaron had AIDS.

Having a sick child is devastating and draining under the best of circumstances, but the family can usually count on a support system of relatives, clergy, and friends. Not so with AIDS—or at least, not back then. The climate was quite different. Ryan White was just emerging as a "champion," having won his own battle to return to school. Elizabeth Glaser had not yet become a spokesperson for pediatric AIDS. And the Ray family was looking for a new residence, because their home had just been burned down.

So the Weisses kept their secret. "We chose secrecy to protect our children and ourselves, but especially to protect Saul. He was in the first grade at the time, and we were terribly afraid if this came out he would be cast as a pariah," Linda proclaimed from the *bimah* during her *D'var Torah* on the day of the Bar Mitzvah.

She continued, "So, we kept our mouths shut, except we told my parents and a few close friends . . . who showed *rachmones* (compassion) and gave us *gemulit hasidim* (acts of loving kindness) and none of them revealed our secret."

IV and oral medication became a routine part of the day. Routine, if you call being hooked up for four and a half hours out of the day "routine." Routine, when minor ailments can mushroom into critical infections. Routine, when your life is ruled by the clock—time for this drug, stop that drug, hook up this, or flush that one out. Nurses became familiar fixtures in the house. In spite of this hectic routine, Rob and Linda tried to keep life as "normal" as possible. Whenever Aaron wasn't sick, he went to school. His parents were grateful that although his attendance record hasn't been perfect, he's been in more than he's been out. Because of a learning disability and a partial hearing loss, Aaron attends a special program. He is small for his age, so people tend to treat him as being less capable. In spite of that, he is inquisitive and forever taking things apart to see how they work. He has a great sense of humor and is musically gifted. He is extremely observant and compassionate, and people are attracted to him.

When Saul was preparing for his Bar Mitzvah, Aaron's medical staff was invited. Rob and Linda felt that since these dedicated people shared their sorrow and pain on a daily basis, they should also share in the family's joy. The family was swept up in the moment of Saul's Bar Mitzvah and proclaimed "Six years from now, we will be back together again to celebrate Aaron's Bar Mitzvah." The die was cast.

And, then at the age of 10, what his parents thought was a simple ear infection nearly ended Aaron's life. The infection turned out to be an uncontrollable fungus that started in his ear and ate its way inward toward his brain. It would kill him. The medical team said that if it couldn't be arrested, they didn't have much time left. Aaron had put up a brave fight. He'd already beaten the odds and lived longer than the maximum expected lifespan of five years. Out of all of the kids who had started with them at the pediatric AIDS clinic, only two had survived—Aaron and another little boy.

But like the "unsinkable Molly Brown," Linda Weiss refused to give up. Sleep-deprived and exhausted, she and her husband couldn't, wouldn't let go. She would do whatever she could to keep her son alive. But if they had only a short time left, she couldn't devote all of her energy to caring for Aaron and keep their secret at the same time. So, they went public. The story was published in the Denver *Jewish News*, after Linda participated on a panel about AIDS. And a miracle happened—most people supported them.

Most people, except for the school system. After spending a good deal of the winter in the hospital, fighting the infection, Aaron was not only well enough to go home, but he went back to school with only five days left in the year. At the end of his first day back, Linda went to pick him up. She was confronted by the principal in the hallway, amidst the pushing and shoving and the din of children's voices hurrying for the bus. "Is it true what I heard?" demanded the principal. When Linda answered in the affirmative, she was told that Aaron could not come back to school. Now, this was in the late '90s when all of the myths and misconceptions *should* have been clear to educational personnel.

Linda arrived home and shared this news with Rob. He immediately called the principal. After being told that Aaron was a "health risk," Rob asked him if the children were "having sex in the classroom or sharing needles on the playground" or if it was vice versa. The principal said that during the year, Aaron had presented with a nose bleed and that was dangerous. Rob reminded him that Aaron had taken care of the nosebleed himself, and that if the teacher had used "universal precautions," as she was supposed to, there would be no danger. The Weisses gave the school one day to get its policy on AIDS in order, and, true to their word, Aaron was back in school the day after that.

He beat the odds. He passed the anticipated lifespan and survived a near-fatal infection. The Weisses certainly had something to celebrate. What better way than the very public affirmation and acceptance of Aaron into *Am Yisroel*, the Jewish People? Because of Aaron's learning disabilities, they had to come up with an alternative way for him to learn the *brachot* and his *Maftir*. Since he is very musical (like his big brother, Saul), the *brachot* and his *parasha* were put on tape. There were seven of them. With the help of tutor Hil Margolin (a bankruptcy lawyer in real life), Aaron listened to those tapes over and over for more than a year. Even his Catholic home-health-care nurses heard him practice so many times that they were able to correct him if he said, "*B'nai* this" instead of "*B'nai* that."

Now, he also needed some type of visual clue, some pictoral representation of what he had to do. His speech therapist, Mary Lou Johnson, and his mother came up with an ingenious way for a nonreader to "read" his speech. Using a program on the computer called "Boardmaker" © by Mayer-Johnson, they put the *brachot*, *Maftir*, and Aaron's speech on paper. If the Hebrew word was "boo something," there was a picture of a ghost. If it was a *raq*, there was a picture of a rake. They incorporated some sign language, too. The sign for "thank you" is an open hand coming off the mouth—very easy to show on paper. For the part of his speech when he thanked friends and family, Aaron just looked down at the "prepared text," and this visual clue helped him to remember.

For the rest of the service, friends and family were recruited to take other *aliyot* and prayers. Linda's brother, Stephen, who had not read Torah in forty-three years, did one part. Her other brother, David, did another *aliyah*. Every single person who was invited had a vested interest and in some way was involved with Aaron's life.

Linda made the *tallisim* for her boys, Rob, Saul, and Aaron. These were beautifully designed. All of the participants, whether male or female, also wore special *kippot* or headcoverings. In this way, the participants were very easy to locate during the service. Aaron wore his special "Superman" tie on that day, because it helped him to feel less afraid. His friend Hil also sat on the *bimah* next to him, for moral support. With a little prompting, Aaron recited the *brachot* before and after the Torah reading, read his *Maftir*, and then said the *brachah* before the Haftorah.

His brother Saul was called up for this part. Without missing a note or taking his eyes from the paper, he gently reached out, drew Aaron in under the protective fold of his *tallis*, and held him while reciting the Haftorah for both of them.

Linda then continued with her *D'var Torah*. She was not nervous about the public speaking, but rather about the personal nature of the speech.

> This *sedra* deals with slavery, secrecy, disclosure, reconciliation, and the importance of having and being part of a community. It could serve as a metaphor for my family's life.
>
> In the portion, Joseph and Judah (both Jacob's sons) will meet and confront each other (in Egypt) for the first time in twenty-two years. Each of these men has a pretty checkered past.
>
> Keeping a secret and having AIDS is like being enslaved. You have chains around your tongue, for you can never say what is going on in your life. And having AIDS puts you in bondage to a schedule. There is no spontaneity to your life. You have to always think ahead. Do I have the right medicine? Is it the right temperature? Is it the right time?
>
> . . . here we stand today. We have truly lived this portion. We have been enslaved, kept a secret, disclosed it, and now have, are part of, and are reconciled to the Jewish community.

Aaron's Bar Mitzvah was more than a coming-of-age ceremony; it was a celebration of life. And many people helped him reach that point. It took the whole village. As for Aaron's prognosis—well, the family has been successful so far. This wasn't supposed to happen—it's been a miracle, so far. The family made it to the Bar Mitzvah, they made it to London, Aaron skis every winter and goes to camp every summer. It takes a little more than the village. Now, it's in God's hands.

15

FAITH

Pinchas Gutter—Autumn, 1944
(by Pinchas Gutter, as told to Arnine Cumsky Weiss)

Pinchas Gutter lives in Toronto, Canada. After a successful career in banking, he is now an honorary cantor and hospital chaplain, ministering to the aged. He continues to reunite annually with the "Boys".

I was born in Lodz, Poland, when the war broke out. I was 7 years old and had a twin sister called Sabina. She was my only sibling. My grandfather, Itche Meir, was one of the notables of the Jewish community in Lodz, and my father, Menachem Mendel, was a partner with my grandfather in the business, a wine-making concern. According to our tradition, the business was approximately 400 years old and was known as Zlote Grono in Polish, which means "Golden Grape."

When the Germans entered Lodz, within a few days they started rounding up the notables of the town, both Polish Christians and Polish Jews, priests, rabbis, lawyers, doctors, and nobility. My grandfather was on one of those lists. When the Gestapo game to take him away, they found him in bed, having just undergone a kidney operation. He was 78 years old, and my father was at his bedside. The Gestapo took my father down to our wine cellars, beat him up, and left him for dead. Later that same evening, the caretaker went down to the cellar and found that my father, despite being unconscious and badly beaten, was still breathing and alive. The caretaker carried him to our apartment, where he eventually recovered.

We then decided that it was too dangerous for us to stay in Lodz, and as we had an aunt—my father's sister, in Warsaw— we thought it best to go to her. Jews by that time were not allowed to use public transport, but my mother, Helena, was blonde and blue-eyed, and so were we, the two children. We thought it would be safe for us to go by train as Christian Poles. But my father had to walk from Lodz to Warsaw, and it took him about three months to arrive in Warsaw.

We were in the Warsaw ghetto together until approximately three to four weeks after the Warsaw ghetto uprising. We were there right through the fighting, hidden in a bunker. When the fighting subsided, we were betrayed by an informer.

> Threatened that if we did not evacuate the bunker immediately gas would be pumped in, we crept out to face the Germans who stood waiting for us, armed to the teeth, and shouting "Hande Hoch! Nicht Schiessen!" (Hands up! Do not shoot!)
>
> As we emerged, every person was patted down for arms that might be hidden under clothes. It was the end of the day. The sun was going down as we were marched to the Umschlagplatz (the railway siding in northern Warsaw) through the streets of the Warsaw ghetto. Fires burned on both sides of the long column of Jews, a parodic image of the Hebrews leaving Egypt, marching through the divided waters on their way to liberation.
>
> When we arrived at the Umschlagplatz we were immediately set upon by auxiliary SS of all different nationalities,

Ukrainian, Polish, and others. We were chased up a stairwell and squashed into rooms packed so tightly there was hardly space to sit. My parents managed to get to a small corner where the four of us could huddle. Water was being sold by the bottle, but only for gold and diamonds. After several days we were loaded onto cattle trucks and taken to Majdanek.

The journey to Majdanek was horrific. [We were] Squeezed into the trucks in such numbers, it was not only difficult to find a place, one had to fight for every breath of air. It was even more difficult for the children. My parents shielded us as best they could. They had conserved a sock filled with sugar, and from the time we left the bunker until we reached Majdanek, my sister and I were fed teaspoons of sugar. My parents did not touch it. As soon as we arrived in Majdanek we were immediately torn apart. My sister looked more like a child than I and my mother would not leave her. They were taken together. I went with the men because I was quite tall. My father told me to say that I was eighteen years old. All the men were chased into a building and stripped naked. We had to throw our clothes, except for our belts, into some kind of wooden contraption in the middle of the room. We then had to run with our belts high over our heads. We were directed by an SS doctor to go either right or left, one way to immediate death, the other way to a lingering life.*

My father, Menachem Mendel; my mother, Helena; and my twin sister, Sabina, were killed by the Germans the same day we arrived.

After about six weeks of the most horrendous existence, with daily selections to the gas chamber, I was chosen for the one or two transports that left Maydanek for a so-called working camp. The only difference between the death camps and the work camps was that in the death camps you were gassed

_____

*Author's note: The long quote describing Mr. Gutter's journey to Majdanek was taken from *The Boys, Triumph Over Adversity*, by Sir Martin Gilbert, published by Holt, New York. These recollections were in a letter from Pinchas Gutter to Sir Martin Gilbert, dated 23 March 1996.

to death, whereas in the work camps you were worked to death, beaten, or shot to death. The aim of the Nazis, *Jemach Shemam* (may their name be erased forever), was to exterminate us by one way or another. It is a miracle and Providence any of us survived.

In the autumn of 1944, I was sent from one camp called Skarzysko Kammienne to another camp, Chestochowa Zelazna Chuta, owned at that time by H.A.S.A.G., a German firm. We worked in the iron works. This was hard labor, loading and unloading pig iron, and doubly hard for children.

The only difference between this camp and all of the others that I had experienced was the kindness shown by the Jewish camp commander who ran it. He chose kind *kapos* and somehow managed to work with the German administration in such a way that it did not interfere too much in the running of the camp. Some said that he bribed the German *kommandant*. Also, he especially went out of his way to help the children. In most camps we wore rags, but in Chestochowa, the Jewish camp *kommandant* cut up blankets and made clothing for the youngsters, which lasted until the end of the war. This made conditions in this camp more bearable than those in other camps. But, nevertheless, hunger was still rife, life hung by a thread, and one never knew from moment to moment what could happen. The German guards were "Lords of Life and Death," and any transgression of their rules was usually punished by flogging—and often by shooting.

It goes without saying that any type of religious observance was strictly forbidden and punishable by death. This, however, did not stop religious Jews from continuing to practice their religion against all odds.

When I arrived in Chestochowa, I found Rabbi Godel Eizner there, a great Talmudist. He had been a friend of my father's, and they had studied together in the yeshiva. He decided to take me under his wing. The first thing he said to me was that I should hold onto my faith, and with God's help I would survive the war. The next thing he told me was that he had been present at my *Bris Milah* and that as I was now 13 years old, I was ready to make Bar Mitzvah. I looked at him as if he were mad, because by that time I had lost all hope and had long neglected any form of religious observance.

I ran away from him and tried to keep out of his way as much as I could, partly because I was afraid and also because my friends were all completely irreligious and we stuck together all the time.

Rabbi Godel Eizner, however, was very determined and used every opportunity to keep at me about my Bar Mitzvah. He constantly reminded me of my background as a son and grandson of Gerer *Chasidim.* Finally, he prevailed and I agreed. I could not imagine how the ceremony would be carried out, and he said nothing to me for some time.

Then one day he took me aside and told me that I would have to come and stay in his barracks, as he had arranged a *minyan* (assembly of ten men needed for communal prayer) for later that night. This was very dangerous because I was in a different barracks and we had regular *appels* when we would be counted. I now had to arrange with the boys to cover for me, and just before curfew I went across to Rabbi Eizner's barracks.

I lay under his bunk until all was quiet and the men he had organized for the *minyan* rose from their bunks. As if by magic, a *tallit* and *tefillin* materialized. To this day, I have no idea how he managed to smuggle these into the camp. I repeated the benedictions after him. The whole *minyan* prayed, and I was caught up in the great Chasidic fervor of their devotion that night. It was as if I were born anew, and I began to believe that with God's help, I might indeed survive the war. Shortly after that, we were taken our separate ways.

It seemed almost a miracle that after many trials and tribulations, I met up with Rabbi Eizner once again, this time in Colditz, a camp in Germany, where I was fortunate to work in the kitchen. I was therefore privileged to be able to help the rabbi with my soup portion, which was given to those who worked in the kitchen at night. Rabbi Eizner survived the war as well and became a famous *rosh yeshiva* in Israel.

I was in six camps, all of them extermination camps. I was liberated in Theresenstadt, Czechoslovakia, in August 1945. Then I was taken to England with a group of young children, who now call themselves the "Boys." Sir Martin Gilbert wrote a book about us, entitled, *The Boys.*

After the war I lived in several countries—England, France, Israel, Brazil, South Africa, and finally Canada. I married an understanding South African Jewish lady in 1957. We have three children and two grandchildren, *Baruch Hashem* (praise to God). I am an honorary full-time cantor, which happened quite by accident, and have been for the past twenty-five years.

I feel spiritual always, but especially when I conduct services and do ministering work for the aged. My advice to anybody and everybody is to remember what Hillel said, "Love your neighbor as thyself" and the rest will fall into place. The Holocaust not only defines you, but brands you. And yet Judaism and spirituality are part of every sinew in my body. I grew up in a Chasidic home and imbibed my Jewishness with my mother's milk. I have no idea how I kept my faith. I think it's the other way around. Faith kept me.

16

STEPP'N UP

Eric Perlyn—November 10, 1990

Eric Perlyn graduated from Duke University in 2000. At Duke, he was the recipient of the Lars Lyon Community Action Award for his efforts at distributing new shoes to needy kids in the Raleigh/Durham area. He has since moved to New York City where he is an analyst with Morgan Stanley. Eric's organization, Stepp'n Up, is still active and, to date, has distributed over 14,000 pairs of shoes. He is an active member of the The Heart of America Foundation in Washington, DC, an organization that seeks to promote and encourage volunteering for youth. Eric has been recognized in numerous books, including Be the Light *by Bill Halamandaris,* Well Done *by R. David Thomas, and* Growing Up Feeling Good *by Ellen Rosenberg.*

Photo by David Eric Studios

In *The Wizard of Oz*, when Dorothy wanted to go home, all she had to do was click her ruby slippers three times. She could have sailed back "over the rainbow" at any time. She just didn't know she had the power—on her feet, of all places. Our modern-day ruby slippers appear in the form of Reeboks,

81

Nikes, and Adidas, with the promise that they, too, can take us to places of which we have only dreamed. Eric Perlyn is a young man who understands that power and that promise. He knows the importance of shoes—new shoes.

Rabbi Merle Singer, from Temple Beth El in Boca Raton, Florida, suggested a tradition for the young members of his congregation who were becoming B'nai Mitzvah. Singer strongly encouraged them to donate a portion of their Bar and Bat Mitzvah gifts back to the community in a form of *tzedakah*. Many of these students choose to perform their first "adult" mitzvah by writing a check to the charity of their choice. For Eric Perlyn, the idea of a remote, anonymous donation offered little sense of gratification. He really wanted to *do* something.

Coming from a very community-oriented, active family, Eric was no stranger to volunteer work. He was a regular visitor at the Children's Home Society* in Fort Lauderdale. Being a sport's enthusiast, he thought he'd like to buy new sports equipment for the society. He met with the director to discuss what kind of equipment was most needed and was shocked by the response. They had all the equipment they needed. Unfortunately, many of the kids couldn't play because they didn't have shoes to wear!

With that, the director told him of a family that had six boys, aged 2 to 13, none of whom had proper shoes. The oldest boy started off with a "new" used pair and then passed them down to his younger siblings. Their shoes were torn and dirty, with the soles literally falling off. Eric made arrangements to pick up the boys, take them out to lunch, and afterward surprise them with a trip to the mall, where they could each pick out their own brand-new pair of shoes.

Lunch was a sullen affair. In spite of the efforts made by Eric and his parents, conversation lagged, and the kids were up-tight. When they got to the shoe store, however, the mood lightened considerably. When Eric announced his intentions, the kids stood rooted, unblinking and unbelieving. It took the

---

*A statewide agency that provides care for abused, abandoned, and neglected children and their families.

lack of inhibitions of their 2-year-old brother, who walked over to the wall and helped himself to a tiny pair of Reeboks, before the older boys started exploring the store. Each child picked out his favorite, regardless of price. When the kids put on their shoes, it was like witnessing a transformation. They loosened up, started to laugh, jumped all over Eric, and ran around the store.

Eric was awestruck by the impact of the kids merely putting on new pairs of shoes. He realized that shoes are more than a basic foot covering. They provide a sense of pride and self-esteem and an overall feeling of well-being. He paid for the shoes with cash and left the store, resolute with the idea that whatever had just happened was going to happen again.

That's how "Stepp'n Up" was born. Eric and his family brainstormed and came up with the name of this organization, whose sole purpose (forgive the pun) was to provide shoes for underprivileged kids. To get things off the ground, he went back to the Children's Home Society, where he asked for a list with every child's name, age, and shoe size. With the help of his family, he drafted a letter and started his quest. His mom, Marilyn, drove him to the mall every weekend and he went from store to store, asking for donations that would specifically match the needs of the children on his list. He didn't want to end up with a random collection of shoes in assorted shapes and sizes. He wanted to find shoes for each child that would match that child's age, size, and gender.

The response of the store owners and managers was amazing. Maybe it was because the solicitor was a polite, forthright, well-intentioned 13-year-old. Maybe they recognized what a good idea this was and wanted to become part of the program. From September to November 1991, going door to door, store to store, Eric collected 175 pairs of shoes—a retail value of almost $6,000!

In December, a special Christmas party was hosted for the children from the Children's Home Society at a nearby restaurant. There, they were treated to a holiday meal and presents were distributed. When the kids boarded the bus for the return trip, most of them thought that the festivities were over for the evening. As they approached the home, the kids started hanging out the window. Waiting for them in front of the building was the Perlyn family, surrounded by stacks of beautifully wrapped packages (which they had wrapped themselves). When the children realized that there was one gift apiece with each person's name on it, they started scrambling for their personalized packages. As recognition dawned about the contents of each box, they abandoned their other gifts and immediately donned their new shoes. There was such excitement—the kids started to strut, dance, jump, and karate kick. Anything to show off their new footgear.

Eric's very personal store-to-store solicitation continued, but was supplemented with a letter-writing campaign. At first, letters to large companies yielded only impersonal rejections; however, as the program grew, so did the responses. Several leading shoe manufacturers, such as Sam and Libby and Sebago, along with JC Penney, Payless, and The Limited Too, have sent shoes to the Perlyn home, to be distributed by Eric and his family.

Eric continued the program through high school, and it grew exponentially. He and his family received national recognition for their efforts. He has appeared on television and radio, been recognized in newspapers and magazines, and received, among other prestigious awards, the "Point of Light" award, for which he was saluted by General Colin Powell. Eric was grateful for the publicity, only because it gave the project more credibility and enabled him to successfully continue.

When he entered Duke in the fall of 1996, he "franchised." Eric not only brought the program with him, but his sister, Amanda, a high school freshman, also minded the store at home. In addition to "Stepp'n Up," Amanda had founded her own program called "To Have and to Hug," which distributes stuffed animals to sick and needy children. She began her volunteering career at the age of 7 and believes strongly that no matter how old you are, you're old enough to make a difference. When they split the program, they realized that other kids might like to set up their own "franchise." So Eric and Amanda wrote a manual detailing how to get started.

Little did Eric know that the chanting of the *parasha Chaye Sara*, on the morning of his Bar Mitzvah, would be the beginning of his public speaking career. In order to do fundraising for the program, he has talked to a myriad of auxiliary programs, associations, and companies. One wonderful option that he offers his audiences is, in lieu of a donation, they can "adopt a child." That means, they pick the name of a child, and when they are out buying shoes for their own children, they can buy a second pair for their "adopted" child. In this way, they can involve their own children in the selection process, but, more important, in the awareness of the program.

Eric graduated from Duke in the spring of 2000, with a degree in economics. However, he has hardly started his new career at the "entry" level. He enters the field with an impressive ten years of marketing, soliciting, and promoting experience.

A mitzvah begets another mitzvah. Lois Pope, a Palm Beach County philanthropist, donated $10 million dollars to the Miami Project to Cure Paralysis at the University of Miami medical school. Her motivation was a story that she read about Eric in a 1993 newspaper article. Eric's brother Chad, a student at the medical school, was on hand for the presentation. In keeping with the family tradition, Chad had started his own project entitled DOC ADOPT, which matches needy patients with doctors and dentists who provide free medical and dental care.

From the humble beginnings of 6 lovingly purchased pair of sneakers, Eric Perlyn and "Stepp'n Up" have collected and distributed over 12,000 pairs of shoes. It's impossible to calculate the emotional impact of this contribution. These new shoes translate into walking taller, standing straighter, and feeling prouder—perhaps taking the wearer to places that he may only have imagined. If Dorothy had met Eric Perlyn on the yellow brick road, he would have had her home in no time.

17

NEVER TOO LATE

Sam Wolkoff—December, 1981

This story was shared by Rabbi David Rosenberg, the "young rabbi," who is now the executive director of the Scranton Hebrew Day School. He still loves to bring flowers to his wife. Sam Wolkoff is 85 years old, retired, and living in Florida.

The young rabbi entered the florist shop tentatively. He had purchased flowers before, but this time it was different. Living in the dormitory of the yeshiva, he was often invited to one of the rabbi's homes for *Shabbos* or a holiday meal. Growing up in a secular, rather than in a traditional, home, he depended heavily on the instructions of his teachers, both in and out of the classroom. They advised him that it was appropriate to send flowers to his hostesses before *Shabbos* or the holiday. But now, he didn't need a token to thank someone for her extension of hospitality. After a five-week whirlwind courtship, he was engaged. Today's purchase would be for his *bashert*, to enhance her first *Shabbos* as his intended.

The florist immediately recognized him as a yeshiva student by his black garb and wide felt hat, which were offset only by a stark white shirt. The rabbi had only a few dollars to spend, but when he excitedly spilled out who would be the recipient of the flowers, the florist prepared an arrangement costing far more than the proffered amount

This *Erev Shabbos* purchase of flowers became a routine. Even though the young rabbi was in a hurry to complete his preparations before sundown, he always made time to shmooze with the older man behind the counter. One Friday afternoon Sam, the florist, leaned forward and in hushed tones confided that he had a confession to make. He added that when the rabbi had some more time, he would like to talk. The rabbi assured Sam that when he was ready to talk, the rabbi would make the time.

A month passed before the subject was brought up again. On that day, when the rabbi arrived for his weekly purchase, Sam ushered him into the back room. The young rabbi gave the demeanor of having all the time in the world, even though he was still unprepared for *Shabbos*. Compared with the lovely lively showroom, the back room was stark and drab. There, the older man started, "I'm 63 years old and I never had a Bar Mitzvah. My parents were communists and they didn't believe in it. I don't feel fully Jewish. Something is missing." This confession led to the query, "What do I have to do to become a Bar Mitzvah? And will you teach me what I need to know?"

With Sam having not even elemental knowledge of the alefbet (Hebrew alphabet), they started with a primer. After a day filled with creative ways to motivate, stimulate, and excite his young pupils at the local day school, the rabbi would arrive at the flower shop and switch gears to teach a man who brought his own motivation and enthusiasm. The young rabbi had an innate sense for teaching very basic concepts, while recognizing and respecting his student's lifetime of experience.

They set a goal of Sam's 65th birthday for the Bar Mitzvah date. Since the Torah is read during morning services on Mondays, Thursdays, and Saturdays, they chose a Thursday morning, because it seemed less threatening. They worked hard for two years, and Sam progressed from the alphabet to words, then sentences, and finally moved up to prayers. The *Shema*, the basic precept of the Jewish religion, was the first prayer that he learned in full.

On a cold day in December of 1981, Sam Wolkoff, World War II veteran, college graduate, and owner of his business, was called to the Torah as a Bar Mitzvah. He sang the blessings before and after the Torah reading, then led the prayers until the end of the service. He had not just rotely memorized it, he was reading it!

Sam did not embark on this undertaking alone. His wife, Jean, who had strong family ties to an Orthodox *shul* in town, knew how important this was to her husband. She had lovingly woven the *tallis* that he wore. She sent out invitations and hosted a beautiful breakfast for their guests. She was beaming as the community congratulated her husband on fulfilling his dream.

During the two-year tutorial, the subject of payment never came up. However, during that time every holiday table at the rabbi's home was adorned with an arrangement from Wolkoff's florist. The *Shabbos* flowers for the rabbi's wife were silent barter for his many lessons. And a week after the Bar Mitzvah, Sam arrived at the young rabbi's house bearing a special gift, a set of *Mishnah* (the Oral Law) inscribed "From your most difficult student," signed Sam Wolkoff.

Over the years, Sam's artistry had enhanced many a *simcha*. While into every floral arrangement he put his heart and soul, he himself felt incomplete—that is, until a kind and gentle young man took the time to listen. Maybe it was looking into the young rabbi's intense brown eyes, which possess a hint of sadness and a glint of mischief, that compelled Sam to reveal what was missing in his life. On his 65th birthday, five times later than tradition dictates, Sam Wolkoff became a Bar Mitzvah, finally feeling complete.

18

THE KING'S EQUAL

Ramsey Sullivan—December 1, 1990

King Saul, the father-in-law of King David, ruled for a scant two years. He was benevolent, humble, handsome, and tall—head and shoulders above most men. He unfortunately did not follow what God had commanded him to do and suffered the consequences. His line would have been established as the Kingdom of Israel forever. He disobeyed God's orders not only once, but twice, and for that not only was his reign terminated, but his son Jonathan, a good and loyal man, would never become the king. In spite of this,  *Jonathan remained a faithful son, a fearless warrior, and a devoted friend.*

The night before his Bar Mitzvah, Ramsey Sullivan couldn't sleep. He wasn't worried about being up in front of everyone. He played baseball and a crowd often watched his Little League and junior high school games. No—being in the limelight didn't bother him. It was more than that. He didn't want to mess up. He didn't want to make any mistakes. No—it was more than that . . . he had something to prove. As one of the youngest members of an aging Queens, New York, congregation, he knew that the elders would be primed to yell out corrections during any part of the service. But he didn't want that. He needed to do it by himself, and he needed to do it right. After all, he was Joe Sullivan's boy. Joe Sullivan—the handsome, bright, charismatic man who could light up a room by just making an entrance. Joe Sullivan—the caring, loving father who was intently interested in anything and everything related to his family. Joe Sullivan—who was serving two life sentences in the Sullivan County Correctional Institution for murder.

Even Joe will admit that he is two people. That sense of duality has led to his family filtering out his behavior. They focus on the loving, caring man whom they visit almost weekly. And three times a year, they have trailer visits where they are able to spend the weekend together. In spite of the physical distance that separates them, Joe is an integral part of his family. As his sons grew up, Joe was the one who fine-tuned their athletic skills during their Sunday visits. Athletic prowess, however, ran in his family. His Uncle Joe Sullivan had played football for Notre Dame in the 1930s and was captain-elect of the team when he was struck with an illness and died. The younger Joe, too, could've been a contender on the outside. Instead, his football skills were honed during many seasons of playing ball behind bars. Both of his sons, Ramsey and Kelly, inherited their father's speed and natural agility. Ramsey played every sport, but excelled in baseball. Kelly emulated his father and uncle with his talent for football.

Their mother, Gail Sullivan, is an amazing woman. Joe has been away for the past 17 years of their 23-year-old marriage. Gail made some conscious choices about how her boys would be raised and what kind of family life she would have. She could have chosen to be filled with anger and resentment at the hand she was dealt. But instead, when you meet her son Ramsey Sullivan, you encounter a young man who is filled with grace and dignity. He is sensitive, loving, emotional, and proud. And he credits both his parents, but especially his mother, for who he is.

His father has had tremendous input into his life, as well. If Ramsey had a question or needed advice, he could call the prison and leave a message. When Joe was able to, he would call them back. As Ramsey prepared for his Bar Mitzvah, Joe was very involved. He and Gail planned the guest list together and he helped his son write the speech that Ramsey would deliver from the *bimah*. Joe, of course, couldn't attend the service, but he was an integral part of the planning and interested in the outcome.

Ramsey was well prepared for his Bar Mitzvah, due to the efforts of another strong, wonderful woman in his life—his grandmother Sylvia. Because Gail worked, it was Sylvia who was there to greet the boys when they came home from school. She would sit in her folding chair outside of the apartment, and the boys would race to see who could get to her first. Sylvia was so proud of her grandsons and looked forward to Ramsey's Bar Mitzvah. She was the one who listened and practiced with him. However, several months before the big day, Sylvia died unexpectedly. On the day of the Bar Mitzvah, Ramsey looked down from the *bimah* at his mother and younger brother seated in the front row. He was used to the idea that his father wouldn't be there—but next to his mother there was an empty place saved for his grandmother. She, more than anyone, had wanted him to have this ceremony, and he felt that she was there with him.

When he finished chanting his Haftorah and reciting the blessings, he was ready to sit down, but the cantor indicated that he should keep going. At first hesitant, he thought of this little hitch as just a "curve ball," and, though unprepared for the next part, he continued on with the service. Many people expected very little of him. His dad was in jail—he'd never make anything of himself. Well—they were wrong! He had proved himself on the baseball field, in the classroom, and once again at his Bar Mitzvah. He pulled it off well and handled himself with style and grace.

Later at the party, his mother addressed the crowd and talked about how proud she was of her son; how much she, too, missed her mother; and how glad she was that all the people who had supported her family over the years were there to share in her joy. Since it was a fairly Orthodox community, they could not have a candle-lighting ceremony on Saturday afternoon, so Ramsey called up special friends to place flowers in an arrangement. Ramsey Clark, the former U.S. attorney general under President Lyndon Johnson and a close family friend for whom the Bar Mitzvah boy was named, was one such honored guest. And since it was an integrated neighborhood, the mostly black and Hispanic kids who attended were also called up to place flowers.

Ramsey Sullivan is a faithful son, a fearless competitor, and a wonderful friend. He is indeed any man's equal and better than most. He demonstrates a beautiful gentility and asks only that he be judged on the basis of his own merits and accomplishments and not for the sins of his father. He is attending graduate school in Albany and hopes one day to teach, but, more important, to coach. He has valuable lessons to teach young people about honor, loyalty, and pride—about setting your goals really high and then working hard to reach them.

For Ramsey felt that when a boy becomes 13, reading from the Hebrew is not the most important lesson of becoming a Bar Mitzvah. There is no automatic entrance into manhood. You have to first search for and find self-respect, honor, and belief in yourself. No one just hands it to you.

Growing up, Ramsey loved "Popeye" because he was a really nice guy, but when confronted with danger or evil, he always rose to the occasion. "The sailor man" unconditionally defended his girlfriend and was able to summon his limitless reserve of strength with something as benign as a can of spinach. Time and time again, he was called on to prove himself, and without fail, he faced each new challenge and prevailed. He always got his girl and, though remaining humble, seemed just a teeny bit smug. Like his cartoon friend, Ramsey has felt that need to prove himself repeatedly. However, he doesn't need spinach to find his strength, for it comes from a different place—strength of character. "Character, not circumstances, make the man" (Booker T. Washington). If armed with only that arsenal, Ramsey Sullivan will surely succeed.

19

BROOKLYN PROJECTS

William Silvermintz—August 24, 1963

Bill Silvermintz is the Director of the Barbados Tourism Authority. He is preparing for his newest role—grandpa.

During the early 1950s, the stage was being set for the Civil Rights Movement. With *Brown vs. The Board of Education* and the Montgomery bus boycott that began with Rosa Parks's refusal to give up her seat, racial unrest was becoming apparent all over the country. However, in a tiny corner of Brooklyn, New York, race was not an issue back in the late '50s and early '60s. From Batchelder to Bragg Street, flanked to the north by Avenue W and the south by Avenue X, stood the Nostrand City Housing Project. Built in the early

1950s, these apartments were predominantly meant to provide inexpensive housing for World War II vets who couldn't afford to buy a house. An entrance criterion was based on income, but usually once you got in, you stayed in.

Florrie and Lou Silvermintz—he, a decorated WW II vet—were thrilled when they were awarded their apartment in Nostrand City. They had been living with Florrie's grandmother since their marriage, but because her house had been sold, they were forced to find other living quarters. While Florrie was in the hospital delivering their second child, Lou went to city housing to apply for an apartment. They were delighted to finally have a place of their own. In December 1950, with Susan, 18 months old, and Billy, 4 months old, the Silvermintz family moved into their new home.

"From the beginning," Bill recalled, "there was no black, no white, no Jewish, no non-Jewish . . . what was important was the neighborhood. Color didn't exist. We were all *just friends*. We had our own little universe and never crossed Avenue W!"

Their world was encompassed in five 6-story buildings that circled a grassy park. The "No Playing on the Grass" rule was enforced by housing police. So, the kids picked a "look-out" and proceeded to play a daily ball game in the prohibited area. Whenever this housing officer approached, the "look-out" gave a signal, and the kids scattered.

Baseball was an integral part of the kids' daily activities. From the apartment house's grassy field, most of the kids ventured the few blocks away to join Little League teams. Billy first played both pitcher and catcher for "Buddy's" team, named for the amusement park on Flatbush Avenue. The pinnacle of Bill's ball-playing career was being chosen as the starting pitcher of the All Star Team and throwing two "no-hitters" during the 1962 season.

Though baseball was the primary occupation of the day, cards dominated the night. During the summer, the kids would drag card tables outside and played pinochle and bridge until the first of their parents would summon them up to bed.

At age 9, Bill started Hebrew School, three days a week, at Young Israel of Bedford Bay. This Orthodox congregation was

an unusual choice for a family with a limited level of observance; however, young Bill could be found seated next to his
father during the High Holy Days. He started fasting for Yom
Kippur at age 12 and fondly remembers the meal to break the
fast. The family cleaned out bread products on Passover, but
did not celebrate the seders.

The goal of Hebrew school was the ultimate culmination of
becoming a Bar Mitzvah. "It was a real 'pain' to go. I didn't like
Hebrew School. For years I resented that I was praying, but I
didn't know what I was saying," remembers Bill. Six months
before his 13th birthday, he started with intense Bar Mitzvah
lessons taught by one of the teachers from his school. Since so
many children were in the congregation, it was pretty typical to
share a Bar Mitzvah with another young man. Bill found out
that he would be splitting the Haftorah with an unknown kid
named Stuart. They each studied separately and each learned
only half of the Haftorah, silently depending upon the other to
complete his obligation.

On the morning of the Bar Mitzvah, a sweltering day in
August, Bill found himself sweating, unrelated to the weather.
Attired completely in a new suit, *tallis*, and yarmulke, all
purchased by his father, he kept wondering if he'd heard the
rabbi right. "I was only supposed to learn half of the Haftorah,
right?" he silently and relentlessly questioned himself. As the
sanctuary started to fill, he was comforted by the sight of his
friends from the neighborhood. Unself-consciously, the kids—
black and white, Jewish and non-Jewish—donned the satin
yarmulkes and found seats. These were the kids whom he'd
shared everything with for the past thirteen years; of course,
everything was going to be okay.

However, Bill did not take his first deep breath until he
actually saw Stuart and his family enter the *shul* and knew
that he was not mistaken. He was only supposed to learn half
a Haftorah and that much he could chant without a hitch!
When the service was over, the families provided a light
Kiddush for their guests.

Later that night, the much-awaited celebration for Bill took
place . . . the party. Held at Le Versailles Restaurant on
Nostrand Avenue, there was music, food, and dancing. Bill

knew that it was not easy for his parents to pull this together and really appreciated that the party was just for him. One of the special moments happened during the candle-lighting ceremony, when Bill's great-grandmother came up to light a candle. All of the same friends with whom he shared school, baseball, holidays, and summer nights came up collectively to light candles, as well.

At Sheepshead Bay High School, Bill had the "advantage of the alphabet." In tenth-grade homeroom, he found himself seated next to Barbara Weiss, who was not only bright and athletic, but also beautiful. With her waist-length chestnut hair, sparkly eyes, and easy laugh, he couldn't take his eyes off her. Getting over his initial shyness, he found her surprisingly easy to talk to.

Sometime during one of their morning chats, he told her about his band, the Jesters. She mentioned that she was looking for a band for her sweet-16 party. The five-man band, some of the same guys from the neighborhood, shlepped all of their equipment to Ocean Avenue and auditioned in the Weiss's two-bedroom apartment. The Jesters were hired for the job and split the princely sum of $50.

Bill and Barbara did not see each other as juniors because Barbara was in academically accelerated classes, and Bill didn't bother to apply himself. They re-met as seniors, once again with help from the alphabet. They were both scheduled for senior pictures at the same time. They resumed their old friendship while they waited for their photographs to be taken.

Through a mutual friend, Bill found out several weeks later that if he asked her out, she would say "yes." He finally got the nerve to ask her out for New Year's Eve. He was delighted when she accepted, but somewhat disconcerted when they arrived at the Golden Gate Inn for dinner, only to find that Barbara's parents were there, as well. It didn't, however, put a damper on the evening, and they had a wonderful time. Two weeks later, she was wearing his high school ring around her neck.

Twenty-eight years and three children later, Bill Silvermintz is as much enamored of his wife as he was when he first met her in high school. Through job changes, moves, and never-ending travel, she remains the constant in his life. Judaism is important to Bill and his family, but more from a sense of heritage than from a level of observance. Now a college instructor and travel specialist, he fondly remembers what is at present called the "cultural diversity" of his early years. Back then, they were "just friends."

20

FROM BAGHDAD TO BETH ISRAEL

Heskel M. Haddad—September, 1941

Dr. Haddad went on to train at Harvard University in Cambridge and Washington University in St. Louis. A renowned ophthalmologic surgeon in New York City, he is also a prolific writer, both in his medical specialty and on behalf of world Jewry and Israel.

eskel Haddad did everything early. To start with, he arrived two months prematurely. Already having a son and a daughter, his mother lost her third baby at birth. That loss, coupled with Heskel's unexpected arrival, caused her to dote on and spoil her second son. Second, he started school a year earlier than dictated. Not only was he in a hurry to learn the mysteries that were imparted to his siblings who left the house early every morning, but he thought that his entrance into school would afford him the respect worthy of a student, rather than the dismissive disregard bestowed on "babies." He was precocious and bright and, though small, found strength in his intellect and wit.

Iraq is the modern nomenclature for a country that was known in ancient times as Babylonia. After World War I, the southern part of Turkey (Assyria) was included. It has the distinction of being the birthplace of Abraham and the settling place for Jews exiled from Israel after the destruction of the First Temple. There has been a Jewish community in Iraq for at least the last twenty-five centuries. It is recognized as having the oldest continuous Jewish community in the world. The Great Synagogue of Baghdad is the oldest in the world. It was build almost six centuries before the birth of Christ. And yet the story of the Jews in Iraq has become all too familiar.

In 1935, three years after Iraq's independence, "Zionist" activities were declared illegal. The interpretation of what constituted Zionist activities varied greatly and gave rise to dismissals from positions, as well as banishment from the country. Like a virus that spread, anti-Jewish feelings intensified, allowing thugs to attack and kill innocent Jews whose only crime was being in the wrong place at the wrong time. In June 1941, at the time of the pro-Nazi uprising of Rashid-Ali al Kailani, the Jews of Baghdad became open prey for the Arabs, leaving over 900 dead and thousands injured in a single night. Children and women, along with their fathers and brothers, tried to defend themselves from thousands of attackers, but sticks and stones were no match for their enemies' artillery.

From the rooftop of their Baghdad home, Heskel, at age 11, along with his parents and siblings, fortified themselves with a pile of bricks—effective ammunition, given their strategic position. Heskel's immediate family survived the carnage. Not so his beloved first cousin, Haron, who went to the aid of a friend being attacked by a group of hoodlums. As Haron pulled his friend to safety, the group turned their wrath on him and stabbed him in the back. Because of the danger and distance to the Jewish Hospital, he was brought to the clinic of a Christian Arab. Despite the pleading and bribes of Haron's family, he was allowed to die an agonizing death of septicimia (blood poisoning) over the course of a day and a half because no staff member would attend to him. Haron Haddad was buried according to custom, covered only with the soil of the country that murdered him.

Heskel was distraught and furious at the slaughter of his people and the death of his older cousin, who had always been his confidante and adviser. He felt conflicted and confused. His family was strictly observant and followed the age-old customs with joy and respect. His father and mother enhanced every mitzvah by celebrating them with beautiful objets d'art, rather than mundane ritual objects. And yet Who was this God Who allowed His people to withstand such suffering? Who was this God to whom Haron prayed dutifully and lovingly, and yet was not there in Haron's time of need? Where could this inquisitive 11-year-old find the answers to such baffling questions? The yeshiva.

The yeshiva. There he could study and learn the lessons of the Torah and the Kabbalah. There he could try to unravel the mysteries of the God of his forefathers, especially Abraham, who had inhabited the very same soil. There was only one hurdle for his entrance into the yeshiva—his Bar Mitzvah. Bar Mitzvah, the son of the commandments, the age of responsibility, happened when a boy became 13. There was only one way around it. They needed special permission to hold Heskel's Bar Mitzvah early, and then he would be permitted to enter the yeshiva. His father approached the rabbi with the request. The rabbi said that if Heskel was willing to accept and understand the commandments, he would waive the age requirement. After quizzing Heskel, he was so satisfied with the responses that he allowed the family to proceed with plans for the Bar Mitzvah.

There was another reason that Heskel wanted an early Bar Mitzvah. In the wake of the pogrom, the slaughter of innocent people, he was not in the mood for a big party like his brother's. Iraqi Bar Mitzvahs were lengthy, joyous celebrations. Only in light of the current sadness would his father consent to limited festivities. His mother and older sister Nazima had made all of his clothes up to this point. There was no time to make a new suit for the occasion, but they devoted all of their spare time to sewing and embroidering his prayer shawl (*tallis*). In Iraq, the custom of putting on *tefillin* is very private and is concealed under the *tallis*. During the week, Jewish men don *tefillin* every morning before prayer. His father reminded Heskel that even though putting them on would become routine, they could never be bound without Heskel's thinking about the process. There were two small square boxes that contained lines from the Five Books of Moses, attached to long leather straps. The leather straps were natural on one side and dyed black on the other. They represented night and day, and God and man. One set was fixed to the brow, while the other was bound to the left arm.

Surrounded only by his family and the rabbi, Heskel began his Bar Mitzvah ceremony by kissing his phylacteries. He surrounded himself with his shawl so that this age-old ritual taught by his father could now be witnessed only by God. He affixed the first cube to his left arm, closest to his heart. He wrapped the strap seven times, one for each day of creation, and then added three more for our forefathers, Abraham, Isaac, and Jacob. To symbolize the four corners of the earth, he gathered the fringes on the four corners of his tallis. He then placed the second cube in the center of his brow to symbolize knowledge: "Torah given by God to crown the head of man." In his own words, he describes how he felt at that moment:

> I'd risen, as prescribed, to place the second cube. In sitting down again to pray, I shook beneath the shawl, over-whelmed by the immensity of the occasion. In this, the single biggest step I'd ever take, I'd bridged the gap between the boy I'd been and the man I'd now become. In this single act, I'd taken on the obligations of adulthood—those of man to man and those of Jew to God—and I prayed to God that I was ready.
>
> On standing up and kissing Baba's [his father's] hand, I saw his pride in me—and also sadness that I'd grown up sooner than he would have wished. His speech was very short and emphasized what I already knew. From this day on, I was accountable.

He entered the yeshiva and studied with some brilliant scholars. However, while other students took their afternoon break to rest or study, Heskel used that time to fulfill another promise. He had been involved in the underground movement before he hit double digits, but now, in earnest, he organized for the defense of his seven-member team (Haron was the honorary seventh member). They began with makeshift weapons, some stolen from their mother's kitchens, and worked their way up to learning how to shoot a real gun. This band of unlikely rebels remained active in the movement, helping the emigration of Jews to Israel from Iraq, while the situation became increasingly dangerous.

Heskel graduated, and even though there was a strict Jewish quota (ten Jews per year from the whole country), he entered medical school at the age of 15. He was admitted because he received the highest score on the entrance exam in the country. He completed the four-year program and would have graduated at the top in his class, but because he was Jewish, the school refused to give him his diploma. Iraq became even more dangerous for Jews, and because of his work in the underground, he was forced to emigrate immediately to Israel. A budding country trying to house its hundreds of thousands of refugees, Israel was just creating a medical school. Without credentials, Heskel had to take an exam and, after completing a one-year internship, was given the first diploma from the Hebrew University, Hadassah School of Medicine. He was 20 years old.

When Heskel Haddad first entered the yeshiva, his teacher Rabbi Ezra asked why he was there. Heskel responded that he wanted the rabbi to teach him "all about the Lord and our religion." Rabbi Ezra responded with the following, "Before a man can know the Lord, he must know his fellowman. And to know your fellowman, first you have to know yourself. You must look inside yourself with honest eyes." Heskel learned that the answers at the yeshiva were elusive. Unlike the exact and precise responses in math and spelling, he learned that there were no shortcuts in the Torah to learning the truth. But, rather, the search and the attainment of the truth would take a lifetime.

Author's note: This story was written with information provided during an interview with Dr. Haddad. In addition, the background information was found in both of Dr. Haddad's books, *Flight from Babylon* by Dr. Haddad, as told to Phyllis I. Rosenteur (published by McGraw-Hill Book Co.), and *Jews of Arab and Islamic Countries* by Dr. Haddad (published by Shengold Publishers). The direct quote is taken from *Flight from Babylon.*

21

#22

Tamir Goodman—December 31, 1995

There is a traditional Ashkenazi custom of naming a child after a deceased beloved relative or respected friend. The Goodmans chose instead to name their only red-headed son "Tamir," translated as "tall, palm tree," simply because they liked the name. How fitting that the palm grows tall and straight, has deep roots, thrives in the light and warmth of the sun, and has leaves that point heavenward.

Goodman is playing professional basketball for Israel's top team, Maccabi Tel Aviv.

Our tradition is filled with the pairing of "the bitter with the sweet." At Jewish weddings, amidst the joy, the groom breaks a glass, remembering the difficult times in our history. Every year during the Passover seder, while we revel in our freedom, we still eat the *moror*, bitter herbs, to remember our suffering as slaves in Egypt.

This tradition held true for Tamir Goodman on the day of his Bar Mitzvah. The day before he was to be called to the Torah for the first time, his paternal grandfather, who had been ill for quite a while, died. Instead of a home filled with cheers of "*Mazel Tov!*" and other congratulatory greetings, family and friends gathered at their residence to offer condolences to Karl Goodman on the loss of his father.

In Baltimore, Maryland, where there is a veritable smorgasbord of *shuls* to choose from, Tamir and his family daven (pray) at the Chabad *shul* connected with the ultra-Orthodox sect, Lubavitch Jews. Although not Lubavitch themselves, they attend this tiny *shul*, because of the beauty of the davening, the kind and gentle rabbi, and the cloistered life of the other members. Most of the Lubavitch community avoid the mainstream of everyday life and do not watch television or read the newspaper. Therefore, many of the congregants know Tamir only as a tall, humble, respectful yeshiva student, rather than as a whiz kid on the basketball court. They see him as a young man who delights in the joys of Judaism, rather than as someone who averages 37 points a game. No one in the *shul* offers criticism of a recent game or pointers on improving his jump shot. No one in the *shul* cares that he was recruited to play basketball by the University of Maryland in his junior year in high school from a small yeshiva. No one cared when there was an equal amount of hoopla when Tamir decided to matriculate at a different college. No one cared when he transferred in his senior year to continue his secular studies at a Seventh Day Adventist School, where he still would not play on the Sabbath. The members of the little *shtebl shul* see him only as a devoted son who idolizes his older brothers and sisters and is fiercely protective of his younger twin brothers. And when he comes to *shul*, they leave him alone to pray and thank God for his many gifts, including for his basketball talent.

In spite of the death of his grandfather, Tamir and his family would have gone to *shul* anyway on *Shabbas* morning, so they proceeded with his Bar Mitzvah. Tamir led the entire service, which included the davening and reading the *parasha Va'eira* and the Haftorah. The *shul* is tiny and sparse, lacking any fancy adornments. But the spirit runs deep and the warmth is pervasive. It felt as if there was a Bar Mitzvah happening. The *aliyah* to the Torah was important, not the theme. There was no chatter, petty politics, or fashion competition. When Tamir completed the chanting of the Haftorah, he ran over to the women's side to embrace his mother, who was silently shedding tears of joy and pride.

Tamir felt a sense of relief when the service was over, because training for his Bar Mitzvah was a chore for a kid who would much rather be playing basketball. While other classmates chose to have lavish parties to celebrate their coming of age, Tamir chose instead to visit his grandmother, who lives in Israel, and while there to attend a basketball camp. However, he takes his responsibility of manhood very seriously, in that he puts on his *tefillin* and davens every morning. Not only once, but he follows the Chabad tradition taught to him by his older brother Chen, and he *lays* a second pair of *tefillin* daily. Whether in school or on the road, he plans to continue this obligation proudly and, if necessary, publicly.

His mother, Chava, born in Israel, has served as his spiritual role model, teaching by example. She taught her children that whatever they do is between them and God. People will make judgments on you based on what they see and think. He (God) is the only One they have to please.

Chava's whole family flew over from Israel to celebrate Tamir's Bar Mitzvah. Also in attendance was Tamir's coach, Chaim Katz, who has been his mentor and remains a valued family friend. With Katz's encouragement, Tamir's raw talent was polished and honed through many hours of practice, and together they shared the joys of success.

And successful they were. This young man, nicknamed the Jewish Jordan, was splashed all over national television and magazines—not so much for what he could do, but rather for what he wouldn't do. This young man, a joy to watch on the courts, is a committed Orthodox Jew who refuses to play ball on the Sabbath. For Tamir, the practices of Orthodoxy are as second nature as waking up and brushing your teeth. But at a time when popular culture is riddled with violence and obscenities, a young man who has deep convictions is seen as the exception rather than the rule. Some detractors in his own community also see a yeshiva student as one who should devote himself solely to the study of Torah, with no room for extracurricular activities. They see sports as frivolous and unnecessary. Tamir and his family are conventionally unconventional and remain true to their tradition, without being swayed by opinions on either side.

Tamir looks up to his parents, but also finds a sense of pride in the accomplishments of many other successful Jews. When he was in Israel, he marveled at the powerful soldiers whose job it was to defend and protect that small country. As for himself being a role model, he didn't look for that status, but he's happy to share several messages with kids to try and help. The first thing he tells his young audiences is to *listen* . . . really listen to what parents, teachers, or coaches tell you, and you can become successful. His other messages are less generic and really geared to Jewish boys and girls who live in a secular world. "I'm not afraid of being Jewish. Kids are ashamed to wear a *kippah*. If you are shaky about who you are, then you'll get stomped on. I'm so proud about who I am. I wear my *kippah* and put on my *tefillin* in front of anyone. I want to share that pride."

22

SEVEN BAR MITZVAHS
AND A WEDDING

The Kirshner Family—
February 1964–February 1977

The Kirshner family, though spread out geographically and substantially larger, remains close and in constant contact. The eight children have all made significant contributions to the field of medicine. It is believed that they are the only family in the country in which three brothers are heart surgeons. Obviously, all because of Sid and Bobbie.

Photo by Mark Cohen

I n a faraway kingdom in the land of Wilkes-Barre, Pennsylvania, lived a beautiful queen with her kind, cerebral king. Their castle was spacious, and the queen wanted nothing more than to fill it with children. She turned to her king and said, "Sydney, let's have ten." In his wise way, he responded, "Let's start with one." So, that's just what they did.

And a cry went up around the land, when a little red-headed boy (just like his father) was born. He was bonny and bright and his parents loved him dearly. Holding this child for his mother, the queen, was like holding heaven. She left the affairs of the kingdom to her husband, for she knew in her heart she'd found her calling. She turned once again and said, "Sydney, let's have another."

In his wise way, he knew it was important to keep his queen happy, so, lo and behold, a second child was born. This time the boy was raven-haired like his mother and more serious and intense than his brother. Ah, he, too, was much loved by his parents.

And so it went every time the queen turned to her husband and said, "Sydney, I . . . ," he responded with a twinkling smile and the family grew to eight. Eight—a perfectly symmetrical number, both horizontally and vertically. Eight days of Chanukah. Eight days of Passover. The *Bris Milah* is performed on the eighth day. Eight—seven boys and one girl. Three redheads, two blondes, two with brown hair, and one with jet black. A veritable rainbow of children.

The old wives' tale that children bring their own good luck was multiplied exponentially. There was magic in the castle. Although there were servants, the queen herself attended to the needs of her children. She loved holding them as babies and, as they grew, marveled at each new phase. She cooked in pots the size of cauldrons. Her familiar quip "This is not a restaurant" assured that everyone in her family ate together each evening. There was hustle and bustle in the castle, but not the din and chaos that you would expect from such a large brood.

On Friday afternoons, when the royal carriages brought the children home from school, the smells of *Shabbos* greeted them as they crossed the moat. The queen would spend the day preparing all of their favorite foods, making every Sabbath a wondrous occasion. On *Shabbos* morning, the children would line up like imprinted ducklings and follow their father to the *shul.*

The king led by example. The children, respecting him greatly, did what he did. He never forced them to go to the synagogue. He went, so they went. During the week, Sydney *layed* his *tallis* and *tefillin* every morning. He often woke the children for school by tickling them with the fringes of his *tallis*.

If *Shabbos* was a weekly celebration, the holidays were pure enchantment. On Chanukah, there were ten menorahs lined up on the mantel, and when all lit, the room blazed gloriously. The gifts were color-coded so that each child could find his (or hers) easily.

In the kingdom school, United Hebrew Institute, the children spent half of the day on secular subjects and the other half studying the Hebrew subjects of Torah, Prophets, Laws, and Gemarah. Sydney chose to arm his children with the best tool he could provide, a good education. The school was filled with good-natured competition, where excellence was encouraged, embraced, and achieved.

The eighth child was born only weeks before the Bar Mitzvah celebration of the oldest son. There was great preparation and anticipation for this coveted event. While his mother attended to every detail of the joyous occasion, her son studied and practiced. He was one of the youngest boys in his class. His friends had already become Bar Mitzvah. If he made a mistake, they would know and he didn't want to be embarrassed in front of them.

The Bar Mitzvah boy was called to the Torah. He was the oldest of eight. His father and each of his uncles were honored with an *aliyah*, and he stood there surrounded and protected by the men he admired most. Rather than thinking of it as the culmination of years of study, he marveled at this new beginning. He thought, "Now, I can put on *tefillin*. Now, I can fast. I can be part of the congregation. I can get an *aliyah*. I can be counted!" Becoming a Bar Mitzvah was really special.

Before the party, his mother took him aside and taught him how to shake hands. Demonstrating, she advised him never to give a "dead fish" handshake and always shake as if you mean it. When he entered the party, he couldn't believe that all of this fanfare was for him. The room was ablaze in decorations of red. Red is bold, happy, uplifting, and the color of the crimson ribbons his mother so lovingly tied to each pram to avoid a *kineinahura* (the evil eye).

As each male child came of age, he followed the same ritual. They studied, practiced, and aimed for excellence. Now, along with their father and uncles on the *bimah*, each new Bar Mitzvah was welcomed into the fold, surrounded and embraced by his older brothers.

Each celebration proceeded without obstacles until the Bar Mitzvah of the seventh son. He was as ready as his brothers, when his appendix flared up. Because he required an appendectomy, followed by convalescence, the Bar Mitzvah had to be postponed. The disappointed young man not only needed to recuperate, he had to learn a whole new *parasha!* The new portion, *Terumah*, was the same one his oldest brother had chanted thirteen years before. Bookends! In order to commemorate the Bar Mitzvahs of both his oldest and youngest son, their father sang that Haftorah every year in *shul* on the anniversary.

At that time in the kingdom, young ladies came of age as a matter of course, without any fanfare. The wedding, however, was a different story. As the first of eight to be married, and the only girl among seven boys, the wedding of the princess was a grand spectacle. The beautiful bride carried two roses. She presented one to her new mother-in-law and one to her beloved mother. Now unencumbered, each brother approached and presented her with a rose (red, of course) and a kiss. They all took their places around the *chupah*, just as they had encircled each other during the Bar Mitzvahs.

The children grew, and the time came for the youngest to go off to the university. After seeing him safe, his parents returned to the empty castle. Facing the fire, with his back turned to his wife, Sydney quietly said, "We should have had ten."

The king and queen provided a magical, marvelous childhood for their children, filled with love of family, respect for each other, pride and love of Judaism, and a strong sense of who they are. The education that they provided enabled each child to enter the medical profession. Their varied choices within the same field affirm their individuality, anchored in their unity. Their only strife, now, is related to conflicts of professional opinions. Whereas the surgeons might choose a course of treatment that involves removal of an "offending" organ, their brothers, the chiropractors, might take a less invasive course of action. Though geographic distance separates them, they still try to get together often. Expecting only 4 of her children this past Thanksgiving, their mother was shocked when all 8 (and their families—a total of 32 people) showed up to combine the holiday with a birthday surprise for her.

Still regal and elegant, the queen lives alone, now, in the castle. Every inch of the house is filled with wonderful memories of her children and her husband. However, there is very little time for melancholy reverie. Every evening her phone rings repeatedly with little voices asking, "Grandma, are you there?"

Dr. Bruce Kirshner—optometrist—Kingston, PA
Dr. Ronald Kirshner—cardio-thoracic surgeon—Rochester, NY
Carla Dawn Breitman—former medical technologist (currently employed in an art museum)—Philadelphia, PA
Dr. Todd Kirshner—chiropractor—Ann Arbor, MI
Dr. Drew Kirshner—cardio-thoracic surgeon—IN
Dr. Cory Kirshner—chiropractor—Allentown, PA
Dr. Rand Kirshner—anesthesiologist—Washington, DC
Dr. Merrick Kirshner—cardio-thoracic surgeon—Phoenix, AZ

NACHAS!

23

THE RIGHT STUFF

Allen Feuer—August 29, 1981

From the parasha *we learn that "Man is the only creature, earthly or heavenly, who has been granted this treasured gift of being able to choose his own destiny. Nevertheless, God desires that we make the correct choice. . . .* On the day that Allen Feuer "became a man," he made a choice that would set the framework for the rest of his life.*

The vibrant colors of Gerber daisies adorned the *Kiddush* tables. The oranges and yellows were a perfect choice for this festive occasion. The fragrant aroma of whitefish, lox and bagels, and coffee wafted upstairs into the sanctuary.

The Torah Anthology, Rabbi Shmuel Yerushalmi, Maznaim Publishing Corporation, New York, Volume 17, page 108.

Steven Feuer sat in the front of the *shul*, near the *bimah*, and glanced around the room. With a nod and a smile, he acknowledged friends and family who came to share Allen's Bar Mitzvah—but, more important, where was Allen? They'd arrived together, but as *Shacharit* (morning prayers) began, Allen disappeared. Steven knew his son to be a conscientious, responsible young man, so, more than concerned, he was curious as to the whereabouts of his son, the Bar Mitzvah boy.

Meanwhile, shortly after arriving in the *shul*, Allen had been silently summoned into the hall by his Bar Mitzvah and classroom teacher, Rabbi Chaim Tatel. In a very calm voice, almost casually, Rabbi Tatel explained that a mistake had been made. Different companies publish yearly calendars that correspond the date with the weekly *parasha* (portion) from the Torah and the subsequent Haftorah. According to Rabbi Tatel's calendar, he'd taught Allen the correct Haftorah, *Ariah So'arah*, for that week. However, Rabbi Groner, the congregation's rabbi, disagreed. His calendar stated that a different Haftorah, *Machar Chodesh*, was the appropriate one for that week.

With his normal jaunty demeanor, Rabbi Tatel gave Allen a choice: He could proceed and recite the Haftorah that he had diligently studied for the past several months, or he could quickly review the "correct" Haftorah, according to the pulpit rabbi, and recite that one.

Allen took a minute to look over the new Haftorah and quickly replied that he would chant the "right" one. He used the half hour or so, while the congregation was davening *Shacharit*, to learn his Haftorah, *Machar Chodesh*.

When the morning service was completed, family members were honored by being called up to the *bimah* to remove the Torah from the *Aron Kodesh* (Holy Ark) and place it on the podium. Allen would now read from the Torah, in front of the congregation, thereby initiating him as a Bar Mitzvah, a son of the commandments. As he proceeded through the melodic chanting of the Haftorah, he felt himself stumble a time or two on the unfamiliar words. However, to the ears of the congregation and Rabbi Tatel, his recitation was flawless.

Allen chose not to discuss this situation with his parents until the service was over. He didn't want to worry them unnecessarily and didn't want to mar this happy occasion for them in any way. His maternal grandparents had survived the work camps in Germany during World War II. His mother, Dora, was born in a displaced person's camp after the war. Allen was the firstborn son and the first in his family to become a Bar Mitzvah after the war.

His parents were impressed not only with his decision to read the right Haftorah, but also with his performance. They knew that Allen was a bright student, but for him to learn and recite a Haftorah in a matter of minutes in order to "do the right thing" gave them further insight into his character.

As the guests reassembled in the social hall for the *Kiddush*, Steven and Dora Feuer were *kvelling* ("swelling with pride"). They found themselves greeting their friends and family and repeating this story of Allen's accomplishment.

As Allen grew older, so, too, did his list of accomplishments. At awards night of his senior year at Vestal High School, his parents were thrilled to find that Allen was singled out as the only student to maintain a 93+ average for seven consecutive semesters. As an economics major at Brandeis University, Allen graduated with honors.

Steven's only disappointment with his son was that Allen did not follow in his footsteps. He had hoped that Allen, too, would become a pharmacist and take over the family business, the Clintwood Pharmacy, a cornerstone in downtown Binghamton, New York.

Meanwhile, Allen had dreams of his own. He has taken many of his personal strengths and incorporated them into a career. Being soft-spoken, strong-willed, organized, discriminating, and articulate, with the ability to pay meticulous attention to detail, he has chosen to remain behind the scenes as a production manager at the Discovery Channel in Washington, D.C.

While at Brandeis, Allen was introduced, by a mutual friend, to his wife, Melissa. Melissa says that prior to the introduction Allen was described as "extremely loyal, helpful, and would do anything for anyone." As for the Bar Mitzvah story, which has now taken on folklore status in the Feuer home, Melissa added, "I'm not surprised that Allen learned the 'right Haftorah.' He is stubborn and has to do it right or not at all."

24

DOR L'DOR

The Yunker Torah—1958–present

Since 1958, the Yunker Torah has been used by eight members of the Yunker family for Bar and Bat Mitzvahs.

Michael, the first to use the Torah, is a dentist in Rochester, New York. Both of his daughters, Jessica, a graduate student at Touro College in Manhattan, and Molly, a student at Case Western Reserve University, followed their father's example by reading from the Yunker Torah at their Bat Mitzvah ceremonies.

Photo by The Prism

M olly Yunker felt that her Torah portion for her Bat Mitzvah fit her well, because she is artistic, creative, and not afraid to go new places. In her portion God tells Abraham, "Go to a land that I will show you." Even though Abraham didn't know his destination, his faith allowed him to follow God's command. There were risks and dangers along the way, but Abraham faced them all courageously.

Molly probably inherited her adventurous nature from her grandfather or maybe from her great-grandfather. The Yunker family lived in the small town of Neustadt on Aische, in the Bavarian section of Germany. In the late 1920s and early 1930s, Sigmund Yunker could feel the town's growing unrest and more blatant anti-Semitism. He recognized sadly that this country, which had been home to both his and his wife's families for generations, was no longer safe. Not wanting to find himself in a similar predicament elsewhere, he sent his four sons to scout out new lands.

Edwin, the third son, arrived in New York first. Being sponsored by a distant relative, he boarded a cross-country train, with a typed letter as his only means of communication. Unable to speak English, the letter identified him, outlined his destination, and listed a contact person in case of emergency. He sent back glowing reports of this new country to his family, because he started a new job, met and married a California girl, and became Americanized rather quickly.

Meanwhile, back in Germany, the situation grew more ominous. Subtle acts of anti-Semitism had now become outright. Public policies became vehicles for terror. Former factory workers, bank tellers, and store clerks transformed themselves with their new attire—the uniform of the Third Reich. The outward metamorphosis gave people license to release long-held feelings of hatred toward their Jewish neighbors. Later they would claim that they were just following orders, but they carried out their ministrations with a delight and enthusiasm that belied this lame excuse.

As part of the "final solution," Hitler ordered all Jewish schools, businesses, and places of worship, along with their contents, to be destroyed. Bands of hoods, approaching their work with relish, torched and demolished these structures. They paid little heed to the historic role played by some of these buildings. With only destruction of a culture and people in mind, they had little thought of architectural preservation.

The synagogue in Neustadt was burning. The townsfolk recognized that, if nothing else, they must save the Torah. The Torah—the Five Books of Moses—was hand-lettered on parchment. Our history, our law, our heritage. So holy, that every letter or marking must be perfect. Someone rushed into the building and was able to save the precious scrolls. Knowing that the Yunkers were a religious family, the Torah was brought to them.

In this atmosphere, Sigmund obtained affidavits for himself, his wife, and their two remaining sons (Arthur, the second son, had already left for America), but couldn't get visas to leave. Daily, someone from the family went to the minister's office, but every request was met with denial. That is, until Max's (the oldest son's) wife, Beatrice, went one day. She waited in the queue at the office until she noticed a high-ranking officer exit through a side door. She demurely approached him and explained her request. As she was a beautiful woman, the officer was quite taken with her. The family was given its visas!

The Yunkers were allowed to leave, but were permitted to take nothing with them. They were told that everything they had was the property of the "state." They couldn't take their money out; however, they were allowed to book passage. Without taking any chances, Sigmund lined up first-class transportation to several different ports. Knowing the plight of the Jews and the immediacy of their need to leave, profiteers commonly extorted money for passages that didn't exist. The family flew to Amsterdam on a Friday in 1938 and found that the only legitimate voyage would take them to the United States. Luck was with them. The following Monday, the Gestapo came to round up Max and his family because of the sensitive nature of his work. When the Yunker family embarked on that ship, the Torah was with them.

Since Arthur had arrived a few months earlier, he arranged a business for himself and his brothers. Once again, with the aid of a relative, they founded a children's clothing factory in New York City. After several years, the business, along with the family, relocated to Parkersburg, West Virgina. When they had first arrived in New York, they placed the Torah "on loan" in the Hebrew Tabernacle Synagogue in Brooklyn. However, after their relocation, Max felt that the Torah should follow the Yunker clan wherever they gathered for prayer. In 1953, in a special Torah service, the Yunker Torah was placed in the *Aron Kodesh* of their *shul* in Parkersburg. Along with the Torah having a new home, the brothers had a new velvet cover embroidered to read, "In loving memory of our parents, Sigmund and Gitta Yunker."

In 1958, when Michael Yunker, the first grandchild in the family to become a Bar Mitzvah, was preparing for his service, the Torah took on even more significance. Of the fifty Jewish families from Neustadt on Aische, the Yunkers were one of the few to survive. When Michael read from the Torah on the day that he assumed adult responsibilities, he did so with much more than himself in mind. This Torah represented not only the survival of one family from a remote town in Germany, but it symbolized the survival and the continuity of the Jewish people. *Dor L'Dor*—from one generation to the next. Michael stood with his father and his uncles in this foreign place that had become home. His family had been transplanted by necessity, and his Bar Mitzvah represented the perpetuation of a tradition, language, culture, and heritage that traces its roots back thousands of years.

Now living in Rochester, New York, Michael's daughters both read from the Torah on their Bat Mitzvahs. For Jessica, the oldest, Michael made the long trek to Parkersburg to collect the Torah. In Jessica's speech she said,

> Although over 6 million Jews were killed during the Holocaust, some of the religious articles are still being passed down and used by the next generations. This Torah may be one of the last remnants of that small Jewish community in Neustadt, Germany. An entire culture can be destroyed, but its memory still lives on through its descendents. Therefore, I am very proud to be able to read from this special family Torah at my Bat Mitzvah this morning.

After the Bat Mitzvah, Michael shlepped back to Parkersburg and returned the Torah to its home of almost forty years. When the time came for Molly's Bat Mitzvah, four years later, Michael decided to effect Max's wish that the Torah follow the Yunker clan. Michael and Molly made their final trip to Parkersburg. Because no family remained in West Virginia, they moved the Torah to their temple in Rochester, permanently.

Unfortunately, the Torah, which is estimated to be 130 years old, is no longer kosher for use and is impossible to repair. It is still honored as part of the family tradition. The next generation, Sigmund and Gitta's great-grandchildren, Ruth and Samuel Ginsburg, both incorporated the Torah into their Bar and Bat Mitzvah ceremonies, even though they could no longer read from it. The Torah was lovingly and carefully transported to these events and treated with the well-deserved respect of a prominent guest. Its presence is a constant beautiful reminder of our endurance, tenacity, and strength.

Like our patriarch, Abraham, the Yunkers had to leave the home of their fathers and move to a new land. Their move, however, was prompted by the malice of man, rather by than divine order. Nonetheless, in each case faith played an important role. Faith allowed Abraham to follow God's order and in the process undergo severe trials and tribulations. He emerged from his ordeal with the promise that his future generations would be like the "stars in the sky." The Yunker's journey, too, involved great peril. Their faith was demonstrated by the preservation, custody, and care of the Torah, even though this involved tremendous risk in smuggling it out of Germany. In turn, the Torah represents the failed attempt to extinguish Abraham's descendents and the promise that our stars will continue to light up the sky.

25

DESERT SNOW

Ari Klionsky—December 1979, February 1980

Ari currently lives in Mill Valley, California, with his wife, Nicole, and daughter Ally Ray. He is the co-founder and vice president of Business Development for CYGENT, Inc., of San Francisco.

There is an old joke: Mr. Schwartz, a wealthy business-man and a bit of a show-off, wanted his son's Bar Mitzvah to be special, unparalleled, and one-of-a-kind. So he arranged for an African safari where his party would be transported deep into the jungle. They loaded up the Torah and prayer books onto their pack animals for this unique service. The parade of jeeps was flanked on either side by elephants festooned with flowers and colorful decorations. No expense was spared to keep the guests happy, as they made their way to a remote site where the ceremony would take place. As they neared their destination, they were alarmed and surprised to hear the sound of a horse galloping in pursuit at breakneck speed. Its rider, weighted down with cases haphazardly strapped about his neck and bouncing with each stride, appeared nervous and tense. Sensing imminent danger, Mr. Schwartz approached the man and asked, "May I help you?" Grateful to see this party, the man replied, "Is this the Plotkin Bar Mitzvah?" (APPLAUSE . . . strike the cymbals . . . cha ching!)

Okay, fast forward to the Klionsky Bar Mitzvah. By the time Ari Klionsky had reached fifth grade, a schism had appeared in his class of six boys and two girls at the Hebrew day school in Binghamton, New York. Three of the boys wanted more *Chumash* and less rest periods. Ari and the two other boys wanted less *Chumash* and davening and more baseball. They were all bright, but a wedge was driven between the factions. Ari just said "phooey" to this business and literally ran away from school. Trying to be a reasonable man, the principal sat down in the Klionsky kitchen to discuss the situation. In a somewhat paternalistic (and maybe a little patronizing) voice, the principal began, "Now Ari, tell me what you don't like." Not one to be shy, Ari boldly responded, "Everything, starting with you." The principal quickly agreed that Ari would be happier in the public school system.

In spite of his other siblings either remaining at the day school or having already graduated from there and his father being a chairman of the board, Ari forged his own path in public school, now having more time to devote to sports and his favorite, baseball. His father hired one of the teachers from the school, Rabbi Tuvia Pearlman, to tutor Ari for his Bar Mitzvah, which was to take place in February of 1980. And then someone got a bright idea. The dialogue went something like this:

"But we are going to be in Israel, anyway." (Dad)

"I don't want two Bar Mitzvahs. It's hard enough to learn one *parasha*, let alone two." (Ari)

"But won't it be wonderful? We'll be at the Wall. You only have to learn the *brachot* and one *aliyah* for the service on Monday morning." (Dad)

"But I don't want to do it." (Ari)

"Great, we agree and it's all decided!" (You can guess who)

Sometimes a great notion . . . Ari's older brother, David, was spending a year in Israel studying with the young Judea program. The family, en masse, would visit him and spend some time in Israel during their winter break. Sy Klionsky (Ari's dad) got the idea that since they would be in Israel anyway and this was Ari's Bar Mitzvah year, wouldn't it be just great if they could celebrate there, and Ari would be called up to the Torah for the first time in this holy place. Sometimes a great notion, indeed!

It snowed . . . in the desert. It never snows in the desert. That's why it is a desert! Dry . . . little rainfall . . . no *water* . . . let alone snow. But it snowed. It snowed about six to eight inches in a country that is not prepared for this type of inclement weather. Sandstorms, yes . . . snow—definitely, not. The buses were not running, the city was immobilized, but Ari Klionsky was going to have his Bar Mitzvah in Jerusalem on that day. They carefully steered, plodded, and maneuvered their way through the streets and made their way to the Western Wall. Always bustling with the faithful from all religions, the wide-open plaza now stood empty and snow-covered. Wearing only street shoes, they stood up to their ankles in snow. Their rabbi in Binghamton had arranged for a rabbi to meet them there, but due to the weather, he was late. Ari's mother and sisters stood on chairs in the women's section and looked over the *mechitza* (partition). Normally, this is done so that the women in the party can watch the ceremony. The Klionsky women were more enterprising. They stood on chairs trying to keep their feet dry!

As the menfolk stamped their shoes, trying to keep their now soaked feet at least warm, if not dry, they were approached by a stranger in the deserted surroundings. He was obviously a photographer, with the tools of his trade hanging from each shoulder; they anticipated that this was the man they had hired. He approached rather tentatively and queried Mr. Klionsky, "Is this the *Goldberg* Bar Mitzvah?" Despite being freezing, wet, and alone, the Klionsky boys rolled with laughter, realizing that in spite of their own "unparalleled situation," with the Wailing Wall blanketed in eight inches of snow, they, too, were about to be upstaged!

Yes, the rabbi showed up. Their photographer eventually arrived, as well. They went ahead and had the service. Wearing his *tefillin* for the first time, Ari wrapped himself in his brand new *tallis*, more for warmth than for religious significance. Ari had his first *aliyah*, there was a short service, they posed for pictures at the Wall, and the family left quickly for a celebratory brunch (and hot coffee) in the Old City.

Two months later, in a sanctuary adorned in red and white in honor of the Cincinnati Reds, Ari was called up to the Torah, once again, and this time, because it was a *Shabbos*, he chanted a Haftorah. He delivered a speech that started: "This is the most unusual Bar Mitzvah you ever attended because today is not my Bar Mitzvah. I had that two months ago in Jerusalem. . . ."

Ari's uncle, an Orthodox rabbi, presented an unusual *D'var Torah*. Noting that everything was decked out in red and white, including Ari's mother, he compared the Jewish people to the Cincinnati Reds baseball team and each new Bar Mitzvah to a rookie. He noted that the veterans need to teach their newest members the ropes, but that each new addition keeps the team alive, viable, active, and ensures the future.

It's funny—for a kid who wanted nothing to do with his day school education, Ari had not only one, but two Bar Mitzvah celebrations. At least, at the second one, his feet were dry! He'll tell you that once is enough, but the special, unusual day in the snow at the Wall made the double obligation unforgettable. If he ever finds the Goldberg kid, he's sure that boy feels the same way.

26

A SURVIVOR'S STORY

Samuel Rosen—November 28, 1934

After sharing the following story, Sam's beloved wife Olga passed away. He now has a great-grandaughter, Olivia, named to honor her memory.

Samuel Rosenwasser got a new suit for his Bar Mitzvah. Not the store-bought kind, but one that was tailor-made from specially selected fabric sewn just for the occasion. Following the protocol of the day and place, the rest of the event was a lot less grandiose. Sam was called to the Torah on a Thursday morning. The Torah is read three times a week: Mondays, Thursdays, and *Shabbos*. There were so many boys of Bar Mitzvah age in the town of Secovce, Czechoslovakia, that in a given week on each of these days a boy might be called up to the Torah for the first time. Sam read the *Maftir*, said the *brachot*, and chanted the Haftorah. He received congratulatory handshakes and "*Yasher Koachs*" on his way back down the aisle. His mother sent in homemade *kichel*; his father provided the schnapps. The men drank to his health and went on their way to work; the young boys left for school. Sam, however, went home with his father and two older brothers to a special meal provided by his mother. The rabbi and the cantor joined them for this special occasion. Every meal in the Rosenwasser household was an event, with twelve children to feed, but his mother treated it like an art form and served a beautiful repast. Sam basked in the additional attention from his parents and siblings and accepted their kind gifts of pencils, a *Chumash*, a *siddur*, and some writing paper. Some friends stopped by to offer good wishes and bring simple gifts, as well.

Czechoslovakia in 1934 was a democratic country. Bernard Rosenwasser, Sam's father, owned a grocery store where wine and whiskey were sold. The family members got along well with their non-Jewish neighbors, and often they invited each other over to share in the different holidays. Knowing that the family kept kosher, gentile friends always made sure to provide food that the Rosenwassers could eat. All of the kids adored the same soccer and tennis players and aspired to play just like them. The president of the country, Masaryk, educated in America, was well respected by his countrymen. It was a beautiful country. And then the world fell apart. . . .

Sam was drafted into the Czech army at the age of 18. The first sign that things were awry was when Jewish soldiers were singled out by being made to wear blue uniforms and asked to return their traditional green ones. Then they had to trade in their guns for shovels and were put on road-building detail. In 1943, Sam heard from the underground that Jews were being exterminated. His unit was really a staging area for transfer to the concentration camps. Sam made plans to escape, but before he did, he wanted to go home and warn his family. Knowing that he would be caught immediately in the blue uniform, he persuaded a fellow soldier to loan him a green one. He arrived at his parents' home on Passover, the first seder night. His father had aged drastically, and his mother was crying. All of the children over the age of 12 had already been rounded up and taken away. Sam begged his parents and the remaining children to "disappear." His father looked at him quizzically and said, "I am a Czech citizen. I was a soldier for the Czech army during the first World War. I didn't do anything wrong." His parents refused to leave. That was the last time Sam saw his parents and his younger siblings.

He returned to the army and was fortunate to secure false papers identifying him as a Catholic. His luck ran out when the Gestapo challenged his papers, identified him as a Jew, and transported him to a concentration camp. He was in the Novaki camp for about a month when he decided he had to escape. He couldn't take the mental and physical torture any longer. One night he walked right through the gates that opened from one barracks to another. He didn't care if they caught him or killed him. He sold his meager possessions for the cost of a train ticket, about $8. He had just missed the train by ten minutes and needed to wait two hours for the next one. The wait seemed like twenty years. Luckily, he made it onto the train and slipped by unnoticed, without having his papers examined. He arrived in Presov, Czechoslovkia, and from there the underground helped him through the woods into Hungary, but not without incident. A young boy on a bike, no more than 11 years old, threatened to turn him in if he didn't turn over everything he had. He was being blackmailed by a prepubescent hood. With no choice, he gave up the few coins he had left and headed into town.

In dire need of papers, he was able to learn the few Polish phrases necessary to answer the basic questions posed by the authorities. He spent the next year as Jan Postawsky, a Polish Catholic. Ironically, he found a job in a grocery store. Not long after he was hired, he found out that the owner was a prominent Nazi supporter. When Jews were rounded up and their businesses abandoned, Sam's boss would confiscate the food and sell it in his own business. He also rented a truck to the Nazis who were transporting the luggage of Jewish children and old men who were being deported to the concentration camps. The luggage was carried in the trucks, while the human cargo was forced to walk alongside. Sam was given the task of driving the truck. Feigning the need to do his job quickly because he got paid by the truckload, Sam let the weakest ride in the truck, despite the protests of his boss and the Gestapo. It was the only kind thing he could do. He couldn't do anything about the crying children who had to wait in line for water or the bathroom, while the Nazis stood by and laughed. The Jews were completed degraded—treated worse than animals. Bald and starved to mere skeletons, they were completely dehumanized. Not only were Jews fodder for the gas chambers, but those strong enough were forced to clear the ashes and bone fragments in preparation for the next load. Sam observed these horrors and stood by helplessly, always fearing the worst for his family.

The Germans were given notice that some people in town had false papers and promised a roundup. This time, not only would papers be checked, but each man would be inspected to see if he had been circumcised. The thirty to forty young men who were summoned to headquarters drew lots to see who would go first. The unfortunate loser went into the interrogation room. Luckily, a bribe had been made by the underground, and only papers were checked!

The terror was the worst part. Sam lived with the unrelenting, stressful anticipation that at any moment he would be found out. Every day that he went undetected was a miracle. People never knew when it would be their time. They didn't know what their fate would be the next minute. Informants were unpredictable. An 11-year-old would turn Jews in for sport, or Jews might give themselves away with the wrong answer to a simple question. One day a young Polish woman came into the store and asked for "Pomidori." As a supposed "landsman," Sam should have been able to fill the order. He gave her potatoes instead of the tomatoes she asked for. She looked at him suspiciously, but kept her doubts to herself.

In 1944, the Russian army entered Hungary, and this time the Nazis were rounded up. With proficiency in several languages, including Russian and Hungarian, Sam became an interpreter for a Russian captain. Sam told them about his former boss, but by the time they got to the store, the owner had fled, leaving behind his wife and children. His wife was left to face the consequences alone and was deported to Siberia. Sam stayed with the Russian army until 1945.

Sam returned to his town, hoping that someone would be there. The first greeting he heard was "We thought you were dead. Why did you come back?" His family home had been purchased from the Germans. He went to court to win it back, but the victory was bittersweet. He was unwelcome and his family was gone . . . his parents, eleven brothers and sister, aunts, uncles, and cousins. Almost 250 members of his family were destroyed in the Holocaust. He was the sole survivor of a beautiful, vibrant, and now nonexistent family.

He heard that a young Jewish Czech girl was being held in jail on a trumped-up charge. She also had lost most of her family in the concentration camps. Sam and a friend were able to arrange for her freedom. In the process Sam fell in love and married her—his wife, Olga. As the threat of communism closed in around them, they were able to arrange passage to the United States. While they were waiting for their visas, Sam learned the fate of his beloved older brother Joseph, who had been an ordained rabbi. Living in a bunker with two other people, it had been his turn to search for food. When he left the bunker, he was shot by a retreating German army on February 9, 1945. His two companions were also shot, and all three were left to bleed to death. Someone crudely buried the bodies near the bunker. Upon learning this, Sam made arrangements to re-bury the three of them in the Jewish cemetery. The three were buried together because it was impossible to distinguish the remains of the decomposed bodies.

When Sam and Olga came to the United States, the new couple was greeted by Sam's uncle, his only living relative. Sam and Olga were diligent about learning English and became American citizens in 1953. Sam started working for his uncle's business, the National Pretzel Company. Even though the company has been purchased several times and now trades under the name of Anderson pretzels, Sam remained and has been a top salesman for almost fifty years.

He and Olga have two sons, Raymond and Steven, and five grandchildren. In 1994, they dedicated a Torah scroll that was brought to the United States by Memorial Scrolls Trust of

London, in memory of their family members who perished in the Holocaust. The Torah, from Czechoslovakia, was donated to the Scranton-Lackawanna Jewish Federation Holocaust Museum. The Torah is a memorial to those Sam and Olga lost, because they have no cemeteries or gravestones to visit. On the plaque accompanying the scroll, the Rosens inscribed the names of both sets of their parents, along with the names of Sam's eleven brothers and sisters. The Torah was dedicated during a Kristallnacht commemoration in a moving speech given by Lisa Rosen, their oldest grandchild. She told the crowd:

> The other reason (I came here to address you) is that it fulfills a very special promise that I once made. A long time ago, I made a pledge to my grandfather that one day, I would take over his responsibility of engraining the memory of the Holocaust into people's minds. That is why the dedication of this Torah is so significant. My grandparents have always been my living reminder of the Holocaust. Now, as I begin actualizing my responsibility, perhaps they have fulfilled theirs by giving this Torah to all of you, so that it may function as *your* reminder.

Recently, Sam and Olga had the pleasure of traveling to California to attend the Bar Mitzvah of their only grandson, Brat Rosen. The most poignant moment for Sam was Friday night as he sat around the *Shabbos* table with his family. His family. Almost fifty years ago, they came here with no one. Two survivors clinging together, trying to carry on after witnessing the unimaginable and unthinkable. They could never replace the hundreds of family members lost to an unmentionable tragedy. But they started again and built their own little family. Where there were two, there are now eleven healthy, thriving members of the Rosen family. Sam shared some advice with his grandson on the eve of his Bar Mitzvah: "Follow the Jewish traditions, stay with them. I've seen many boys become Bar Mitzvah and a month later they don't even know that they are Jewish. I want you to continue studying to be a Jew and then you are going to make something of your life. Then you are going to respect everybody. Just follow that tradition. Then, you'll be a mensche."

Sam has searched for answers and, coming up empty, he is still haunted. They had lived like everyone else, in a comfortable home with a loving mother and father, and the Holocaust changed everything. It's important for him that children and future generations will hear this story. The Holocaust happened. He was there. As he gets older, the memories are even more vivid and just as painful. Sam finds comfort in his family, his work, and his daily 3½ mile walk around the lake, where he brings peanuts and bread to feed the squirrels and chipmunks. He believes in God his own way. "Be a mensche . . . that covers all religions. That's my religion. I'm a mensche. I try to do as much good as I can, and I try to help. Don't listen to people when they say the Holocaust never happened. Speak up. Don't be afraid because the same thing can happen. Don't be afraid any more."

27

A STRONG CONNECTION

Danielle and Ari Rosenbaum—February 13, 1999

Ari and Danielle are in high school. Ari is a junior, still interested in acting and theater. He is starting to take a look at colleges. Danielle is a sophomore in the same school, in a special program.

Photo by Russell Smock

anielle and Ari—the Rosenbaum twins. Ari is a not-so-typical kid, very bright, mature, and a talented actor. Danielle is a not-so-typical kid, beautiful, funny, autistic, and mentally retarded. There was never any question that they would celebrate their B'nai Mitzvah together. It's a twin thing.

These twins—inexorably intertwined in each other's lives. Share a womb . . . share a room . . . share a life. Fraternal twins—one boy, one girl . . . one light, one dark . . . the yin and the yang. Somewhat opposite, yet connected by a bond others don't understand and too strong to be broken. No singular pronouns—no *I*, *Me*, *Mine*. . . . Rather, *We*, *Us*, *Our*, always.

They chose a *Havdalah* service. On a regular *Shabbat* morning, the Hebrew Educational Alliance in Denver, Colorado, has about 300 congregants. The crowd would be overwhelming for Danielle, who has problems with distractions and staying on task. The service would also be too long. So, they settled on an afternoon service, with Ari doing the "lion's share" and Danielle preparing to say the blessings before and after the Torah reading, read one line of Torah, and make a speech.

Because they chose an afternoon service, Ari realized that he would not be reciting a Haftorah. He liked the idea that reading the Haftorah was something the Bar/Bat Mitzvah gets to do by himself or herself, and he wanted that opportunity. So, he decided to tackle both the *Shabbat* morning services, alone, and the joint *Havdalah* services. This meant that he learned one *Maftir* and Haftorah for the morning, and because the next day begins at sundown, he learned a different Torah portion for the evening service. He was up to it and prepared for months to do twice the work.

Danielle studied for over a year for her Bat Mitzvah. She doesn't read or write, but has very good auditory memory skills. Her mother, Jane E. Rosenbaum, with her long-time college friend Susan Gluck, created a speech in rhyme that explained the Jewish holidays and several mitzvot. They designed a picture book, with photos of Danielle and family engaged in Jewish rituals and celebrating the holidays. The corresponding text was printed next to the pictures. The speech was then recorded, and Danielle listened to it and looked at the pictures endlessly over the course of the year. Everyone who came in or out of the house during that time memorized it right along with her. Her mother tried to accentuate her strengths to help her learn her part for the Bat Mitzvah.

For the day of the B'nai Mitzvah, Ari had a chance to shine singularly during the morning service. His mother commented that he sounded as if he read Torah every week, rather than for the very first time. Later that evening, he and Danielle lit up the room. They each wore a new *tallit* with a special *atarah* (collar) embroidered by their mother. Ari led the *Mincha* services. Even though Danielle is one minute older, Ari was first to make a speech. He explained the *parasha*, detailing the different levels of *tzedakah* and where and how he plans to donate a percentage of his gifts. He then turned his thoughts to a more personal nature:

> Danielle, I love you. You are the only one I want to share this B'nai Mitzvah with. I can't remember a time that I was mad at you. You are so beautiful. Don't let anyone push you around. People's imperfections make them special. . . . You already know that. . . .

It was then time for Danielle to make her speech. She was sandwiched on the *bimah* between Ari and family friend Laura Gluck. There were many old and new friends in attendance, and Ari was a little apprehensive. He feared that Danielle would ramble on or, worse yet, run off the *bimah* to say "Hi" to someone she might spot in the crowd. He started her off:

> Today I am called to the Torah,
> It makes me feel so proud,
> To stand here, friends and family,
> Before you and God, head bowed.
> For this special day I've learned a lot
> And tried hard to prepare,
> And those things about my Jewish life
> I would now like to share.

For the next several stanzas, Ari delivered the first few sentences, and Danielle would supply the last line. A few times she took over and moved from verse to verse by herself.

Midway in her speech, she paused, leaned toward Ari, and kissed him. He told her he loved her, and they continued. Sometimes it was difficult to understand Danielle's speech, but Ari knew exactly what she said. He gave her time to finish a line, and if it was not forthcoming he prompted her with the next word. They looked so beautiful together, him with his arm around her, so self-assured—completely uninhibited about supplying words like *yummy* and *tummy* so that Danielle would continue:

> Today I am called to the Torah,
> With Ari by my side,
> It's our day to become B'nai Mitzvot,
> And it fills us with pride.
>
> We thank you all for coming,
> How wonderful you have been!
> We thank God for bringing us to this day,
> And let us say, Amen.

As they came to the end of the speech, he leaned over and kissed her.

People were very moved, many to tears, but Ari just didn't "get it." He didn't understand how much they, he and Danielle, had touched people. The rabbi commented that if ever there was an instance when God was in the sanctuary, it was on that day. Ari stood on the *bimah* with his arm around his sister, keeping her focused, lovingly, gently encouraging her—observable evidence of their connection. That is just their life. He doesn't see their relationship as unusual. That's just who he is and just who she is—they are twins.

28

REDEMPTION

Edward Asner—October, 1942

Ed Asner is enjoying a long, prolific career that has spanned over half a century. He has delighted audiences with his work on the stage, television, and in the movies.

Photo by Michael Greco

The "Industrial Removal Office" sounds like a massive effort for extermination and pest control. It was in fact an office set up in the early part of the twentieth century to ease the congestion of Jewish migration in the large cities that were ports of entry. Its goal was to find economic opportunities in America's hinterlands for new Jewish immigrants. More to the point, it was an effort to "fan" out the ever-growing Jewish population. As a result of the devastating pogroms in Russia and Eastern Europe, immigration was at an all-time high. For some of our ancestors, if they had a chance to read the inscription at the base of the Statue of Liberty, it was on the move. They were shuffled from boat to train or wagon as quickly as possible and sent off to less crowded cities in the Southwest. Some never even glimpsed Lady Liberty; they entered the United States through the smaller port of Galveston, Texas. Although we have the stereotypical picture of our grandmothers and grandfathers huddled together in overcrowded tenements, quite a few of our foremothers and fathers were spread out over the plains of the Midwest.

Because he had a "landsman" there, Morris Asner and his brother Itzik found themselves in Kansas City, Kansas, at the turn of the century, after they made their way from Eastern Europe to America. Without any farming experience, they set up a junk yard and proceeded to raise their families in the Orthodox tradition among the 100 or so Jewish families who resided there.

Edward, the youngest of Morris's five children, was the third Asner boy to celebrate his Bar Mitzvah in the Ohev Shalom synagogue. He was the rabbi's prize student. As such, the rabbi felt that young Edward could take on more than the average student, so he assigned the boy the coveted task of conducting the Sabbath services, in addition to reading the Torah. But prior to the Bar Mitzvah, the rabbi left for an extended vacation, giving this young man insufficient time to prepare for his special day.

He probably could have done it, but he let his insecurity take over and his recitation came out high-pitched and much too fast. At one point, he clasped his hands behind his back, close to his hindquarters. His father reached across the bimah, slapped them away, and said in Yiddish, "It doesn't look good." It didn't help that his father and uncle patrolled behind him and kept muttering, "Too fast!" in Yiddish. This constant interference indeed yielded a performance that was high, strident, and produced at warp speed. At its conclusion, he deemed himself a total flop.

Ed Asner would say years later that his Bar Mitzvah was instrumental in his becoming an actor. He was so lousy that he had to become a performer to show that he could actually do the Haftorah and make a speech. From that inauspicious beginning, he redeemed himself in the course of a prolific, varied, and well-respected career that has spanned nearly half a century. He has won seven Emmy awards, five of which are for the character of Lou Grant. These well-deserved honors are for the unique talent, balance, and insight to play the same character in both a comedy and a dramatic series. There are also five Golden Globe awards adorning his mantle. He has graced the stage, screen, and television.

Lou Grant, the crusty, crusading newsman, concealed a soft, sensitive heart. As life imitates art, Ed Asner is an outspoken crusader, unafraid to take a stand for the issues he believes in. He has been the national president of the Screen Actor's Guild twice during the 1980s and is active in many humanitarian and political organizations. He learned some of his earliest lessons about activism while growing up Kansas. When he was in high school, there was a miner's strike. Repeating the platitudes he heard around him, he criticized the miners by spouting off how lucky they were to have a job. It was Ed Ellis, his football coach, who took him aside and provided a valuable life lesson. The coach told him that you can't take away a man's right to strike. That was his first "face-to-face rebellion" that begot justice. Perhaps those words caused Asner to take an active role in the actor's strike of 1980.

Not all the lessons growing up were so easily learned. Being a Jew in Kansas was difficult. He was subjected to prejudice and called a "Dirty Jew." He still feels guilty about caving in to peer pressure and playing football on Kol Nidre. And, despite his football activity, he was blackballed from his high school fraternity. No one had a problem with his personality, just his religion.

He's very serious about his religion, without taking his religion seriously. He loves to hear the *shofar* and the singing of *Aveinu Malkeinu.* His family gathers for the seder on Passover. He goes to the synagogue several times a year. The Steven Weiss Temple in Bel Air, affectionately known as "Our Lady of the Highways," is where he holds membership. He openly exalts his Judaism in his work and during interviews. He views the Bar and Bat Mitzvah as a great moment and an honor, and he would advise young people to relax and enjoy it. It was at his son Matthew's Bar Mitzvah, with the boy's perfect recitation, that Asner finally felt exonerated for his own lacking performance.

And yet nothing has been lacking in his lifetime of performances, which include Emmy award-winning portrayals, as well as voices of cartoon characters, each delivered with the same intense level of professionalism. In addition, he speaks out on various issues and not only as part of his celebrity. He does so as an actor, a citizen, but especially as a Jew, and feels that everyone should get involved. The words of Hillel ring loudly with Asner, "If I am only for myself, what am I?" There have been accolades and honors, tributes and testimonies, with certificates and presentations enough to paper a small house. However, praise doesn't have to come in shiny packages or be delivered in eloquent language. Perhaps one of the most cherished acknowledgments of his work came from his harshest critic. After his father passed away and Ed had kids of his own, his mother confided, "Ve vas wrong and I'm glad."

Background information on immigration was found in *The Shores of Refuge* by Ronald Saunders, Schocken Publishers, 1988.

29

AN UNLIKELY SETTING

Joshua Adler*—Fall, 1987

Rabbi Sara Perman has seen men turn their lives around and others who are entrenched in the prison culture. Rather than the "rookie" rabbi she was when she started in Greensburg, she is now a married, seasoned professional. But even with all of her experience, she still looks back fondly upon the tough young guy who, for all of his exposure to the seamy side of life, went back to an age-old tradition to proclaim his belated sense of maturity and responsibility.

R abbi Sara Perman was a young single woman when she took over the rabbinate of Congregation Emanuel Israel in Greensburg, Pennsylvania. It is a suburban Reform temple outside of Pittsburgh with a membership of 125 families. Being new and excited about the position, she came

---

*Author's note: This story was told to the author by Rabbi Perman. The story is true; however, the name has been changed to protect the privacy of the young man.

141

with many of her own ideas that she learned while a student at Hebrew Union College—Jewish Institute of Religion. At the same time, she was savvy enough to know that she was expected to continue certain established practices. One of these duties included the chaplaincy at the medium-security state facility in Greensburg—the jail.

Rabbi Perman had limited expertise in this arena, having ministered only once before in a high-profile case in a prison in a different state. Feeling rather tentative, she entered the world of clanging keys and locked doors. Sensing her apprehension, the prisoners she visited became protective and subsequently quelled her fears. They became her defenders from off-color or offensive comments made by other inmates. She swiftly settled into a routine of comfortable weekly meetings with "her guys." Most of the men in this "extended congregation" were doing time for drug-related crimes and/or larceny.

Josh Adler was different. A dark-haired young man in his early twenties, he had committed a violent crime—assault. Before his formal arrest, he had tried to escape. He was apprehended in Niagara Falls, trying to go over the border into Canada. He had hoped to get to Israel where his grandmother lived. In spite of being raised in a traditional home, he was a rebellious kid and had an early criminal history. He was already incarcerated when Rabbi Perman started going to the jail.

Her visits with each prisoner were different, based mostly on what they wanted. She provided pastoral counseling to some, while others just wanted to chat. Some industrious souls even used the opportunity with this private tutor to learn Hebrew. Rabbi Perman started meeting with Josh, and at first they just talked about what he hoped to do upon his release. He had his green papers, and he knew he would be paroled, eventually. Josh told the rabbi that what he really wanted before he left was to become a Bar Mitzvah. He felt that he had finally grown up and matured, and he wanted to have a Bar Mitzvah as recognition of his Jewish maturity, as well as of his secular maturity. When he was 13, he was too oppositional to follow the traditional mandates of the celebration. He felt that he was ready now.

He could already read Hebrew, but it was rusty. So, they practiced the prayers, blessings, and his Torah portion. They used their weekly sessions now in Bar Mitzvah preparation.

Traditionally, the Bar Mitzvah boy prepares in advance and on the assigned day goes to the synagogue to face the congregation. In Josh Adler's case, the congregation came to him. Rabbi Perman rounded up a *minyan*-ful of willing congregants who would serve as participants and witnesses of this interesting mitzvah. They loaded up their cars with a Torah, *tallisim*, and *Chumashim* (the Five Books of Moses). The chapel in the jail already had prayer books and yarmulkes.

Arms laden with books, religious objects, and food for the *Kiddush*, each person had to pass through the metal detector. In the prison, these detectors are super-sensitive and a hairpin or a wedding ring will set them off. After quite a bit of commotion, back and forth motion, and the removal of jewelry, belt buckles, and hair ornaments, the crowd made its way to the chapel, which is located deep into the prison, far away from the normal visiting rooms.

Attired in their brown prison uniforms, Josh and several other Jewish prisoners entered the chapel. The guards have a right to come in, but on this day, for this ceremony, they all respectfully remained outside the glass enclosure. Rabbi Perman carried the prison-issue whistle in case a problem arose and was instructed on the whereabouts of the "panic button." Josh donned one of the transported *tallisim* and a black silk yarmulke, which stubbornly remained pointed and never quite molded to his head.

Rabbi Perman began the service and was assisted with some of the prayers by those in attendance. She sang out the call to the Bar Mitzvah "boy," and Josh came forward. He recited the blessings before and after the Torah reading, read the *Maftir*, and read, rather than chanted, his Haftorah. He then made a speech, specifically addressing his father, who, in spite of his son's rebelliousness, legal problems, and ultimate incarceration, had remained involved and supportive. Josh talked about getting caught, serving his time, and now wanting to put his life right. He was quite articulate about how he saw himself as maturing, and this ceremony was the most public demonstration of that change.

They celebrated with bagels, lox, and cream cheese (spread with plastic utensils), coffee cake, and orange juice. For this part of the ceremony, the guards accepted the invitation to partake.

Josh's release from prison came about several months later. He went back to school and looked for a job. He called the rabbi only once to tell her of his progress, and then they lost touch. Rabbi Perman still makes her weekly sojourns out to the prison.

30

THE PANAMA CANAL

Daniel T. Barkowitz—August 2, 1982

Daniel T. Barkowitz lives in Newton, MA, and is the Director of Financial Aid at the Massachusetts Institute of Technology. He and his wife, Rebekah, are the proud parents of Rachel and Caroline, who look forward to having a Bat Mitzvah tutor other than their father.

D aniel Barkowitz was born in a place that doesn't exist . . . anymore. The undoing of his birthplace was not the result of celestial interference, but rather the effect of more earthbound events. On December 31, 1999, the United States handed the Panama Canal over to Panama, after building it nearly one century ago. The former Panama Canal Zone is now simply called Panama's canal. Formerly run by the Panama Canal Commission, a U.S. government agency, the administration of this man-made wonder falls on the Panama Canal Authority, an autonomous corporation.

Daniel's father, Seymour Barkowitz, was fascinated with languages. He studied ancient Greek and Latin, but a professor at the College of Charleston instilled in him a love of Spanish. Completing only his freshmen year in college, he was called to duty during World War II. Taking advantage of the GI Bill upon his return home, he was able to complete both his undergraduate and his graduate education. Winning a Ford Foundation Fellowship allowed him, his wife, Leah, and their first child to live in Spain for almost a year and to immerse themselves in the language and culture. This marvelous experience prompted him to apply for a teaching position in the Canal Zone, a temporary position. Being adventurous, but reluctant to leave her Charleston, South Carolina, home where her family had lived for generations, Leah said she would move only with the stipulation that if she didn't like it after a year, they could go home. That was 1955. Seymour kept that standing promise for the next 28 years.

In the American schools, set up for the children of American servicemen and women, Seymour started as a Spanish teacher. His career advanced, and he ultimately assumed the position of principal at Curundu Jr. High School.

In many ways, their life on Panama was charmed. They enjoyed the luxury of a full-time maid. Because the Panama Canal Commission owned their house, the company accepted the full responsibility for its maintenance. There was a large supermarket and the Army PX, in which they could purchase anything from toiletries to furniture. And the last perk was that every other year the army would fly them back to Charleston in the summer. On alternate years, they took commercial airlines back to the States.

Arriving with two children, the Barkowitz family expanded when their third and fourth were born in Panama. Daniel, the youngest, was teased as the "lonely" child because seventeen, fourteen, and eleven years, respectively, separated him from his three older siblings, Paul, Edith, and Joseph. Daniel was definitely the "caboose," a distinction that enabled him to form a special bond with his parents in an already close family.

United Servicemen's Organizations (USOs) tend to conjure up images of girls in pretty dresses dancing with lonely GIs. But the USO office in the Canal Zone functioned more practically. Offices in the front opened up to a large multipurpose room, which served on the Sabbath and holidays as the synagogue. And being dissatisfied with the available preschools for her youngest, Leah Barkowitz set up her own program in the back of the building.

Leah organized a full-day program that started daily with swim lessons. This early familiarity and comfort with the water was probably the impetus for Daniel's later career on the swim team in both junior and senior high school. Leah's little school also attracted the children of the international bankers who worked in Panama. The diverse nature of the student body enhanced not only the curriculum, but also the daily interactions of the youngsters. It was not just a school for the privileged. Leah convinced Aura, their maid, to send her youngest to the school. The two boys grew up together, and their camaraderie led to fluency in each other's language.

The USO *shul* was certainly not the first injection of Judaism into Panama. Other Jewish families there can trace their roots back to their ancestors' escape from the Spanish Inquisition. There were three well-established synagogues—two Orthodox congregations and one Reform temple. The "congregation" of the USO *shul* was transient, due to rotating tours of duty. The numbers varied, but ranged up to forty families at one point. At one time, an official rabbi served as spiritual leader, but when he made *aliyah*, he was never replaced. With his Orthodox background and beautiful voice, Seymour Barkowitz became the perfect choice for "lay leader." Seymour took over the role, not because he enjoyed the limelight, but because he loved the music. He sang from his heart. At the same time, Seymour started the only English-speaking Jewish religious school in the Canal Zone. Before that, Americans had to send their children into Panama for religious education, studying Jewish culture and laws in Spanish.

When it came time for Daniel's Bar Mitzvah preparations, the responsibility fell to his father, who was already the boy's religious lay leader, as well as his junior high school principal! Actually, Seymour tutored all of the kids in the Canal Zone for their Bar Mitzvahs after the rabbi left. Only this time, the student was his son. Seymour never charged for this service. He always teased that if he were to charge what he was worth, people couldn't afford him. Seymour recorded the entire liturgy, *parasha*, and Haftorah on a series of twelve tapes. They set aside a weekly time slot devoted to Bar Mitzvah lessons, but Dad was around to make sure that his son practiced. Their car rides, with the tapes in the tape player, became the perfect opportunity to supplement his regular study time.

Daniel studied not only for himself. In the Soviet Union there was tremendous anti-Semitism and prohibitions against practicing Judaism. Jews who applied to leave the country were called "Refusniks." The government refused their request and then used their application as a means of persecution. Their employment was terminated, and prison time was often the reward for their audacity in asking to leave the "Motherland." Jews were not permitted to practice Judaism, yet were denied the right to leave. One such family, Ada and Aron Averbukh, from Kishinev, Russia, had a son, Dorman, who was also turning 13. Under Soviet law, anyone under the age of 16 was forbidden to take part in a religious practice, so Dorman was not able to celebrate becoming a Bar Mitzvah. Listening to the tapes and attending to his lessons, Daniel practiced for the two of them, knowing that when he chanted it for real, he was symbolically "twinning" with Dorman. Daniel would share his Bar Mitzvah with a Russian Jewish child deprived of the right to celebrate this age-old custom as if the child were standing on the *bimah* with him, not thousands of miles away.

On the day of his Bar Mitzvah, Daniel stood on the *bimah* next to his father. In spite of his nervousness, he recognized on this day as he entered manhood how special it was to stand next to his role model, his spiritual advisor: his father. His three-piece brown suit was somewhat in contrast to the military uniforms and the Guayevera shirts of those facing him in the congregation. The guest list read like something from Cinderella's ball, with many of the names being prefixed with military ranks and honorary titles. Because Daniel had inherited a beautiful voice from his father, those in attendance who didn't understand the words could still share in the joy of the day and delight in the beauty of the service. As in ancient days, father taught son and passed on not only the rights and responsibilities of adulthood, but the beauty and pride of our heritage.

When Daniel completed the religious part of the service, he shared these words:

> My father told me this is the end of the beginning. . . . long before this wonderful Bar Mitzvah day, a Jewish boy is introduced early in life to the synagogue, and he is allowed to participate in little things that make him feel a part of the Jewish services. . . .
>
> . . . (this) is a deliberate act on the part of the parents to help guide children into becoming an active part in the Jewish way of life . . . "the end of the beginning." Beginning today I stand on my own two feet as a full-fledged participant in Jewish life and customs.

A year after the Bar Mitzvah, Seymour and Leah decided to retire and return to South Carolina. Upon his retirement from working as principal of the Curundu Junior High School, Seymour was presented with a certificate of honor (and a medal) from the Panama Canal Company for years of service. Interestingly, the medal and certificate focused more on his religious contributions than on his secular ones.

For Daniel, entering a southern high school was a culture shock. Having attended school with natives of Panama, the black children of servicemen, and the sons and daughters of international businessman, color lines were blurred. Daniel was startled to discover what an issue race still was in Charleston. Restless and missing the company of young people who had captivated him for his entire educational career, Seymour became a substitute teacher in the city schools. His "second career" was short-lived; Seymour died while Daniel was still in high school. However, he left his family, especially his youngest son, a legacy that would serve him well. Through his various roles, Seymour had prepared his son to indeed stand on his own two feet and become a man. Though Daniel's birthplace no longer exists, the lessons learned there would last a lifetime.

31

MITZVAH 99

Alex Rosenthal—March 6, 1999

Alex does not play on his computer all day. He's an avid science fiction reader. He corresponded with science graduate student Zak Shalk as part of a program called "Science by Mail." He became so close with his "pen pal" that Zak came from Boston to share in Alex's Bar Mitzvah. Alex also plays classical and jazz clarinet.

Photo by Morgan's Photography

As Nancy Taubenslag, Alex Rosenthal's mother, prepared for her son's Bar Mitzvah, she remembered hearing that there was a place to buy yarmulkes where the proceeds went to help poor women. She made phone calls, asked around, and, still, no luck. She couldn't find the yarmulkes. As time grew nearer, she abandoned the idea and ordered *kipot* from a more traditional Judaica printing company.

The Taubenslag/Rosenthal family are members of the Reconstructionist Temple, Bet Am Shalom in White Plains, New York. Rabbi Lester Bronstein offers a ten-week class for the B'nai Mitzvah families, not only for the young man or woman, but for the parents as well. It is a time for the whole family to study and learn more about the prayers and the meaning of the Torah portion. During one of these classes, the rabbi mentioned that he knew of a place in Jerusalem where poor women made yarmulkes and used this source of income as their livelihood. Nancy felt frustrated that this information had not been available to her when she needed it. There didn't seem to be any central place that you could go to find information related to Bar and Bat Mitzvahs.

Nancy's son, Alex Rosenthal, liked to use the Internet and wanted to do a Bar Mitzvah project incorporating *tzedakah*. He wanted to create something of value, something that was important to him. Remembering his mother's frustration at not being able to find information readily, he decided to create a website called Mitzvah99. It became more than just a clearing house for Bar Mitzvah accessories. It is an inspired site that offers sage advice about the kind of Mitzvah projects other kids have done and suggestions for keeping the "mitzvah" in the preparation before, during, and after a Bar or Bat Mitzvah. The internet address is *http://members/aol.com/mitzvah99/ mypage*. Because many parental control programs (including AOL) do not allow teenagers to access any personal Web pages, adult readers might need to let their children use the parents' "adult access" to view Alex's website.

Log on and the following appears:

> Welcome to the Mitzvah99 B'nai Mitzvah suggestions homepage!
>
> The purpose of this page is to inform you what other people have done to have a fun but meaningful Bar/Bat Mitzvah. This page is mainly intended for the kids who are about to have their Bar/Bat Mitzvah and want to make the most out of the experience. I myself had my Bar Mitzvah on March 6, 1999.

This page contains suggestions for projects one can do before the event, for the service, for the reception, and for what to do afterwards. Please remember, and remind your guests to only give things that they would want to receive. Feel free to make your own personalized variations on these projects, as you see fit. If you have any further ideas, or wish to send some feedback, feel free to e-mail me at *Mitvah99@aol.com.*

Four links are listed that are labeled what mitzvahs you can do—"before the Bar/Bat Mitzvah," "during the service," "during the reception," and "after the event."

Where does he get his information? Alex heard Danny Siegel speak about Mitzvah Heroes during a lecture at his synagogue. Alex contacted Danny's foundation, the ZIV Tzedakah fund, and got some leads for stories. He sent a letter to all of the synagogues in the Westchester, New York, area to inform the rabbis of his project, asking them to publicize his website and share any stories they might have heard.

The list of things to do "before" the ceremony is two pages long. One example: "You could learn entertaining skills such as juggling and magic and perform them for hospitals, retirement homes, and disabled people. This would be a good mitzvah to do as a group, with friends or family." (Alex then lists names and numbers of contact people.)

During the service, Alex suggests that you can "invite Jewish elderly people from local retirement homes to come and enjoy your service." For the reception, you can "play games like 'Coke and Pepsi,' having the partners match up clothes. Then when the party is over, donate all of those clothes to a local charity." And most important, to emphasize that mitzvah projects should not end when the Bar/Bat Mitzvah ceremony does, two more pages list what you can do afterward. "You could send food to a less fortunate family for a holiday such as Passover, Purim, Rosh Hashanah, etc., through an agency (like UJA) which will locate a family and give them your food." In addition, "You can do a project such as the one I am doing now, which is informing people of good mitzvot they can incorporate into their Bar/Bat Mitzvah."

The website is dynamic, and information is added and updated. It is even listed on YAHOO under Bar Mitzvah information.

Alex's actual Bar Mitzvah took place on Saturday morning, March 6, 1999, where he read from *parasha Ki Tisa*, which includes the laws of the red heifer. Incorporating the ideas of using the ashes of the red heifer for purification purposes, he shared the following ideas with the congregation:

> The Bar Mitzvah ceremony is a form of ritual purification for Jews, not just now but throughout time. The ceremony starts with a long, steady climb upwards, on which the Bar/Bat Mitzvah is introduced to their Torah portion, Haftorah portion, prayers, blessings, etc. During that period, I became aware of ways I could become purer through mitzvot, charity, and good deeds. The Bar Mitzvah also requires sacrifices, of time, and of relaxation. And as I went through the process, more and more factors and details were added, making the climb harder, similar to the way air thins out when climbing a mountain. It was not an easy or quick process, but one that changed me. Once a person goes through the Bar Mitzvah ceremony, they have the capability to pass and spread purity on to others. They would be able to do this through Mitzvot and being an all-around mentsch. . . . Thus the Bar Mitzvah is not just passage from Jewish childhood to adulthood, but it is also a purification ritual that makes one able to make others pure.

Since Alex's Mom and Dad attended B'nai Mitzvah classes and studied right along with him, his father, Mauri, also presented a very heady *drosh* focusing on the themes of death, taxes, and Reconstructionism. On this day, otherwise filled with joy, there was one sad note. Alex's grandfather, who had never learned Hebrew, studied and learned Hebrew so that he could have an *aliyah* at his grandson's Bar Mitzvah. He was so proud of Alex and so proud to be part of the ceremony. One month before the Bar Mitzvah, he died. As an honor and memorial to her father, Nancy Traubenslag chanted what would have been his *aliyah.*

At his reception, Alex played jazz clarinet with his father and his father's fraternity friends, to a song that the frat made up in college (MIT). It was rather cool, since the song they played, called the "Bruce Tobis Blues" (named after another fraternity brother), is a kind of ritual for Mauri and his friends. This song was played at Nancy and Mauri's wedding, the wedding of every one of the band members, and other events. For Alex, "jamming" with these long-time friends was seen by his parents as a kind of "coming of age ritual" in itself.

The concept of "Bar Mitzvah" conjures up ritual objects made of silver, colorful *kipot*, fringed *tallisim*, and the scent of well-used *siddurim*. That traditional imagery is now upgraded to include a website. Starting out to provide information and publicize others' good deeds, Alex has gone on to inspire upcoming Bar and Bat Mitzvah students and challenge them to follow suit. Mitzvah99 is up and running and will remain viable as long as kids are out there performing mitzvah projects.

32

THE FLOOD

David Warshal, M.D.—June 23, 1972

If David felt disappointed at this scaled-down version of his ceremony, he also recognized with wonderment what was happening. This community—his community—was experiencing a full-scale natural disaster. Rather than the "extravaganza" that a Bar Mitzvah often is, his service was so "real." Out of need, under adverse conditions, a group of people came together to allow one member to mourn his loss, while publicly welcoming another. No pretensions, no show—just a very prepared young man taking life in his stride, following an

age-old tradition in a humble setting. They could have put it off, waited until the water receded and the cleaning commenced. They could have ordered new decorations, chosen a different menu, and finally worn their special clothes. Instead, it felt right to simply focus on the spiritual meaning of the event without worrying about extraneous details.

Policeman wielding bullhorns rolled slowly down the street in their open trucks, waking and warning the sleeping inhabitants to evacuate their homes. The river had risen to a dangerous level and was expected to crest within hours. The cry to "Get out of your houses!" could be heard up and down the Wyoming Valley, as the Susquehanna River raged with a vengeance. Although sheets of rain had slashed unceasingly for days, the idea of a flood was just unfathom-able—preposterous—impossible . . . maybe a little flooding, some water in the basement, a minor inconvenience. But a FLOOD . . . nah, that only happened in the Bible.

The river swept along, carrying with it downed trees, branches, and debris . . . constantly rising. Neighbor woke neighbor, and the town rallied in the early morning hours. All who could help migrated to the river's edge to sandbag and build up the visibly inadequate dikes. They labored in vain because the rain kept falling and the river kept rising. The trucks kept rolling, now with an increased intensity that kept pace with the ever-rising river. "Evacuate your homes. For your own safety, you must leave immediately!" bellowed tinny voices through the megaphones.

Where do you go? What do you take? What do you try to save? The incredulity of the residents prevented most of them from packing overnight bags and gathering valuables and keepsakes. People heeded the warnings somewhat reluctantly and left their homes. However, most thought this was just a temporary displacement and escaped empty-handed, leaving their possessions prey to the muddy waters.

At 10:00 A.M. on Friday morning, the bullhorns ceased, replaced by shrill blasts of an air-raid siren. The worst had happened! The dikes had broken! With power and fury, the water crashed through the dike, ripping the full front off a home opposite its banks. The water then snaked through the town like an octopus languidly stretching its tentacles.

David Warshal lived in a beautiful river-front home. Along with his neighbors, he and his father filled sandbag after sandbag, trying to build up dikes. Focusing on this manual task, he gave no thought to his Bar Mitzvah that was scheduled for the following morning. Scheduled to take place in Ohav Zedek Synagogue, where for years he had sat up front next to his grandfather, where he had "cut his teeth" with the singing of *Ein Kaloheinu*, and where tomorrow he would lead the service as a Bar Mitzvah. Now, there was no time for that. The immediacy of the situation precluded any thoughts of the *Kiddush* that would take place at the Sterling Hotel—a beautiful historical landmark, located across the street from the river.

When the water first broke through, the sandbaggers along the river banks recognized the futility of their efforts. The town of Wilkes Barre is nestled in a valley, so refuge had to be taken at higher elevations. Displaced residents looked to family and friends in nearby communities to put them up or suffered through makeshift shelters at local high school gymnasiums. Those lucky enough to find vacancies at nearby hotels snapped up the rooms quickly. People were loath to leave the area, because the damage from the swollen river and the duration of their exile were all unknown.

The Treadway Inn, located up the mountain and just outside of the city, provided a safe haven from the flooding river. It was a perfect respite for many of the Jewish families because the hotel also operated a kosher kitchen and catering service. Mark Kornfeld, the proprietor, recognized the need for shelter and canceled all outside reservations, making rooms for local residents the hotel's priority.

Mel Warshal, David's father, followed the first warnings and saw his family to safety at the Treadway; then he and David returned to town to resume their bagging. They finally left when they were forced to. Reunited in their hotel room, they began the waiting game—waiting to see what would happen and when they could go back home.

"Necessity is the mother of invention." In this newly created *shtebl* in the Treadway, one resident, Perry Shertz, a prominent attorney, needed to say *Kaddish* for his father who had recently died. Because he was assembling a *minyan* (the ten men needed for communal prayer) anyway, he proposed to the Warshals that they go ahead and have David's Bar Mitzvah as scheduled. A room was provided for this impromptu *Shabbat* morning service, and anyone was welcome to join. Jeans and T-shirts were the morning's attire, instead of the accustomed finery. Someone had a *siddur*, they found yarmulkes, and David's Aunt Connie somehow had the presence of mind to grab a small Torah on her way out the door. More decorative than official, this mini-Torah served them well.

David did all of the davening, and although no cantor officially summoned him to the "*bimah*," he proceeded with the reading of the *parasha* from this Torah. Mr. Shertz even provided a memorable extemporaneous sermon and concluding congratulatory remarks. Mrs. Liebenson brought a cake, and, with a purchased bottle of whiskey, they toasted and celebrated the newest Bar Mitzvah.

The water receded by Monday, leaving in its wake monumental destruction, devastation, and mud. Thick, viscous, smelly mud containing unmentionable debris blanketed every surface. Some shell-shocked residents went back into town, only to find their houses gone—literally swept away and deposited elsewhere. Without any power, refrigerators and freezers were off—leaving the townsfolk with the odious task of discarding spoiled and rotten food. Furniture was waterlogged, warped, and worthless.

And yet it was a captivating, fascinating time. Life was back to the basics. With everyone in the same predicament, there was no competition. The community became cohesive and tight. There were makeshift schools, synagogues, stores, and homes. Mud-covered neighbors pulled together to clean their houses, their streets, and their community. It became a time for tremendous growth and rebuilding. Learning how to see the glass as "half-full" rather than "half-empty," many residents felt that the flood of 1972 was a very enriching experience.

On the one-year anniversary of his Bar Mitzvah, David Warshal had a chance to daven and chant his Haftorah in front of a full congregation in their newly redecorated *shul*. There was the rabbi, and a cantor, and a *Kiddush*, and somehow it was anticlimactic. A year before, he had stood up in front of a handful of people in a makeshift *shul* and learned more about accepting his responsibilities than he could have at any formal ceremony.

Author's note: Story after story of both generosity and greed emerged from the flood. Let me share that the caterer, Mark Kornfeld, and the florist, Lucille Bolin, "Flowers by Lucille," did not charge the family for either the food or the flowers that they had already purchased and prepared for the Bar Mitzvah. Their generosity is to be commended!

33

THE SINGER

Emanuel Genauer—December 1952

*Although Manny Genauer's vo-
cation took him to the world of
finance in New York, his avoca-
tion remains the same—singing.*

Reuben Genauer came to America in the early 1930s from Poland, via Palestine, like most immigrants, looking for a better life. Unfortunately, his dreams of the "streets paved with gold" tarnished all too quickly. He barely squeezed out a living from his yard goods store on Orchard Street on the Lower East Side and, in order to survive, supplemented his income with several additional jobs. In the summer he worked on occasion as a cook in Camp Ramah in upstate New York, but his real gift was a God-given one. He had a beautiful voice and was hired as a *chazan* for *Shabbos* and the high holidays. Even so, money was tight and life was hard.

In spite of hard times, Reuben scraped together enough money when his sons were ages 12 and 8 to take a place for the summer in a bungalow colony in Liberty, New York. Their little cottage consisted of exactly one room with two beds, butted against each other, and a hot plate for the kitchen. Nevertheless, it was out of the city, and most of the day was spent out doors. Reuben, along with the other fathers and husbands, made the commute out to the bungalow colony every Friday afternoon and returned to Williamsburg (after an overwhelming amount of traffic) late Sunday night. Like most of these Orthodox summer communities, they had their own *shul*. There, during services, choir director Mr. Lang first heard Manny sing. He immediately invited Manny, the younger of the two boys, to join his choir. Upon their return home at the summer's end, Manny and his mother would take the weekly trek by subway to Utica Avenue, which seemed to this young boy at the end of the earth.

Manny sang with Mr. Lang's choir for only a few months. His grandfather, Reb Joseph Koller—himself a talmudic scholar—decreed, "If he is good enough to sing with Lang, let's take him to the best: Meyer Machtenberg." Meyer Machtenberg was very famous in Orthodox circles. He was an accomplished musician and a composer of liturgical music. His choir sang with some of the most famous cantors of the day, including the three Koussevitsky brothers.

The audition went well, and Manny became part of the Machtenberg choir. Every week, he and his mother took the subway to 2nd Avenue and 11th Street, to the home of the choir director for voice lessons. At the age of 9, Manny became a soloist with the choir. They were hired at expensive weddings in Manhattan's fanciest hotels. In his white robe and yarmulke, young Manny would slowly walk down the aisle toward the couple already under the *chupah*, while chanting the *ViMalay*. As he approached the *chupah*, perfectly timed, this handsome young boy would raise his hands as if in benediction. Very dramatic and very effective. The choir, quite popular and much in demand, was paid well for its services. For each "gig," Manny earned $15, which was a handsome sum in the late '40s and a big boost to the family economy.

Most of the weddings were held on Saturday night after *Shabbos*, and in the summer that was quite late. Way too late for a young boy to commute alone, so Manny's mother, Ann, would accompany him. She stood in the back of the hall, usually with the orchestra, and became her son's most ardent constructive critic. Rather than patronizing him with a pat "you did a good job," she offered honest, supportive advice. His mother realized that her 9-year-old knew nothing of "falling in love." So, she encouraged age-appropriate ways for him to find the sweet notes needed to convey the emotion between the bride and groom. She suggested he recall something sad that he experienced while chanting the bridal song. The audience never knew that the sweet, melodic sounds emitted by this little boy were inspired by the death of his pet turtle.

The fall after he joined the choir, Manny reached a pinnacle in his young career. He sang a duet during the High Holiday services with Cantor Simcha Koussevitsky in a *shul* on Clinton Street off Delancey. It was the only time his grandfather had ever heard him perform. That day Manny also watched his elegant, handsome grandfather. The older man wore a white starched shirt, draped his *tallis* over his head, covered his eyes for the *Shema*, and sang with an intensity that came from his heart. Manny was struck by the seriousness that his grandfather brought to davening. In later years, Manny took a photo of his grandfather, posed in a *tallis*, to preserve that cherished memory.

As Manny's career continued, his older brother Jerry took over the responsibilities of chaperone for getting Manny to and from the Saturday evening weddings. Capitalizing on the opportunity, Jerry usually brought a date. The cocktail hour was always before the ceremony. There, the uninvited young couple indulged in the "free" hors d'oeuvres, listened to the choir during the ceremony, and then brought Manny home. Jerry rarely complained because it was an inexpensive way to entertain young ladies.

As Manny got older and approached Bar Mitzvah age, his father claimed the pleasure of instructing him for the *Shabbos* morning davening. Because Manny would lead the congregation for the full service, his father started a full year and a half before the Bar Mitzvah and studied with Manny every *Shabbos* afternoon for at least two hours. Reuben was a strict disciplinarian and, having lived in Israel, he cherished *Evrit*, the Hebrew language. He didn't want his son to make a mistake even in the pronunciation of the words. Reuben entrusted the task of teaching Manny his Haftorah to Rabbi Shroit, a rabbi in the community. He hired a private tutor, because he wanted the recitation to be perfect.

The Genauers lived in the La Guardia City Housing Project in a third-floor walk-up. Securing an apartment there was like winning the lottery. Built in the 1930s, the apartment complex was relatively new and clean, complete with open spaces and trees. But even with the rent of $35 a month, they struggled to make ends meet. Now in preparation for Manny's Bar Mitzvah, Reuben and Ann saved every penny. They bought him his first suit. It was a brown flannel from Kleins, and with his blondish hair, Manny felt like the Prince of Wales. This was a big deal. The family didn't even have a phone until he was 14. They had to go to the corner drugstore to make a phone call, and just coming up with the nickel for that call was often difficult. This suit was his first "new" piece of clothing. For years he had either worn his brother's hand-me-downs (which weren't so nice to start with) or the much-preferred hand-me-downs from his cousins, the Ginsburgs.

Manny's Bar Mitzvah became a much-anticipated community event. He had developed somewhat of a celebrity status from his years of singing with the choir. When Manny walked home from school through the projects, people whom he didn't even know would stop him to say that they were coming to his Bar Mitzvah. Manny's parents never bragged about his accomplishments. He never felt inflated, but he felt good about himself and rather important that people wanted to come hear him sing.

On a very cold day in December of 1952, their small wooden *shul* was packed. Rather than feeling nervous, Manny was excited and a bit proud. While he held the Torah, he remembered how Koussevitsky sang, and he belted out the *Shema*, wanting to overwhelm the crowd. He was successful.

The singing, which was certainly beautiful, was not the only memorable part of the day. Traditionally, for celebrations in the *shul*, a cold *Kiddush* would be served. Reuben was so proud of his son that he wanted to do something special. He hired stoves (with the gas tanks attached) for the weekend. On Friday afternoon, he went to the *shul* and prepared a *cholent* for 250 people. The stew, made of meat, potatoes, barley, and beans, simmered all night. Between the aroma of the steaming *cholent* and Manny's enchanting voice, the Bar Mitzvah was a veritable delight for the senses. The invited (and uninvited) guests were pleasantly shocked to have a hot, delicious *Kiddush* on a very cold day. Without the means to put on a "big bash," Reuben relied on his skill at cooking for large crowds, gained during summers of working at Camp Ramah, and "showed off" a little for his son's Bar Mitzvah.

Manny continued to sing until he was around age 16. Then, while he sang a solo during Rosh Hashanah services at a temple in Providence, Rhode Island, his voice cracked in the middle of a prayer. He was very embarrassed, but received good advice. He was told to stop singing until his voice matured and then he could resume his singing career. And "resume" he certainly did. He sang not only High Holy Day services, but he sang every Friday night and *Shabbos* morning at services while he was a student at Boston University. He worked his way through school with this income and he lived rather comfortably in college.

Manny's studies, however, took him in a different direction. He became the president and CEO of United Mizrachi Bank and then a commercial and mortgage banker in Manhattan. He still sings at some religious services and occasionally at the wedding of a friend. His voice is still beautiful. This inherited gift from his father has been passed on to his son Reid, who has chosen, instead of a liturgical arena, to share his talents with the acoustic rock band "Strange Folk." What was originally a means of additional income for Manny has become a livelihood for his son. The *ViMalay* that Manny chanted so often for the many brides and grooms is a prayer that asks God to provide them with a life in which their heartfelt requests will be fulfilled. Hopefully, the newlyweds were granted the same bounty as the little boy who made the request on their behalf.

34

THE SUIT

Eugene Lubin—April, 1933

Eugene Lubin has made a career out of helping young boys come of age and look good in the process. He is now servicing second and third generations of the same family. He makes buying this first suit such a pleasant experience that his customers often invite him to the Bar Mitzvah. He rarely goes—"the suit" represents him, and that's enough.

If you ask a man about his Bar Mitzvah, he may not remember the *parasha*. The food, the flowers, the guests were all part of his mother's realm, so their memory is a blur. But the one feature he can recount in perfect detail is "the suit." The Bar Mitzvah suit remains as much a right of passage as any part of the celebration.

A man who understands this is Gene Lubin, who has been in the business longer and does it better than anyone around. "It's more than selling a suit," says Lubin, "It's part of the Bar

Mitzvah experience." He should know; he's been in business since 1946 and in the same Yonkers location since 1954. In the Cross County Shopping Center, the first of its kind to be built in this country, Lubin's remains the only original occupant. This palatial, stylish store is a far cry from his original place of business.

His father, a Polish immigrant, worked as a tailor in a men's clothing store in the Bronx. To help out the family, young Gene worked there every day after school. In order to save the carfare, he walked the five miles to the shop and was never late. He passed his friends playing "kick the can" or tossing a ball, and as much as he wanted to join them, he just kept on going. It was during this apprenticeship that he realized he liked to sell and had a knack for it. His education took the form of on-the-job-training. When he waited on his first customer, the man was indecisive and told him to hold the suit. As requested, the garment was put on the side. When the boss came over to find out why the suit was out of stock, Gene told him that the customer was coming back. The suit went back into stock and the customer, as the boss predicted, did not return.

When Gene graduated from Roosevelt High School right after the war, he opened his own store, a 6' × 6' masterpiece that he stocked with 100 pairs of pants—50 brown and 50 black. His brother opened up down the road, across a brook. If a customer wanted something that Gene didn't have, he'd ask them to wait a minute, run out of the store and across the brook, and retrieve the merchandise from his brother's stock. He went into New York City every morning by train to fill in what he sold. In the beginning he wasn't successful, so he changed tactics. He'd drive his car into the city, go to ten different places, and vary his stock.

When he first started selling suits, there was one fabric: mohair—black or navy. In one style—single-breasted. In spite of the monotony, Lubin made it special. Lubin made a ritual out of measuring the boy like a young man and treating him with the respect of his soon-to-be-acquired status. He also made it a point to address his young customer, rather than the parent who brought the boy in. The only thing that has changed over the years is the dizzying selection available. Today there are multiple styles, fabrics, and colors, making parents nostalgic for the long-ago simplicity.

As his business grew, Gene brought his father in as his partner. His dad's skills were with a needle and thread, not with people. The first day they worked together as a team, the senior Lubin was off to the side, attending to his tailoring. Gene had the talent and enthusiasm for dealing with customers. The first one came in and Gene waited on him. Pretty soon, Gene was juggling three people trying on clothes. When the fourth customer entered, Gene's dad approached him and asked, "May I help you?" This unsuspecting victim asked a question about the garment. The response was, "What are you—an inspector?"

Gene yelled over, "Dad, I'll take the customer!"

They became successful, with a winning combination of gusto and gumption out front and old-world tailoring in the back. Lubin knows that he plays an important role. "I'm there. My suit represents me. We become part of it. We are part of every Bar Mitzvah that goes out of the store. We're helping in the transition from child to young man. This is an important part of life and we understand the responsibility. We want to make this stage as pleasant as possible."

Gene's own Bar Mitzvah took place during the Depression. In those days a suit cost $8 and came with two pairs of pants. Every store in those days carried both men's and boys' wear. And back then, everyone wore a shirt and tie. Even in the stands at Yankee Stadium, you would find the fans who came to cheer "The Babe" wearing a shirt, tie, and hat.

Gene Lubin's Bar Mitzvah was held at the Fordham Talmud Torah on 180th and Arthur Avenue. The most memorable part of the service was that in deference to his grandfather, Gene made his speech in Yiddish. He felt special then, and that feeling has stayed with him even now that he is a grandfather himself.

When his father retired from the store, Gene still went every Sunday morning to "make a report" over lox and bagels. Inevitably, he would recount new developments to his dad, and his mother would approach and join the conversation. His father would turn to her and, without fail, say, "Can't you see I'm discussing business with my son?" Then he would look at Gene and exclaim in his Polish accent, "Vimmen is a coise!"

While other men his age are spending more and more time on the golf course, the 78-year-old Lubin is still driven. "It's a way of life. A customer comes in and they become a friend," says Lubin. He's never had a complaint, and that's after selling over 100,000 Bar Mitzvah suits! He treats each person as if he is the most valuable individual in the world and goes out of his way for everyone. One day a woman called up and explained that her daughter was getting married and she needed a suit for her disabled son, who had some behavior problems. Lubin opened early to accommodate the family. He once got a frantic call: "If you don't help me, my wife will divorce me!" This was Thursday and the Bar Mitzvah was on Saturday. Apparently, the caller had thought he could do better with custom-made suits. His wife had told him from the beginning to go to Lubin's. When his tailor-made suits arrived and were unacceptable, he called Lubin in desperation. They came in Friday morning at 11:00 A.M. and one and a half hours after lunch were fitted and ready to go.

The same concern he exhibits for his customers has also translated into a lifetime of community service. The walls of his basement office are covered with plaques and citations for his involvement in organizations such as the Jewish Federation, Chamber of Commerce, and the South Yonkers Youth Council.

His fifty-plus years in the business have led to his own study of psychology. He has observed many of his young customers come of age right in his store. For example, they come in at age 5 with their mother and she says, "My son needs a pair of pants."

"What color do you want?"

The kid squeaks out, "Black."

The scene is repeated a year later. "My son needs a pair of pants."

"What color would you like?"

A little more assertively, the kid responds, "Black."

This same dialogue becomes the routine as the boy grows, only now he adds that he wants his pants "tight." His mother has long since been relegated to the background.

Then he comes in one day, a six-foot beanpole with scruffy tufts on his face, and on his arm a pixie of a girl who smiles up at him with brilliant eyes.

"May I help you?"

"Yes, he'd like some pants," the young lady says.

"What color do you want?'

"He'll have them brown and loose," she continues, nodding up the young man.

He blushes, giggles, and looks down at the carpet.

And so this young man, who was so definitive and defiant up to this point, is now deferent as he enters this new stage of life.

35

CHILDREN OF CAPTIVITY

Achbawn Patterson—Spring, 1996

Archbawn Patterson is a student at Community College of Philadelphia where he hopes to continue his basketball career.

After a busy week of work and school, there is a flurry of activity on Friday afternoons as the members of the house bathe, dress, and prepare for the Sabbath. As the sun begins to set, a sense of peace descends while Rabbi Patterson blows the *shofar* (ram's horn), heralding the Sabbath. The family then lights the ancient menorah that belonged to the rabbi's grandfather—seven candles, one for every day of the week. This lovely weekly ritual does not take place in Israel—although the *shofar* is blown there as well to announce

Erev Shabbat—but rather in the Cobbs Creek section of West Philadelphia. The Pattersons are black.

Rabbi Shlomo Patterson was born in Moorestown, New Jersey, but he grew up in Philadelphia. His family can trace its Jewish roots back at least six generations. Only Shlomo, out of his seven brothers, is a rabbi—like his father, Earl. This status was not gained from attending formal yeshivas and training programs, but rather from a grass-roots approach of father passing on sacred knowledge to son and both possessing a willingness to teach and share that information with the congregation. Their congregation, B'nai Gelutah, Children of Captivity, cannot be pigeonholed into a more familiar form of traditional Judaism. Nonetheless, their pivotal focus is on the Torah, the family is the mainstay, and their faith is strong.

Their customs vary somewhat from mainstream Judaism, but overall, there are more similarities than differences. Friday night is a time for the family. With the shofar blown and the candles lit, Rabbbi Patterson, his wife, and five children sit down to a meal together. It is a special time to talk about their week and catch up with each other. Rabbi Patterson also uses this time to go through the Sabbath services, emphasize ideas that he wants to share with his children, and clarify points that they may not understand.

Rabbi Patterson keeps kosher, as dictated by the Torah, and keeps his head covered all the time. The congregation meets at the International House, a large multipurpose building on the campus of the University of Pennsylvania. During the week, Rabbi Patterson can often be seen wearing jeans and a B'nai Gelutah T-shirt, topped off with a jean jacket emblazoned with his congregation's colorful logo on the back. However, for the Sabbath services, on Saturday mornings, he is dressed festively in honor of the day. In addition to his finery, he wears a *tallis* and an Ethiopian-style yarmulke. In their second-floor sanctuary, the men sit on one side, while the women sit on the other. Many of the prayers and songs are in Hebrew, whereas the reading of the Torah and Haftorah are conducted in English. Standards like *Shalom Aleichem*, the *Shema*, and the psalms are complemented by songs like "Go Down Moses" and "Go Back across the Jordan." They have an *Aron Kodesh* (ark) complete with one Torah that is well respected, carried around during the services, and kissed at specific times. The congregation has over 100 members and is made up mostly of people of color. The rabbi keeps a low profile and does not view his job as one of preaching or publicizing. Rather, he sees his duty as a teacher—instructing his family and congregation on how to serve God.

They celebrate Rosh Hashana. On Yom Kippur, the children begin fasting at age 2. On Succot, they build a *succah* outside, where their West Philadelphia neighbors might shrug, but say nothing. On Passover they have bitter herbs and matzoh and serve a whole lamb for their seder in remembrance of the Pascal sacrifice made in Egypt so long ago. They also celebrate Shavuot, the remembrance of the giving of the Torah, but Chanukah is not a holiday that is recognized.

One of their customs that is easily recognizable is the Bar Mitzvah. Just as in a traditional ceremony, the young boy is called up to the Torah for the first time. The only differences are that in B'nai Gelutah, once a boy becomes a Bar Mitzvah, he is also able to open and close the services and blow the *shofar* on Friday nights to announce the Sabbath. Achbawn Patterson, Shlomo's only son, grew up functioning as a kind of junior minister, helping his father with the services on Saturday mornings. He was named after his grandfather, with a name that means "keen of intelligence." As he approached the age of 13, it was time for him to prepare so that he could take on the new and additional responsibility of reading the Torah. His Bar Mitzvah was right after Passover, and his *parasha* was about the holidays. Although well prepared, he was nervous that he would make a mistake, because this was his first time publicly reading the Torah. The day was filled with joy, but he was a little relieved when it was all over. There was a festive, lavish luncheon celebrating Achbawn's Bar Mitzvah, complete with chicken, turkey, beef, vegetables, and corn on the cob, followed by apple pie and coconut cake.

Although an avid basketball fan, with Shaquille O'Neil and Koby Bryant being two of his favorites, Achbawn did not play organized basketball until he was 14, when he joined the team at Philadelphia's Lincoln High school. He had been nervous about playing, but his Dad encouraged him to go out there and not be afraid. He took off quickly and demonstrated great skills. At the 76ers basketball camp in the summer of 1999, he was voted the MVP and won the slam dunk and one-on-one trophies. At this camp, he had an interesting encounter. His coach, Brian Schiff, came to camp one day wearing a T-shirt that promoted the Maccabi games, which are held each summer in various cities around the country, giving Jewish teens a chance to compete in various sports. The games are named for Judah Maccabi, who was a powerful warrior and the hero of the Chanukah story. He and his father and brothers, along with a small group of rebels, defeated the Syrian army, despite their opponents' overwhelming numbers and plentiful armaments. Their victory enabled the Jewish people to rededicate the Holy Temple.

Achbawn noticed the shirt and asked about it. When Brian explained the significance of the games, Achbawn responded with "I'm Jewish." Brian, probably a little skeptical, shot back, "You are!" Suspicious or not, Brian signed him up and Achbawn has played for the past two summers on the Philadelphia Maccabi basketball team. They came home in the summer of 2000 with the silver medal. He is an integral part of the team and gets along well with his teammates. Although very quiet around adults, he loosens up with the other guys. He hopes to attend college and would be thrilled if basketball were part of the equation. His only limitation is that as a committed Jew, he doesn't play on the Sabbath.

Author's note: In addition to information gleaned during an interview with both Rabbi Patterson and Achbawn, additional background information was provided in an article by Ted Silary, sportswriter for the *Philadelphia Daily News*, and Brian Schiff, the Maccabi coach who works for Comcast SportsNet.

36

THE DREAMS OF MY FATHER

Jay Krieger—February 21, 1976

Jay is the director of technology at the Indiana School for the Deaf.

At the age of 6, Alan Krieger won $5 from the *Cleveland News* Beautiful Child Picture Contest. He was indeed beautiful, with sparkly eyes, blond curly hair, and an engaging smile. As he grew up, the beautiful baby matured into a handsome, athletic, intelligent young man. When he was inducted into the National Honor Society, his parents were proud, especially since Alan was profoundly deaf.

Before it was fashionable, Alan was mainstreamed in regular classes. He was a skilled lipreader and had beautiful speech.

Although it was a struggle to lip read all day, especially when his teachers continued talking with their backs turned as they wrote on the board, Alan excelled in school. One of his first frustrations was not being permitted to be Bar Mitzvahed. His family was actively involved in the synagogue, but in the late 1940s, boys who were considered "imperfect" were not afforded the same right to this rite as their nondisabled brethren. Deaf men did not have the same obligations related to mitzvot; therefore, they were excused (or denied, depending on your perspective) from their responsibilities and viewed pathologically as those who should be pitied rather than taken seriously.

But as a very affable young man, Alan took disappointment in his stride and carried on. However, when he was 18, he experienced his next set of frustrations, which propelled him to change his course in life. Where sports can be a great equalizer, dating tends to sharply delineate the "haves" from the "have nots." Mustering up the courage to ask a girl out, Alan was shot down with the excuse that he couldn't "whisper in the dark." Depending on lip reading, this deaf young man needed lights in order to communicate.

Ignoring the old adage that there are "plenty of other fish in the sea," Alan chose instead to look in a different pond. He was deaf. If he was going to be rejected because he was deaf, he'd find a place that accepted him for who he was. He started to go to the Cleveland Deaf Club and became active in the Hebrew Association of the Deaf. At this point, he was first exposed to American Sign Language and started to sign. Through these activities, he met the quick-witted, effervescent Betty Guttman, a die-hard New Yorker. Although Betty was certainly a match for Alan's looks and intellect, she was the deaf daughter of deaf parents, and her first language was American Sign Language. In her family, deafness was so normal and comfortable that it wasn't until Betty went to school (P.S. 47, a public school for the deaf in Brooklyn) that she realized that other people could hear.

When Alan first brought Betty home to meet his parents, his mother's first reaction was "But she's deaf!" Blind to the fact that she was Jewish, bright, attractive, outgoing, and funny, all Mrs. Kreiger saw was that her future daughter-in-law was deaf.

In the 1950s approximately 200–300 deaf printers worked in the press rooms in the *New York Times*. Because the presses were so noisy, deaf boys were often trained to work as printers. You could go into any sizable newspaper across the country and find deaf printers working their presses. Hearing people can do their work and still engage in conversation with their co-workers. With only one set of hands, deaf workers are very focused and visually tuned-in to their task because they can't talk and work at the same time. Of course, in the break and lunch rooms, there were animated conversations and flying fingers, but on the job the deaf workers were all business.

Alan followed Betty back to New York. Complete with a graphic arts degree, Alan joined the legion of deaf printers at the *New York Times*. Life was very comfortable; Alan had a good, steady job, a loving wife, a supportive community, and a growing family. They had eight years together. And then one night, on his way home in the midst of rush hour at Grand Central Station, Alan suffered a cerebral hemorrhage and died almost instantly. Betty, not yet 31, was a widow with two children: Marlene, 7, and Jay, 5.

Five years later, at a New Year's Eve party, Betty met Francis Oshman. He was warm, supportive, steady, and treated Marlene and Jay like his own. For two years, he commuted every weekend to New York from Philadelphia. When it finally became impractical to perpetuate this long-distance relationship, Rabbi Huffman married the couple in Temple Beth Or. The biggest adjustment for this blended family was that Betty had to move from her beloved New York to Philadelphia.

Attitudes and practices toward the disabled have changed in both secular and religious arenas. Some were mandated by laws, while other reforms permutated as a spin-off of the civil rights movement; it was simply the right thing to do, both ethically and morally. Judaism finally became more inclusive. (Christians had reached out to the deaf community long ago.) Synagogues and Hebrew schools have come to realize that it's their responsibility to make services and school programs accessible to those who want to participate.

The Jewish world that Jay Krieger faced as he prepared for his Bar Mitzvah was a lot different from that of his father's. Mrs. Anna Ross, whose own son Paul was deaf, made it her life's work to teach deaf boys to become Bar Mitzvah. Jay eagerly went to Mrs. Ross's house every week, where he learned to not only read the Hebrew, but pronounce it. Jay's first language was American Sign Language, and his second language is English. For deaf people, speech is difficult because you can't hear yourself, so there is no natural feedback system. Speech, for deaf children, is learned with the help of tactile and visual aids, with the result sometimes being unintelligible. Mrs. Ross marveled that Jay's Hebrew sounded better than his English.

Betty contacted Keneseth Israel, a Reform temple in the Philadelphia suburbs that offered signed services once a month. Its rabbi readily agreed to let Jay have his Bar Mitzvah ceremony there. It was officiated by the two rabbis from KI, Rabbi Korn and Rabbi Fuchs, and a special guest, Rabbi Lynn Gottlieb, fluent in sign language, who functioned as the interpreter as well. When Jay was called to the Torah, he spoke in Hebrew and signed in English his Torah portion, the Haftorah portion, and the blessings. His relatives were very impressed with his performance. Many of his relatives had never heard him speak English, let alone Hebrew. Jay wrote and delivered his own speech.

> In my long thirteen years, I have experienced sorrows and happiness, but today is the happiest part of my life. . . . I have achieved the dream of my deceased father, Alan, to be a fine Jewish boy, and to become a Bar Mitzvah, which he never had.

Betty's eyes glistened as she watched her son articulately deliver his speech in his native language, American Sign Language. Seated next to her was her mother-in-law, who was openly emotional as she watched her grandson proudly take his place as a Jewish man. She watched as her grandson was counted in a way that his father never had been. She watched as her grandson beamed in the limelight, knowing that her son had been cheated out of recognition, but remained a proud Jewish man despite the rejection. She watched knowing that her beautiful deaf grandson had achieved the dreams of his father by carrying out the tradition of a son from a Jewish family.

37

A GOOD NAME

Benjamin Briscoe—March, 1947

Robert Briscoe served as a member of the House for thirty-eight years, from 1927–1965, being twice elected lord mayor of Dublin. His youngest son, Ben, succeeded him. Altogether, the two have served over seventy years in the House—the longest father–son continuous holding of one seat. Ben was elected lord mayor of Dublin in 1988.

Robert Briscoe was the first Jewish member of the Irish Dail (Parliament). He was also the first Jewish lord mayor of Dublin. His election came only after he had spent years in service to his country. He was in the forefront of the fight for Irish independence and lived for a while with a price on his head. He was a loyal supporter of Eamon De Valera, whom he affectionately called "Chief." His election to lord mayor in 1956 was a great source of pride to the Irish Jewish community. In a Sabbath sermon, Chief Rabbi Jacobovits delivered the following message at the Greenville Hall Synagogue:

> By his election, he has not only raised himself to a stature of world repute, to be the most prominent Jew ever born within these shores. He has also uplifted our standing and turned the attention and regard of Jewish communities throughout the world to Irish Jewry.

Briscoe and his wife, Lily, had seven children: four boys and three girls—a typical Irish family. While Briscoe tended to affairs of the country, his wife attended to the home and family. She was warmhearted, thoughtful, and sensitive to the needs of her children. Managing to get by on the humble salary of a public servant, Lily nevertheless instilled in her children a love for theater and music. Another favorite pasttime in the Briscoe household was boxing. The four boys joined the Jewish boxing club. The youngest brother, Ben, was a good boxer and went on to become a lightweight champion. Their Dad told them, "Life is like a boxing match. Sometimes you have to hit hard to make your principle. You may get bruised, but never throw in the towel."

The senior Briscoe also infused into his family the sense that two of the most important things in life were their religion and their love for Ireland. In a predominantly Catholic country, being Jewish and in public life had its challenges. Briscoe relied heavily on his sense of humor and his sense of fairness to smooth over uncomfortable situations. When a debate raged in the Dail of whether or not to hang a crucifix that was the gift of a priest, Briscoe at first held back from joining the debate. When he was finally asked his opinion directly, he responded, "If having the Crucifix in the Dail will make you any better Christians, I certainly have no objection." (The Committee, after reflection, decided not to place the crucifix in the chamber!)

The children also, on occasion, faced the challenges of being Jewish in an overwhelmingly Catholic country. Brian Briscoe, now a radiologist in Baltimore, recalls that he was unaware of any differences until the age of 10 or 11. Then, because of a gas shortage, the family moved from the outskirts into the city. They switched to a Protestant school and for the first time faced venomous anti-Semitism. It was a terrible experience.

Rabbi Isaac Herzog, the father of Chaim Herzog, who became the president of Israel in 1983, was the chief rabbi of Ireland. He enjoyed rich relationships with leaders of both church and state. At a state banquet in Dublin Castle, Cardinal MacRory teased Herzog about eating only fruit and not trying the delicious ham. The rabbi quipped back, "Let's discuss this at your wedding." Chaim Herzog once explained, "Ireland had no history of anti-Semitism, and while I did not feel outcast, I did feel different. I was always aware that somewhere in the background I was being judged by different standards." When Rabbi Herzog was later appointed chief rabbi of Palestine and had to leave Ireland, he bestowed this tribute:

> Long before he [Herzog] set foot on Irish soil, he felt a kind of romantic interest in this country, where Jews had never, even in the Middle Ages, suffered any persecution. Its attitude toward the Jewish citizens was the truest criterion of a country's level of civilization, and it was precisely in times of great trouble that the true character of a nation was decided.

The Briscoe family belonged to the Adelaide Road Orthodox Synagogue, and all four boys had their Bar Mitzvahs there. Before his departure in 1936, this synagogue had been the pulpit of Chief Rabbi Herzog. Ben was the youngest of four brothers; his Bar Mitzvah was the last one and very important. Like his brothers, he studied his Hebrew lessons under the tutelage of Mr. Eichenstein, who was quite a character, with a big, bushy moustache. Rather than make the Bar Mitzvah an "affair of state" by inviting government officials, Robert and Lily Briscoe chose instead to retain the integrity of the ceremony and invite only close friends and family. The oldest brother, Joe Briscoe, now a retired dentist in Dublin, recalled: "Ben was very 'plucky' and not nervous at all. He was called up to the *bimah.* He had a very good voice and made the *brachah* before and after the *Maftir*, and then chanted the Haftorah, also with the blessings before and upon completion. He did a good job. I think my Dad and Mom were more nervous."

The service was very traditionally Orthodox. It was only the brogue of the Bar Mitzvah boy that gave away the Irish setting. The whole affair was very modest, compared to today's standards. Ben completed his obligation by delivering a traditional "Today I Am a Man" speech, prepared for him by the memorable Mr. Eichenstein. His first public oration was written by a scriptwriter! A reception following the service was held at the nearby Hibernian Hotel.

Robert Briscoe served as a member of the House for thirty-eight years, from 1927 to 1965, being twice elected lord mayor of Dublin as a member of the Dublin City Council. When he decided to retire in 1965, Ben, who had always been interested in politics, was the natural person to succeed him. All together, the two have served over seventy years—the longest father-son continuous holding of one seat. Ben also was elected lord mayor of Dublin in 1988. Ben has four children, and none of them have expressed interest in continuing in the family "business."

Ben Briscoe and his siblings inherited a proud legacy from their father. He taught them pride in their religion, love of their country, and a sense of fairness, and with the advantage of both an Irish and a Jewish heritage, they learned how to use humor and dry wit. But the most valuable lesson Robert Briscoe passed on to his children was the importance of a "good name." Growing up, he repeatedly reminded them, "Be jealous of our good name." In later years, when he was dying, he told his sons that he had no material possessions to leave them, but rather he was leaving them the most valuable belonging he had—a good name. "When you lose it, you never get it back." Ben, who worshiped his father, has heeded those words and incorporated them not only into his political life, but into his private life as well. In Proverbs 22:1, King Solomon wrote, "A good name is better than great riches." In that case, Robert Briscoe left his family a gift greater than gold.

Author's note: This story was written from an interview conducted with Ben Briscoe in Leinster House, as well as phone interviews with Drs. Joe and Bryan Briscoe. The background information was found in *For the Life of Me*, by Robert Briscoe, with Alden Hatch, published by Little, Brown, and Company, 1958; and *Jews in Twentieth Century Ireland*, by Dermot Keogh, published by Cork University Press, 1998.

38

TWINS TIMES TWO

Zvi and Yizhak Bushwick—December 15, 1997

Zvi and Yizhak Bushwick are continuing their learning in the Bais Medrish at Yeshiva Beth Moshe in Scranton, PA.

In Holland, when Beatrice Brom announced that she was pregnant with twins, her family was thrilled. Not long thereafter, in America, her sister-in-law Maggie Bushwick announced that she, too, was expecting twins. They carried together, an ocean apart, and shared as often as they could their joy, anticipation, and *kvetches* about delivering multiple births. The children were supposed to be born two months apart. But with Beatrice being ten days late, and Maggie giving birth six weeks early, the four boys were born just two days apart. Yotam and Ezra Brom were born Friday, February 7, 1984, and their cousins, Zvi Eliezer and Yizhak Bushwick, arrived on Sunday, February 9. Out of the four boys, Zvi is the only one to carry a middle name: Eliezer. He is named for Maggie's brother Zvi, who died very young. The name Eliezer, which was also Maggie's grandfather's name, means "God is my help" and was added to "boost" the *mazel* (luck) of the namesake. Their grandfather, Mottel Brom, who was blessed with four grandchildren in a matter of one weekend, started thinking about their Bar Mitzvahs even before the *Bris Milah* had taken place.

Strong family ties connected the boys as they grew, but more than geographic distance separated them. The Broms had moved to Israel when the boys were 3 years old, and their cultural and life experiences were completely different from those of their American cousins. Even though Maggie was born in Belgium, raised in Holland, later lived in Israel, and is fluent in five languages, her sons were raised in an American small-town Orthodox environment. With only one Hebrew day school in town, they grew up side by side, grade after grade. In Israel, twins are not permitted in the same class. With many more Jewish educational opportunities, the Brom boys were in the same school, but in different classes. Growing up in Jerusalem, the twins were raised, as were many Israelis, with lots of freedom, whereas northeastern Pennsylvania provided a much more provincial, protected environment.

Nonetheless, despite differences, the boys all approached their 13th birthdays, the age of their Bar Mitzvah. Their respective fathers undertook the preparations. In Israel, Danny Brom, a trauma specialist with a Ph.D. in psychology, taught his sons how to *layn* (read) the Torah. Natan Bushwick, who, in addition to his *smicha* (rabbinical certificate), also has a Ph.D. in philosophy and cognitive sciences, actually started teaching his sons when they were in kindergarten. Every week, he would read with his sons the Torah portion with *trup* (the tune). He stepped up their lessons about nine months before the Bar Mitzvah, when the boys themselves practiced the *layning.*

It was decided that the Bar Mitzvahs would all take place together and in Israel. All of Maggie's family lived there, and there was no question of forcing the family to split across two continents to celebrate a joyous occasion.

As with many of the best laid plans, while the families were planning for a double (or quadruple) *simcha*, they suffered several losses. First, Natan's mother died six months before the joint Bar Mitzvah. Then, to compound their sorrow, Mottel Brom, the grandfather who could barely contain his joy with the birth of four grandsons over one weekend, died six weeks before the B'nai Mitzvah.

With three out of the four parents now in mourning, plans had to be changed. The Jewish people have marvelous rituals and customs related to life-cycle events, which offer a comfortable set of "dos and don'ts" for those experiencing situations for which they have no frame of reference. For twelve months after the death of a parent, mourners do not go to parties, listen to music, or wear new clothes. And yet the Broms and Bushwicks wanted to find a meaningful way to celebrate their sons' rite of passage while still respecting and honoring their departed parents.

Although the boys are only two days apart, with one set of twins born on Friday and the other set on Sunday, they had two different Bar Mitzvah *parashas*. This meant that the four could not celebrate during the same service. The families came up with a wonderful way to incorporate two separate ceremonies and then a combined one in the span of one week. The American contingency arrived in Israel on Thursday, December 11, 1997. Maggie had commissioned a beautiful hand-drawn invitation displaying two *tallis* bags, bearing the names "Yizhak" and "Zvi Eliezer" on a *bimah* leaning against the *Kotel*. Unfortunately, the invitations were not ready in time to send out to relatives. Therefore, from the minute they arrived in Israel until sundown the next day, Maggie and Natan were on the phone calling relatives, inviting them to a double *simcha* (happy occasion), once again separated by two days. Yotam and Ezra were called to the Torah on that Shabbat in their *shul*. As in many communities, their *shul* actually meets in a school building until they can one day claim their own building. A *Kiddush* was held after services.

Early Monday morning, the Brom and Bushwick families made their way to the *Kotel*, the last remaining wall of the Second Temple, which was destroyed in 70 B.C. A feeling of solemnity and holiness pervades the space around the wall. It is a public place, open to anyone who wants to pray there. Although you can "rent a rabbi," this party of learned men and boys was capable of conducting its own services. There is a *mechitzah* (a wall separating the men's and women's section), so Maggie, Beatrice, and the other women stood on chairs and overlooked the ceremony from the women's section. After the *Shacharit* (morning) prayers, the Torah was carried in and Zvi Eliezer, older by nine minutes, was called up first. Because you may not call brothers up to the Torah, one after the other, their cousin Ezra—a well-seasoned, two-day-old Bar Mitzvah—was given the second *aliyah*. Yizhak was next to *layn* his part from *parasha Vayeishev*, which deals coincidentally (or not so coincidentally) with Jacob and his brothers. After the Torah reading, the women pelted the group with candy, another tradition of "showering" the Bar Mitzvah boys with sweets.

It is traditional that while you are in mourning, you do not have a meal with other people. Originally, the family members had planned to go out to breakfast together. A rather creative alternate "meal" was planned. After the services, each member of the party of thirty was given his or her own "breakfast bag" and escorted on a tour of the newly excavated tunnels under the holy city. The party ate and explored. By going "underground," they could virtually see the history of Jerusalem, as layer upon layer, century after century was revealed.

There was one more affair to round out the Bar Mitzvah celebrations of the Brom/Bushwick boys. They rented a hotel in Jerusalem, and over fifty members of their extended family gathered there to spend *Shabbat*. They started on Friday evening with *Kabbalat Shabbat* services, and they all stayed over in the hotel. On *Shabbat* morning, the *Shacharit* services were led by Uncle Yizhak Brom, their grandfather's brother. Then Zvi Eliezer *layned* the whole *parasha*, while his "younger" brother chanted the Haftorah and davened *Mussaf* (additional prayers on Sabbath morning). Their Israeli cousins shared in the services with *aliyot* during the *layning*. The services were concluded and a family luncheon was shared. (There are no prohibitions about sharing a communal meal on *Shabbat*, because on that day you do not have public displays of mourning.) Maggie prepared a rhyming verse in Hebrew that traced the course of the twins, both separately and together. The following is the English translation of the end of the poem:

> We have arrived at the ultimate now
> As we celebrate the Bar Mitzvah
> To each of you
> And all of you together.
>
> Dear honored quadruplets
> The message should be clear
> You have common roots
> Which are your heritage and family ties.
> I wish for you that when you grow up and develop
> You will value your similarities and differences
> And that you will grow up to be good Jews
> With the holy Torah in the center of your lives.

The Bar Mitzvah *parasha* for the Brom boys was *Vayishlach*. It details the story of Jacob and Esau—twins. *Vayeishev* was the *parasha* for the Bushwick brothers. In it, we learn the story of Joseph and his brothers. There is a segue into the story of Judah. His daughter-in-law Tamar gives birth to Perez and Zerah—twins—from whom the line of King David will descend. Two *parashas*, back to back, detailing the stories of twins, from whom a nation and a dynasty are born. Two modern sets of twins, cousins, born two days apart, perpetuating a family, a heritage, and a way of life. Two sets of twins bringing *nachis* (pride) and joy to a family. Two sets of twins realizing their own promise and potential by keeping the holy Torah in the center of their lives.

39

THE HIDDEN CHILD

Henry Rodrigues—March 18, 1986

When Henry Rogrigues read the Diary of Anne Frank some years ago, he was amazed to find similarities between her experiences and his own. They both had lived in the same city— Amsterdam, Holland—and although they'd lived within walking distance from each other, they had never met. The miraculous difference between them is Henry's survival. He just turned 70 on his last birthday. Had Anne lived, she would be about the same age.

Hitler's army invaded Holland in May 1940. It started the systematic deportation of Dutch Jews. Every night after 8:00 P.M. the dreaded police vans would enter the neighborhood. The black-uniformed Dutch police jumped out of the vans, accompanied by the Grune Polizei. They went from door to door, pulling people out of their homes and taking them away. There was no discrimination—they rounded up men, women, children—old and young alike.

191

Anne and her family went into hiding on July 8, 1942.
Members of the Frank family actually walked to their hiding
place, which was in the center of the city, just a few miles from
their home. That famous attic became their new home for the
next two years. In August 1944, they were betrayed, arrested
by the Nazis, and deported to the concentration camps. The
only survivor of the family was Anne's father, Otto Frank.

The Rodrigues family lived in a middle-class neighborhood
in Amsterdam. As a result of the Spanish Inquisition, their
ancestors had fled to Holland from Portugal during the 15th
and 16th centuries to join the already active community
of Sephardic Jews. Henry's father, Abraham, sold textiles
for women's clothes. This job required a great deal of travel.
Being very personable, he made friends and good contacts
all over Holland.

When they realized that at any moment the next "round-up"
would be for them, Henry's father made arrangements for
the family to hide in the attic of Bert Bochove and his wife,
a pharmacist. The store was located downstairs. For eight
months, Henry, his younger sister Elizabeth, and their parents
remained there, without ever seeing the light of day. They lived
in terror of being found out. Every night, they rolled their
clothes up and placed their shoes on top, so that they would
always be ready to escape in a hurry. If the Nazis came at night,
the family members knew to make their beds before they hid.
Even so, they heard that the Nazis would pull back the covers
and feel whether the sheets were still warm.

Although preservation was a priority, Abraham realized that,
war or not, his children needed fresh air and sunshine. In the
summer of 1943, two Christian women, Diet Van Rosendaal
and her sister Nel Pasveer, took the children into their home,
deep in the countryside of central Holland. Their parents
assumed a false name and hid in Utrecht, Holland. After that
summer, the children were split up. Elizabeth remained with a
woman they called Tanta Grie until the end of the war. In
December 1943, their parents were betrayed, arrested in
Utrecht, and sent to the camps. They were able to smuggle a
letter to the children. It was too dangerous to keep Henry in his
hiding place, so he was moved several more times. He fled to

another rural town, where another Dutch Christian took him in. This time, instead of hiding him, they told neighbors that the blue-eyed boy was a poor relation. He lived out in the open and went to church with the family on Sundays.

His sister also lived out in the open and attended school as a young Christian girl. One day, she innocently almost gave herself away. In Bible class, when it was her turn to read aloud, she read the familiar names of our Patriarchs with her accustomed Hebrew pronunciation. The country children didn't even notice; however, the teacher realized that she was a Jewish child in hiding. He informed her "family," but only to keep her safe.

Henry stayed with his "family" until the liberation of Europe. People in the town came over and shook his hand when the war was over. He looked at them, dumbfounded. Much to his surprise, they responded that they had always known who he was. Whether just keeping quiet or actually hiding these children, several righteous gentiles are responsible for keeping the Rodrigueses and other Jewish children alive during the war. Great risk was involved with harboring Jews of any age, and the punishment was the concentration camps. No money was paid to these families. Their good deeds were carried out as part of their religious convictions. Despite the great peril, this was the right thing to do.

When the war was over, Henry was only 15. He completed his education in Holland and emigrated to the United States at the age of 19. He started college in New York, but once again his education was interrupted by war. He served in the United States Army during the Korean War and, ironically, was sent to a military base in Germany. He had met a lovely, feisty young lady at a fraternity party (the only one she ever went to) and married Renee Dubinsky. She accompanied him to Germany, where they lived for two years. Upon arrival back in the United States, he finished his education at night while he started an export business.

Picking up the pieces and moving on physically are difficult enough after surviving a devastating and prolonged traumatic experience, but finding emotional solace and peace is even more daunting and sometimes impossible. For a long time after the war, Henry could not reconcile his feelings about Judaism and a God Who would let such atrocities take place. There were no answers for how the inconceivable could happen. As he read his nightly newspaper, he was always struck by the dramatic response to the local news. If casualties occurred in a fire or an accident, he noticed an outpouring of shock and sympathy for the victims and their families. Where was the outcry for the fate of 6,000,000?

With the love and support of Renee and his two children, Albert and Lea, Henry went on. He was able to focus on the positive and recognize all he had to be grateful for. In Holland, before the war, Henry went to Hebrew school two days a week and attended the Portuguese synagogue. In New York, it was natural that he and Renee would join and become active members in the Sephardic Temple of Cedarhurst. Henry should have become a Bar Mitzvah in March 1943, but the war interrupted his plans. Forty-three years after that date, he decided to formally become a Bar Mitzvah. He wanted to honor his grandfather, Moses Coopman. Coopman, a religious Jew and primarily responsible for Henry's early Hebrew education, had been living out his last years comfortably in an old age home, when the Nazis hastened his demise. They forcibly rounded up the residents of the home and transported them to Aushwitz. Moses Coopman was 85 years old.

Henry studied with Rabbi Arnold Marans and Cantor Abikzer for about six months prior to the date set for his Bar Mitzvah—March 8, 1986. He already knew how to read Hebrew, but needed to brush up on his davening and learn his *parasha* for *Shabbat Shekalim.* While Henry did his part, Renee designed and ordered the invitations, made a guest list, and arranged for a caterer. It didn't matter that the Bar Mitzvah "boy" was almost 56 years old. This was the realization of a magnificent dream and the first adult Bar Mitzvah in the Sephardic Temple.

Henry addressed his guests:

> *Baroech atah adonei elohenoe melech haolam sheche-*
> *chianoe, vikiemanoe, vehigianoe, lazeman haze.*
> Blessed are You, Eternal, our God, King of the Universe,

Who let us live and Who perpetuated us and Who let us reach this day.

How glad I am that I can say these words of praise on my Bar Mitzvah day. These same words were spoken by the chief rabbi of the city of Utrecht, Justus Tal, on May 7, 1945. It was two days after the liberation and at the first service after the war at the Portuguese Synagogue in Amsterdam. Rabbi Tal must have been a remarkable man, indeed, to have been able to praise and thank God amid unspeakable sorrow, ruins, and desolation. At that time, I could not share the rabbi's words of praise. I was too bitter and disillusioned by all that had happened to me and my family in the Holocaust.

But time is a great healer. Now, forty-three years later, I have a different and more positive outlook on life. I am grateful for the blessings and good fortune God has bestowed on me and my family. I am thankful for the opportunity to celebrate my Bar Mitzvah and thereby honor my parents, grandfather, and all my family who perished in the war.

I want to thank my wife, Renee, for her encouragement through her living example of upholding the Jewish traditions.

And I want to take the example of Anne Frank, who wrote in her diary on July 15, 1944, while hidden in Amsterdam: "Despite everything, I still believe in the basic goodness of man."

Henry extended his Bar Mitzvah celebration with a trip to Israel. At the *Kotel* (the Western Wall), he was called to the Torah for the second time. At this very holy place, Henry succumbed to his emotions and wept as he recited the ancient words thanking God for giving us the Torah. A very proud Renee stood on a chair and peeked over the wall from the women's section, as her husband embraced their heritage.

In a good novel, the story would end here with a rapprochement and a happy ending. Unfortunately, the Holocaust has far-reaching and long-lasting effects. In his golden years, when Henry should be enjoying life and his retirement, the opposite has occurred. Since Henry's retirement, the miseries of the Holocaust have plagued him, making it very difficult for him to lead a normal life. Nevertheless, he has tried to overcome the memories of his tribulations of the past. Hopefully, someday he can fully enjoy his life, his family, and especially his young grandson and be the life-guiding force for the boy, just as Moses Coopman was to him.

Author's note: This story was found in *Amit Magazine*, in an article written by Zipporah Marans. Mrs. Marans was kind enough to put the author in touch with Henry and Renee Rodrigues.

40

EVACUATION

Morris Lenchner—March, 1940

Morris Lenchner is enjoying his retirement. He and his wife, Sara, are traveling and spending time with their children and grandchildren.

Sara Shannock wandered the streets in the East End of London. It was September 3, 1939, the day of her birthday party. She had just turned 13. None of the children she'd invited showed up for her party. Her family didn't have a phone, so she went up and down the streets in the neighborhood, looking for her friends. The streets were empty. She sighed, "Where are all of the children?"

They were gone . . . millions of children—gone. Anticipating war, the British government had devised a plan to evacuate the children. About 4 million children, some with adults, were moved from the bigger cities, and another 2 million were evacuated privately.* This was strictly a voluntary program for the safety of the children.

Morris Lenchner was the youngest of four from a family in the Gant's Hill section of Essex, outside of London. His older brother and two older sisters were already grown and out of the house, leaving him the only child at home in September 1939. With war imminent and fearing the worst, Morris's parents agreed to his evacuation to the country. The first set of evacuees left on September 1. Over the course of the next few days, almost one million unaccompanied children left the big cities. Morris Lenchner was one of them.

On September 2, 1939, Morris and about forty other children were put on a train to Hertfordshire, a sweet little village about thirty-five miles outside of London. They gathered in the village hall, where several kind women looked after them and plied them with chocolates and sweets.

The children were next taken to the center of town, where they were paraded down the main street. The townspeople came out to appraise this lot—some merely curious, while others had more purposeful intentions. With fingers pointing, the braver members of the crowd started yelling out that they would take in this boy or that girl. Some of the countryfolk, unfamiliar with Cockney boys and girls, were just cooperating with the war effort to save the children and avoid having young casualties of war. Others, more opportunistic, saw these children as cheap labor and took them in for the work that could be squeezed out of them.

The group shrunk rather quickly, leaving only two boys left to place. Their chaperone, undaunted by this slight, took her two young charges to a nearby home and knocked on the door. She asked the lady of the house if she would be willing to take in a child. The surprised woman appraised the two forlorn creatures facing her, with their haversacks on their backs and gas masks in hand, and said, "I'll have the curly, skinny one." The other young boy was rather plump, and in those days of strict rationing, his size was perhaps a deterrent in his placement. And so Morris Lenchner found a place that would be his home for the next two and a half years, with a childless couple, the Warwicks, who would come to love him as their own.

The first year of the war was called the "phony war" because the bombing didn't start until 1940. With the deceptive calm, many of the evacuees chose to return home, thereby putting them in harm's way once the bombing started in earnest. Morris, however, remained in Hertfordshire, comfortable with his "foster" parents and visited as often as possible by his real mum and dad.

Out in the country, the only Jewish children were those who had been transported by the war effort. There was a "roving rabbi" who would drop into the schools, identify the Jewish children, and if any of them were near Bar Mitzvah age, he would spend a half hour with them, teaching them the *brachot* so they could be called to the Torah. This Rabbi Levin, an earnest young man, found Morris in his country school. Recognizing that Morris's 13th birthday was coming up, he taught him the *brachot*, helped him to figure out the exact Saturday of his Bar Mitzvah, and arranged with the nearest synagogue to give Morris an *aliyah* on this day.

To the Warwicks, Judaism was totally unfamiliar, and the only Jewish person they'd had any contact with was Morris himself. On the night before his Bar Mitzvah, Morris tried his best to explain to them in language that they would understand where he had to go the next morning. He told them that he was being called up to the (Jewish) law, and he was going to become a man. This explanation satisfied them.

The next morning, Morris awoke very early. The nearest *shul* was in Wellewyan, Garden City, nine miles away. In the best outfit he could muster up, he walked about half of the distance and found himself exhausted. Knowing that he was not supposed to ride on the Sabbath (especially, his Bar Mitzvah), nonetheless he spotted a milk floater—a horse and buggy delivering milk—and asked for a ride. In the days of petrol rationing, the horse provided an alternative, if less efficient, means of transportation. At the horse's pace of five or 6 m.p.h., Morris could have walked almost that quickly, but he was seated and enjoyed the bouncy clip-clop of his chariot. He thanked the driver and jumped off near the synagogue. They

were obviously expecting him, because no one looked surprised when this somewhat disheveled, dust-covered young
man entered the *shul.* At the appropriate time in the service he
was asked his Hebrew name, Moshe Ben Eliezer, and called up
to the Torah. He recited the blessings as Rabbi Levin had
taught him, accepted the congratulatory handshakes, and sat
down. When the services were over, several members of the
congregation approached him and invited him to join them for
lunch. Though touched by the hospitality of the strangers,
Morris was quite shy and declined all of the offers. With his
newly acquired status, a Jewish man under halachic law, he
turned around and walked the nine miles back to Hertfordshire and the Warwick home.

His parents could not attend because they were living
underground, contending with constant air raids. However, on
their next visit they brought him a signet ring with his initials,
which he wore for years. Morris stayed with the Warwicks for
two and a half years, at which time he returned to London and
did what he could for the war effort. At the age of 14, he started
working as a machinist in a factory, making army tunics, and
continued until the end of the war. Several years after the war,
he met Sara Shannock, the young lady who had wandered the
streets looking for friends on the day of her birthday party.
While he weathered the war in the English countryside, Sara,
an only child, chose to stay in London with her parents. Her
story is quite a contrast to Morris's. Every evening her family
members grabbed their bedclothes and headed for the shelters. With the constant bombing, it was impossible to stay
above ground. There was great camaraderie in the confined
space. In the intimacy of the sleeping quarters, it was hard to
remain aloof. People from varied backgrounds joined together
in the common goal of survival. Every morning, when they
emerged from their bunks, they dreaded what they would find.
Sometimes, some of their homes would have been destroyed
during the night, while the luckier ones only had to sweep up
broken glass from the bombing raids of the night before. With
school a distant memory due to the war, Sara, too, found her
way to the factories, only she became a dressmaker's model. In
the process of comparing their wartime experiences, Morris

and Sara fell in love. Before they were married, though, Morris brought his intended to meet his other family, the Warwicks. Mrs. Warwick, who treated Morris as if he were her own, was rather possessive of him and needed to meet Sara before the young woman was officially welcomed. The Warwicks, of course, were special guests at their wedding.

In their nostalgia, Morris and Sara lament the lost simplicity and lack of materialism of their wartime experiences. However, while raising their own three sons, when it came time for the Bar Mitzvahs, the Lenchners made lavish affairs. Maybe that was just a reflection of the changing times, or perhaps in a small way it was an effort to make up for the modest event that was Morris's own coming of age.

With their children grown, Morris and Sara find many different ways to keep busy during their retirement. However, three or four times a year, Morris makes the now-familiar thirty-five-mile trip to the lovely Herfordshire countryside. And there, in the Woolmer Green Church yard, Morris places flowers on the gravesites of Mr. and Mrs. Warwick. Although more than sixty years have passed, he can still hear her first words and they never fail to evoke a smile, "I'll have the curly, skinny one."

41

JEWISH HUMOR

Sam Finesurrey—March 18, 2000

Michelle Fine is a professor of social psychology at the City University of New York, Graduate Center. As part of her work for the college, she teaches and does research at the Bedford Hills Prison Facility. The pregnant women at this maximum security facility are allowed to keep their babies up until 18 months. Without benefit of baby showers and helpful families, these babies start with little. Hearing the stories from his mom, Sam donated a chunk of his Bar Mitzvah money to the day-care program established  *for these children. Another chunk went to Jersey City Headstart. He wanted to give a start to people who don't have any help. He didn't just send a check, he presented his gifts in person.*

A what?? Baaaaa Mitzvah?? What do we do?? Sam Finesurrey lives in many worlds filled with multiculturalism and ethnicity. Therefore, many of the invited guests for the upcoming Bar Mitzvah were respectful, yet clueless, about what was expected of them, what they could expect, and what they were supposed to do before, during, and after. So, in their own way, Michelle Fine and David Surrey prepared a veritable "Cliff Notes for the Uninformed." The following insert accompanied Sam's "formal," but unconventional, Bar Mitzvah invitation:

Sam Finesurrey's Bar Mitzvah
Frequently Asked Questions

1. **Do I really have to attend both the service and the reception?**
   Stop whining. Between our lips and God's ears, we won't be taking attendance at the service.

2. **How long is the service?**
   Two hours and twelve minutes, but we are not sure if that is human or cat minutes.

3. **Won't I be hungry after the service?**
   Yes. However, for an additional fee, there is an *Extended Kiddush* in the synagogue immediately after the service at which you will be served challah, bagels (6 Weight Watcher points), wine, and other refreshments.

4. **Won't I be hungry at the reception?**
   For what we pay the caterer, you better not be. Between music, talks, and games, there is a sit-down meal with knives, forks, and napkins.

5. **What do I wear?**
   We encourage something. Our idea is that no one be uncomfortable so we suggest anything from *casual to formal.* In other words, do not overdo it.

6. **What is this Mitzvah project?**
   Well, the after-life is not a central, or even clear, belief in our religion. Nonetheless, we hedge a bit by encouraging good deeds. Therefore, each Bar/Bat Mitzvah child is encouraged to ask his/her guests to help with a project that will make the world a better place.

7. **What music will I have the pleasure of listening to at the reception?**
   Wars have been fought over less. The compromise, or the blend, is Klezmer, Country, Hip-Hop, R&B, and Pop.

Suggested Activities for Intermission: 1 P.M. until 7 P.M.

For the creative:
Go to the theater in New York.
Visit the Montclair Art Museum.
Delight at the Newark Art Museum.

For relatives:
Flop in on Rose and Jack unannounced—and watch their faces!
Reflect on the trauma and joys of your own Bar/Bat Mitzvahs.

For the procrastinators:
Go to the Willowbrook or Livingston Mall for a present for Sam (or shop for yourself).

For obsessive types:
Check your e-mail somewhere at Montclair State University.

For the wise:
Nap
Write an Op Ed piece protesting the March 17th St. Patrick's Day parade exclusion of lesbian and gay organizations.

For leftist, feminist comics:
Draft a short story, satire, memoir, or tragic-comedy about designing a "Bar/Bat Mitzvah or coming of age" event—multiracial and multi-ethnic stories, with good politics, encouraged; authentic dialogue with grandparents will get special attention.

For the ambitious:
Learn Hebrew.
Practice Random Acts of Justice and Kindness.
Think about why Jews do what we do.
Try to guess who all those people were on the *bimah* (podium, stage).
EVERYONE MUST—
Kvell (Yiddush for "spill over with joy") in the sunshine of Sam and the sixty-year marriage shared by Rose and Jack.

Who is Sam Finesurrey—this kid with the well-merged name? A study in opposites. A product of contrast. A funny kid with a deep social conscience. A kid whose family experienced struggle, death, and loss—whose members use humor not to deflect it, but to remember the past, recast their lives, and re-imagine a better future. A blending of two families that couldn't be more different—not in values, but in background and upbringing. Michelle Fine's (Sam's mother) parents are the "Jack and Rose" in the invitation—celebrating sixty years together! Jack lost much of his family, including his mother, in the Holocaust. He arrived in this country with only his grandmother and started as a junk salesman on the Lower East Side. His wife, on the other hand, was surrounded by family, being the youngest of eighteen children. Despite hardships, their family survived with integrity—humor—and love of the world.

In contrast, David Surrey (Sam's father) lost his father when he was only 12—that pivotal year before his Bar Mitzvah, which then never took place. The Surreys were one of the few Jewish families in Missouri, and the nearest synagogue was forty miles away. His mother passed away only a few years later, when David was just 19. He began his college career virtually alone, with only the memory of his father's short, but successful, academic career as a professor at Northwest Missouri State.

Sam lives in an ethnically and culturally diverse world, making the cast of characters not only at his Bar Mitzvah, but also in his everyday life, well . . . colorful. The Finesurreys, in addition to their two sons, Sam and Caleb, have an African-American foster son, Demetrius, and an "adopted" (lovingly—not officially, because of her age) young Vietnamese woman, Lin. Caleb's godfather is African American, and their first cousins are adopted and hale originally from Colombia and El Salvador. Amidst this variety, Judaism is a "place to work out of"—with its history, culture, Yiddish, and strong sense of social justice.

David was ambivalent about the Bar Mitzvah. An archaeology professor at St. Peter's College, active in the struggles of urban education, he didn't like the materialistic direction that Bar Mitzvahs, in general, had taken. What started as a simple rite of passage had become a forum for public showiness and a flaunting of wealth. But in watching the dedication and enthusiasm his son put into the preparation, David learned a deeper respect for the ceremony. Because Michelle and David have only a rotely learned Hebrew base, Sam was on his own in learning the Hebrew. Watching him was a source of pride for his parents, but as two academicians, they found it tough knowing he was out there on his own, and the most they could offer was moral support.

It was some ceremony! On his mother's side, eighty-two close relatives (first cousins, nieces, and nephews) attended. On his father's side were an aunt (by marriage) and one special guest, a former student of David's father who came to honor his old professor and his professor's family. There was a real presence of the past and those who were no longer living. Not only was a candle lit for departed relatives, but large posters also chronicled events of Sam's ancestors. Sam felt this deep connection to a past he didn't know firsthand and had only heard about in stories from his family.

Sam's *parasha, Vayikra*, from the book of Leviticus, is multi-faceted and touches upon many issues related to questions of sin and guilt. In his *D'var Torah*, Sam reflected on the sin of withholding testimony in the face of witnessing transgression:

> We live in a world surrounded by injustice. As such, we have an obligation to help those in need, to help the suffering, to help the many, to help the world. We must testify about the oppression that has survived within our nation. In my Torah portion, it is written: "One who is able to testify by having seen or learned of the matter, and does not give information, is subject to punishment."
>
> Our Torah teaches us: Do not stand idly by the blood of your neighbor. How could silence be considered anything but a crime?
>
> I recently read a book titled the *Narrative of the Life of Frederick Douglass*. Mr. Douglass was an abolitionist, a former slave, and an author who expressed the pain and the wrongdoing of this nation. He told a story of a man whose life revolved around this disaster of American history—slavery. He gave the truth to people all over the

world about his saddened times and a nation's horrible crimes against humanity. Douglass ended his narrative by explaining, "I felt it my duty to testify."

. . . He wrote this narrative with racism staring him right in the eye. With death hiding from him behind every door, in every alley, in every tree, and in every racist's heart. His testimony expressed the brutal hardship that came with slavery to the world.

Douglass might not have been giving witness to our religion, but he was giving testimony across the globe. To be a Jew today, as Jews have been required to do for the better part of 4,000 years, means we, too, must tell of those who have suffered. We must tell those of the future about past wrongs, to help in the mitzvah of *Tikun Olam*, which means repairing the world. We shall always serve witness so that wrongs of the past will not be repeated as wrongs of the future.

> Don't weep, testify
> For Jewish people, for all . . .
> We must testify.

Sam's speech, written by himself (with the admitted assistance of spell check), incorporates thoughts and feelings that he practices, not just talks about. He is outgoing, optimistic, and co-president of his middle school. He ponders social and moral issues. When Sam was about 4, he witnessed friends of the family spanking their child. He asked his father to please intervene and tell them not to hit. While David was still pondering this surprising request, Sam took action himself. He went right over to the other child's mother and told her not to hit her child. Very practically, he explained to this woman twenty-plus years his senior that hitting scares the boy; it might hurt him, and it doesn't work. Sam offered that his mother and father would buy the family a rocking chair so they could use that for time out. The open-mouthed woman complied with his request.

Sam did not arrive at his conclusions on social injustice on his own. In his mother's words, "It takes a very large multicultural *shtetl* to make a child. Many of the people in attendance had a role in the making of Sam Finesurrey."

In honor of his grandson's Bar Mitzvah, Jack Fine made a few remarks: "Sam was always a brilliant child; a heart of gold, a friend to all. His acquaintances always know that Sam will help and defend them. A heart full of love and affection. But he has no vices. I said to myself, 'I must teach him a vice.' So, I taught him to play gin rummy and made a gambler out of him!"

If you polled the now "informed" guests for the top ten reasons for going to Sam's Bar Mitzvah, the list might look like this:

10. We now know what *kvell* means.

9. Although the service was long, there was enough action and variety to keep it interesting.

8. The food was great, plentiful, varied, and no one left hungry.

7. The music and dancing were a hoot! So, that's Klezmer music.

6. We celebrated not only Sam's Bar Mitzvah, but Rose and Jack's 60th. A double whammy!

5. Seeing eighty-two Fine cousins on the right and one lone Surrey relative on the left.

4. Sam's Mitzvah project—way cool!

3. Sam's speech—so much knowledge from one so young.

2. Sam's first public reading of the Torah (he was great!)

1. Sam.

42

VALEDICTORIAN

Alexander Goretsky—September 9, 1989

Victor and Alex graduated together, Alex from high school and Victor from the school of radiology at CMC. Alex went on to do his undergraduate work at the California Institute of Technology in Pasadena, completed a master's degree at Berkeley, and now works as a chemical engineer in Silicon Valley. Through a circuitous route, Victor became a radiation inspector for Einstein Hospital in New York City. Julia is the aquatics director and swim team coach at the Jewish Community Center in Scranton. They have a long-distance marriage and see each other on weekends. Willing to do anything once they arrived, no one is more surprised than Victor and Julia that they are engaged in similar occupations to the ones they left behind—only now they are free.

Alex Goretsky graduated as the valedictorian of the Class of '94 of Scranton High School. Graduating as the valedictorian is a noteworthy and distinctive achievement for any student. It is a monumental accomplishment for a young man who arrived in the United States only three years earlier, speaking almost no English. The Goretsky family emigrated from Kiev in the former U.S.S.R. in March of 1991.

Alex's grandmother, Lidia, was an outstanding student of chemistry. She hoped to pursue a college degree in the subject. The day before she was to matriculate, she was told that she had not been accepted into the university. The reason given was that her papers did not arrive on time. Alex's mother, Julia, had hoped to study medicine. In spite of getting top grades and deserving the gold medal that would mean automatic entry into college, she was given only mediocre recognition and denied access into medical school.

Lidia grew up hearing from her parents to just "be patient, and when you grow up things will be better." She then shared the same rhetoric with her daughter, telling her to be strong and "hang in there." "When you grow up things will be much better." These platitudes were now being handed down to the third generation, and Julia and her husband, Victor, decided that "the buck stops here." They were not going to pass on the same empty words to their children. In spite of her family being active, productive citizens of the Ukraine for many generations, the space for "nationality" on her passport was stamped "Jewish. She learned also that her "nationality" was the reason for the dirty name-calling in elementary school and her denied access to desired schooling and jobs. Victor and Julia were not about to let their children experience the same frustration and limited options. They applied for emigration.

The late 1980s in the former Soviet Union were a time of flux. Gorbachov had set up his policies of glasnost and *perestroika*. There was a supposed new "openess," but people who had never trusted the government were wary. People were expecting things, but didn't know what to expect. In this atmosphere, Victor received a letter from his brother, who had emigrated to Israel in the early 1970s and was now living with his family in New York. He described in glowing terms this thing called a "Bar Mitzvah" that his son just had. There was a party and a celebration and now his son was a man, according to Jewish tradition. They even included a photo of the gala event. While

Julia had at least some basic information on Judaism, the traditions had been lost completely to Victor's family. This concept of entrance into manhood, celebrated with a ceremony, was something they felt that their son Alex deserved, too. Since Alex was almost 13, it was the perfect time to have a Bar Mitzvah. But what were they supposed to do?

To supplement his income as a radiation inspector for the government, Victor was a tour guide for the beautiful city of Kiev. He knew all about the architecture and history of many of the former churches in the fair city, but very little about the synagogues. It wasn't possible to just open the yellow pages of the phone book and turn to the heading marked "Synagogue." While stories of the new tolerance and openness were splashed across the international press, in reality the open practice of religion did not fit into a communist society. Nonetheless, Victor took a train ride to a synagogue that he knew existed some forty minutes away from their home.

In contrast to the ancient building, Victor found a young rabbi with a nice smile. The rabbi was a Ukrainian-born Jew who had been educated abroad. Victor told him that he would like his son to have a Bar Mitzvah. "What do we do?" he asked. The short, round rabbi was surprised with the query, but then explained that Alex had to study and learn the Hebrew blessing. The rabbi transliterated the Hebrew into Russian letters and set up an appointment to meet with Alex the following week. They met a few more times and set the date for September 9, 1989, Alex's 13th birthday.

Several members of their extended family came to celebrate, although none of them really knew what it was all about. Alex was the first in his family to have a Bar Mitzvah. Julia, her mother, and some cousins found themselves in the women's section upstairs in the synagogue. Downstairs, Alex and Victor were surrounded by strangers, a few old men who were the keystones of the building. Even the books with the words from the Torah were archaic, having been printed before the revolution. They had Hebrew written on one side and the translation in Old Russian on the opposite page. Alex was called up to the *bimah*, located in the center of the room. He was wearing the new *tallis* that the rabbi had given him. It had somehow been delivered to Kiev through the rabbi's connections. Alex recited the blessings from memory as he held the *yad* (the silver pointer) to the Torah. His father then joined him on the *bimah* and also recited the same "magic" words. When the service was over, Julia provided cake, wine, and candy. Since the women had been segregated during the service, she assumed they were not permitted to eat together, either. She set the table and then she and the other women waited outside. No one invited them to stay.

In the weeks after the Bar Mitzvah, Alex brought photos in to school to show his friends and tell them all about his Bar Mitzvah. Julia didn't know that he had taken the pictures into school. She found out when she received a call from the principal. The children had told their parents, who in turn called the principal. He phoned to tell Julia that religion was "not appropriate" and that Alex was being dismissed from the school. Every cloud has a silver lining. Alex transferred to a new school that was farther away from their home. However, it was academically superior, and there Alex demonstrated that he was gifted in both chemistry and math

A little more than a year later, the Goretskys finally were given permission to leave Kiev. Julia's aunt had already settled in Scranton, so the family was relocated there. Alex was probably the most excited in the family to leave. He had nothing to lose and everything to gain. Julia and Victor, committed to providing a better life for their children, were prepared to do anything necessary to survive once they arrived. In the Soviet Union, Julia was on maternity leave from her physical therapy job, having given birth to a little girl, Yasya. Victor, who has two master's degrees, lost his job as a radiation inspector when he reported unusual amounts of radiation one month before the Chernobyl nuclear accident. He was later hired by another company to assist with the clean-up. When they arrived in Scranton, Julia was hired almost immediately as a lifeguard. She has a strong background in physical education and had swum competitively in Kiev. In the beginning, Victor did not fare as well, but nothing dampened his good-naturedness and his sense of humor. He plucked and cut chickens at a kosher chicken plant, hauled furniture, chopped ice in a refrigerated meat packing-plant, and worked in a paper cup factory. The problem with manual labor is that the risk for injury is high, and the Goretskys had no health insurance. Victor applied for the Community Medical Center's school of radiology program and was accepted. Only four students were in the two-year training program, and the hospital paid a stipend that included medical insurance. The best part of the program was that although Victor already knew the physics and the anatomy, he learned English.

Meanwhile, in high school, Alex quickly worked his way out of the ESL (English as a Second Language) program. By his second year, he was the only sophomore in a junior elementary analysis honors calculus course. He continued to take accelerated courses all the way through high school. His insight into math was phenomenal, and his questions stimulated the rest of the class. He became Americanized very quickly, while at the same time he recognized the need to keep his own identity. He was somewhat self-conscious about his accent; the other kids teased him and he learned to tease them back. His teachers found him to possess an incredible determination, a strong work ethic, and a desire to succeed. He not only concentrated on academics, but also demonstrated the same skills on the swim team that he did in the classroom. Although everyone found it incredible that a boy who had been here only a little over three years became the valedictorian, Alex had distinguished himself early on, so that no one who knew him was surprised.

Alex shared some very poignant words during his valedictory address:

> What awaits us in the future is a new life, different from the one we know now because through a slow process we have to learn to live as one great world community. . . . only by putting aside our differences—by concentrating on our similarities, and by an unhampered cooperation, will we be able to improve and progress humankind to the highest stage of its development in which peace, trust, and harmony will be our guide.

Alex and his family knew firsthand what it was to live in a country where there was no peace or trust, and where by virtue of "nationality," access to education and position was granted or denied. They had struggled to leave their Mother Country, and the trials and tribulations continued in the process of assimilation and acculturation. They came to America forsaking all that was familiar and forged a new path. Like the early pioneers, they asked for nothing but the chance to try. And as it did to our ancestors, this country offered them renewed hope for joy and prosperity in the future. But the relationship is reciprocal. These new immigrants have contributed back tenfold, adding greatly to the cultural, social, and economic base of this country.

43

A LONG TIME COMIN'

Lonnie Calvin Childers—January 6, 1997

Since his Bar Mitzvah, Lonnie has learned how to read the Megillah *of Esther and has read it on Purim eve. He never wants to stop learning, for he feels as if he has a lot of time to make up. His son Andrew has started to demonstrate a little of his father's independence. Permitted to make the choice, Andrew told his parents that he feels most comfortable in an Orthodox* shul *and would like to have his Bar Mitzvah there. Since Lonnie's long-awaited conversion was Conservative, he would not be permitted an* aliyah *at his son's Bar Mitzvah. Un-*  *daunted and determined as always, Lonnie and Fran adopted an Orthodox lifestyle to pave the way for an Orthodox conversion. They had always kept a kosher home, but now Lonnie walks the several miles to* shul *on erev Shabbos and Shabbos morning. If his construction business hadn't kept him in shape, the walking certainly did. Lonnie was converted, again, circumcised, again (only ritually speaking), and married for the third time to the same woman. But he will tell you that all of this has been worth it. When Andrew was called to the Torah in August 2000, Lonnie stood proudly beside him. Maybe it was that funny line in the palm of Lonnie's hand that led a country boy from West Virginia to the* bimah *at Beth Shalom. Nevertheless, without a trace of bitterness or a moment's regret, he remembers instead the deep kindness of strangers, making the best of every situation, and thoroughly enjoying the journey.*

215

A strong line in Lonnie Childers' palm veers off to the left, while the others all run parallel to the right. A palm reader once told him that meant that an event would happen that would change his life. In a life dotted with a succession of remarkable events, it's difficult to claim only one pivotal moment as being responsible for his extraordinary ride. More likely, it is the compilation of these experiences, rather than a single one, that accounts for a life less ordinary.

At age 4, when his parents split up, the kids were divided, too. His sisters went south with his mother, his older brother headed out with his father, and as the youngest boy, he was packed off to Cedar Grove, West Virginia, with his grandparents. Whether "nature" or "nurture," young Lonnie favored his grandpa in demeanor: easy-going, slow to anger, patient, and good-natured. He easily adapted to their "on-again," "off-again" life of working on a riverboat. "Rolling with the punches" became less a of cliché and more of a survival tactic. That is, until his grandmother died. Feigning concern for their welfare, his aunt moved into their home, en masse with her family, and banished Lonnie and his grandfather to a small sewing room. Even that was tolerable until his grandfather started to fail. Lonnie would sit with him for hours. One day, as Lonnie held his hand, the old man said quietly, "I'm ready to go with Mom." He died with his grandson at his side.

Lonnie's mother couldn't come for him until the summer, and when his aunt realized there were to be no future support payments for the young boy, she told the county authorities to pick him up the following Monday. Overhearing the phone conversation, Lonnie was determined that he would never go to a county home. He packed his grandfather's suitcase, stashed the $75 from his paper route, and headed out in the middle of the night. He was 12. He headed toward Maryland because he knew that his stepmother's people were from there. Without knowing her maiden name, he was relying on instinct and luck, more than on any clear recollection from his visit there several years earlier.

He first encountered a state policeman, who wondered where this young boy was going in the wee hours of the morning. Lonnie answered honestly that he was going to the bus station. Worrying more about his safety than about propriety, the officer drove him to the station. When Lonnie arrived in Laurel, Maryland, the first thing he saw when he got off the bus was a construction site. Having some rudimentary knowledge of woodworking, taught to him by his grandfather, he approached the owner about a job. The skeptical man, R. C. Troxell, took one look at this boy and asked him how old he was.

Lonnie retorted, "How old do I have to be to work here?"

Troxell replied, "16."

"Then, I'm 16," Lonnie shot back.

Troxell told him that if he could haul a pile of lumber up close to the building, the job was his. Lonnie not only got the job, but this benevolent proprietor rented him his first apartment for the princely sum of $25 per month!

He hung out at the fire company "with the boys" to have some company in the evening. After a few weeks, the chief called him outside to talk privately. The chief's day job happened to be truant officer. He confronted Lonnie, assuring the boy that he didn't want to make trouble. He only wanted to see this obviously bright young man complete his high school education. Making a promise that he would, Lonnie enrolled in night courses. He began a routine of a full day's work, followed by classes from 6:00 to 10:00 P.M., Monday through Thursday.

After about a year of driving Lonnie to and from work, Troxell suggested that the boy buy his own car and start transporting himself. Lonnie told him quite honestly he didn't have enough money for a vehicle. The next day after work, Troxell threw him the keys to a little box of a car. "This is for you," was all that he said. Lonnie spent the next few hours acquainting himself with the five speeds on the column. He drove home rather tentatively. He was 14.

The gift of the car came with strings. Lonnie now had additional responsibilities of driving at the construction sites. He was careful and conscientious. He just didn't have a license. When he was finally of age to get a license, he walked over to the Department of Motor Vehicles. Unfortunately, his boss was a good friend of the testing officer. Troxell had dropped by for a chat. When he saw Lonnie descending the steps, Troxell asked the boy in front of the officer what he was doing at the DMV. The officer, having seen Lonnie's papers, responded that this young man was here to take his driving test. Troxell looked up incredulously and said, "This boy's been driving for me for the past two years. I didn't know how old he was!" The officer, hearing the words of his friend, stamped Lonnie's papers and told the boy he had his license. Lonnie never even had to get into the car!

These driving responsibilities turned out to be most fortuitous. On one haul to pick up gravel, he started conversing with the quarry owner, who said that he looked familiar. When Lonnie told him his name, the man let out an audible gasp. "We thought you were dead!" Standing in front of him was his stepmother's brother, whom Lonnie had started to search for four years earlier. By a stroke of luck, he'd happened to be in the right place at the right time. This meeting led Lonnie to phone calls with both parents and his siblings, and they made plans to meet. However, he continued to live on his own until he got a high school diploma, got a fixed wing license, married (at age 17) and was drafted into the army right after he turned 18. He spent four years in Vietnam flying helicopters and came home to his bride at the age of 22.

Three children later, his first marriage ended in divorce. In the meantime he continued making a name for himself in the construction business. He met his second wife, Fran, and was immediately taken with her. He gladly agreed to a Jewish wedding and started his own journey to become Jewish. He approached the rabbi who had married them, asking for help with the conversion process. This young rabbi, with other plans on his mind, exchanged a few lessons for construction work on his house. When the rabbi sold the house, he left the area without a backward glance at his most enthusiastic student.

Lonnie then approached another rabbi in Baltimore, where they were living. The rabbi was sympathetic, but denied him conversion lessons. He felt that Lonnie was only doing it for his

Jewish wife and not for himself. The denial came again after two more appeals for lessons on Judaism and conversion. Disheartened but not defeated, he finally found a champion in Rabbi David Geffen. Fran and Lonnie had moved back to Fran's hometown of Scranton, Pennsylvania, so that they could raise their son near her family. Rabbi Geffen immediately detected the sincerity in this man. After all, Lonnie had been trying to convert now for almost fourteen years. Geffen was also undaunted by Lonnie's thick West Virginia accent, for after all, Geffen was originally from Atlanta and a southern accent felt like home to him.

Between the cantor and the rabbi, Lonnie not only learned the *aleph bet*, but he studied intently about Jewish laws and customs. When it came time for his conversion, he first had to face the rigorous questioning of a board of rabbis, a ritual circumcision, and a trip to the *mikveh*. After the conversion, he was called to the Torah for an *aliyah*, to make the *brachot* on the wine and bread, to open and close the ark, and especially to take the Torah in and out of the *Aron Kodesh* (the Torah is very heavy, especially when it is weighted to one side).

Feeling pretty comfortable with the ritual of *Shabbos* and holidays, Lonnie decided that it was time to have a Bar Mitzvah. He and the cantor picked out a *parasha*, *Vayachi*, and he started working on the *trup* and the *brachot*. On January 6, 1997, Ariyeh Leib ben Avraham Avinu—the Lion, son of Abraham, our father—was called to the Torah as a Bar Mitzvah at the age of 50. This Hebrew name had been Rabbi Geffen's father's name. When the rabbi realized that Lonnie's birthday was in August, making the new convert a Leo, he knew that the name was a perfect fit. In an emotional speech Lonnie talked about the sixteen years that it had taken him to arrive at this day, about the kindness and compassion of the rabbi and Cantor Wolkenstein, and, most important, how he could now share with his son what it was like to become a Bar Mitzvah. "Nothing is hard if you set your mind to it. Just keep on doin' it," he told the congregation filled with his wife's family and their good friends.

44

DOSVEDANYA

Peter Block—November 12, 1994

Though very Americanized in his appearance and actions—Peter Block plays the bass guitar in a "hard-core" rock band—he still describes himself as a Russian Jew. For his high school graduation present, his father took him back to Moscow for a visit. Peter couldn't believe how different it looked from the images he remembered. This was his first time back and it felt odd; so much had changed. Maybe some of the changes were in him and in the way he viewed his former homeland. It had been more than a decade since he left, and he returned as a full-grown man. One of the most startling realizations he had on his trip was that this country, which for almost a century had banned religions and persecuted Jews with blatant anti-Semitism, was no longer threatening. Russia was left with new ideologies and a crumbling economy. And Peter, a distant descendent of Abraham, has picked up the traditions that were lost, but not forgotten, and continues the covenant.

When the former Soviet Union finally let the Block family leave in 1989, the government didn't make it easy. There were no direct flights from Moscow to New York. Only permitted to take two suitcases each, the family members left for Austria, where they remained for two weeks. From there it was on to Italy. Once they arrived, they were not sure how long they would remain. Living like nomads with a group of people, all under the same circumstances, they went nightly to meetings with HIAS (Hebrew Immigration Aid Society) representatives to find out who had been lucky enough to find a sponsor and who would be able to leave. Their sojourn in Italy lasted four months. The Jewish Family Service of Northeastern Pennsylvania agreed to sponsor them and bring them to the United States.

Luba and Gregory Block arrived in Scranton, Pennsylvania, in April 1990, five months after leaving their home in Moscow. Their sons, Peter, age 8, and Boris, age 5, enrolled in the Scranton Hebrew Day School. At first, their greatest difficulty was the language barrier. Boris was silent for the first three months. Peter credits the "Teenage Mutant Ninja Turtles" for being instructive not only in colloquial language, but in American culture. After the first few months in school, the boys went to the JCC camp, and in that free, uninhibited social atmosphere their English skills improved.

The former U.S.S.R. was a communist country where the practice of religion was illegal. Luba and Gregory knew they were Jewish, but for them it really meant more of what they were *not* permitted to do. Luba was denied entrance into medical school. They were not allowed to attend certain schools and were banned from several jobs. Overtly, reasons were always given for the denials, but everyone understood it to be their "Judaism" that had caused the prohibitions. When the Blocks arrived in Scranton, their first task was to find employment. Previously a nurse in a Moscow ambulatory clinic, Luba accepted a position as a nurse's aide in the Jewish Home. Gregory, an engineer with a background in computers and clock repair, was able to find a job in "Ye Olde Clock Shoppe."

Boris and Peter faced their own challenges. They wore yarmulkes and *tzitzit* to school every day and studied a dual curriculum. They had secular subjects for half a day and Hebrew subjects for the other half. They were immersed in an Orthodox environment, where they had to learn the "do's and don'ts" of observant Jews. They were forced to conform, at least on the outside. However, when Peter, at age 9, studied *parasha Lekh Lekha* and learned about Abraham, our Patriarch, circumcising himself at the age of 99 in order to fulfill God's covenant, the boy was moved. He went home and told his mother that he would like to be circumcised. Luba, herself learning about Judaism in the Jewish home, contacted the rabbi. She had very little hesitation, because after all, she asked herself, "Isn't this why we came here?"

Arrangements were made for a *bris*, a ritual circumcision, for both boys. A local urologist, Dr. Jeffrey Weiss, made arrangements with a surgical center to allow Rabbi Avraham Herman to co-officiate, a highly irregular request. There are state rules about who is permitted to do what in the operating room, but somehow Rabbi Herman was granted "temporary privileges." Because anticipation of the surgery increased the anxiety, Peter let Boris go first. Different from the *bris* of an infant, these boys were anesthetized, and both procedures were successful. Like any Jewish celebration, it would not have been complete without cake, schnapps, and a little singing. In the nurses' lounge, a small group of rabbis and learned men gathered together with Rabbi Herman, dressed in surgical scrubs, Dr. Weiss, and Luba to made a *Kiddush* and signify the continuing of the covenant. There was a larger community celebration held the next night at the Scranton Hebrew Day School, and Peter was well enough to attend.

The last Bar Mitzvah held in the Block family was Gregory's uncle, held before the Russian revolution. After 1917, communism took over the status of "higher power." So, it was with great pride and awe that Peter prepared for his Bar Mitzvah only several years after his *bris*. Already knowing how to daven and read Hebrew from his attendance at the day school, he started studying with Cantor Wolkenstein at Temple Israel. It really is a small world because when Luba arrived in Scranton, she learned that she was distantly related to the spiritual leader of that temple, Rabbi David Geffen. Peter's Bar Mitzvah was very much a community affair. All of the people there had some role in his reaching this goal—from Peter's teachers and classmates, to members of the Jewish Family Service and Jewish Federation who were instrumental in their resettlement, to friends who just made their adjustment that much nicer. Peter was fortunate to have both sets of grandparents in attendance. They all had taken quite a journey to get there. Peter was excited and nervous at the same time, while his mother experienced a broader range of emotions. In Moscow, they had never even thought about attending a synagogue, yet here was her child standing in front of the whole congregation, so poised and so comfortable. She looked over and saw her mother crying. Luba had never even known what a Bar Mitzvah was, and here was her son, connecting the whole family back to its roots.

When the service was over, Peter felt different, perhaps more mature. He had already had life experiences that surpassed anything his peers might sustain in a lifetime; for him, this rite of passage was more spiritual and emotional than physical. His mother and father also experienced a variety of changes. Luba completed a two-year X-ray technology program and Gregory completed a program in computer programming. They moved to the Philadelphia suburbs for better job opportunities. Peter continued his Jewish involvement in USY while in high school and became the president of his chapter.

45

DOWN UNDER TIMES FOUR

Victor Fonda—November, 1926
David Fonda, M.D.—July, 1963
Michael Fonda—July, 1993
Victor Fonda—November, 1996

Michael, 22, is a medical student at Melbourne University. David, 52, is the Director of Aged Care Services in a large health network. He is internationally recognized for his work. Victor, at age 89, remains active maintaining an interest in community affairs, and a very keen interest in his family.

Though Israel is called the "land of milk and honey," Palestine of the late nineteenth century was more like the land of "swamps and deserts." Jews went there to be buried, not to build. Searching for a livelihood, Victor Fonda's grandfather emigrated from Palestine to Melbourne, Australia, at the turn of the new century. He brought with him most of his family, except for a young daughter who was of marriageable age. He knew her prospects of finding a suitable husband were more likely in Palestine than in the rough young city of Melbourne, so she remained behind. Years later, as a married woman, she came to visit, bringing in tow her 2-year-old twin daughters. Her husband, 12-year-old Victor, and Victor's older sister joined them two years later. They never went back to Palestine.

So, there was Victor Fonda, two and a half months before his Bar Mitzvah in a new country. Coming from the Holy Land, he spoke impeccable *Evrit* (Hebrew), so his lessons, three in all, consisted mostly of learning the tune to recite his Haftorah of *parasha Vayeitzei*. The Bar Mitzvah was very low key, as was the tradition of the day. Victor was called up to the *bimah* in the "Stone *Shul*," so named for Mr. Stone, an English Jew, who was the *shul's* founder. This was the ghetto *shul* of the new immigrants and was reminiscent of an Eastern European *shteble*. Victor chanted his Haftorah with his father and a few uncles in attendance. His grandfather was in Palestine at the time, and the rest of the congregation consisted of strangers. A small *Kiddush* was held in the *shul*, and a reception for the family took place in the kitchen of their tiny cottage.

There was a huge influx of Jews into Melbourne immediately prior to and right after World War II. In the early part of the twentieth century the city contained approximately 8,000–10,000 Jews. Its population then multiplied to 50,000 Jews. David Fonda was prepared to come of age in 1963 in a thriving traditional Jewish community, much different from the one his father had first encountered. Many of his peer group were first-generation Australians, with their parents arriving in the country only after the Holocaust. David attended the Jewish day school Mount Scopus Memorial College—the largest Jewish day school in the southern hemisphere. Here a Bar Mitzvah teacher was provided as part of the school's curriculum.

In the summertime is a mourning period of several weeks, culminating with *Tisha B'av*, a full day's fast. It is a time of grieving over the destruction of the Second Temple. Weddings, Bar Mitzvahs, and other celebrations are prohibited. The *Shab-*

bos immediately following *Tisha B'av* is called *Shabbos Nachamu*, the *Shabbos* of Comfort, when *simchas* may resume. The *parasha* for that week is *Va'eschanan* from the book of Deuteronomy. It is a long and significant portion, containing both the Ten Commandments and the *Shema*, the central prayer of the Jewish religion proclaiming our monotheistic faith. Traditionally, the Bar Mitzvah boy recites only the Haftorah as part of his ceremony. It was suggested to David that because of the significance of his *parasha*, he might like to learn the entire portion for his Bar Mitzvah. Aiming to please and loving a challenge, David decided to take it on. It took him a full year to study the entire *parasha*, and in his determination to succeed, he had extra lessons with the rabbi of the *shul*.

By the time of his son's Bar Mitzvah, Victor Fonda had retired from law practice and had gone into commerce with his wife's family. Their business encompassed the full gamut of the women's dress trade, from manufacturing to marketing. A very proud Victor watched his son chant the entire *parasha* in the Kew Shul in Melbourne, surrounded by his large family. Three out of four of David's grandparents were in attendance. There was a family-sponsored *Kiddush* and that evening a huge party, shades of "Goodbye Columbus," with 300 people in attendance for all of the fuss and pomp.

As it happened, David's son Michael's Bar Mitzvah fell on the same *Shabbos*, thirty years later. The family, though not religious, cherishes the tradition, and Michael decided to read some of the *parasha* because his father had done it so many years before. In addition to all of the pride and joy a father and grandfather have in watching the tradition continue, David had the extra pleasure and sense of déjà vu at knowing this relevant *parasha*. They celebrated the following day with a casual get-together in their garden, where friends dropped by to mingle and offer good wishes. This celebration was followed several months later by another one, when the family made one of its frequent trips to Israel to visit relatives still living there. Michael had a second Bar Mitzvah at the *Kotel* on a Monday morning, when he recited an additional portion that he learned. It was Succos, and there was the excitement of many B'nei Mitzvot taking place simultaneously. It was a lovely event, with both Australian and Israeli family members in attendance. The entire party continued its celebration with a special trip organized by a cousin who worked for the Ministry of Tourism. He arranged for a tour of the tunnels under the *Kotel*, where the wall can be seen underground. Holding Michael's second Bar Mitzvah in Israel at the *Kotel* was very special and offered the three men a distinct connection to their history and the past. More than just reading about it, they were standing in the place where all of our history has taken place. And related to more recent history, this was where their own patriarch, Victor, had originally come from.

With the three men, it is the tradition that remains important. The Bar Mitzvah marked their personality, their entrance into Jewish life. It's like being branded in a good way: "I'm a Jew." From grandfather to father to son, the birthright has been passed down. Although none of them are very religious, they have deep respect for the tradition. They still get together weekly to celebrate *Shabbos*. Michael is following another family tradition. He is studying medicine, as did his father—an internationally recognized geriatrician.

Although David and Michael make only rare appearances in the synagogue, Victor goes regularly and finds a sense of peace and connection. He has also chanted his Bar Mitzvah portion every year for the past seventy-five years. Those three Bar Mitzvah lessons were a very small investment whose benefits he has reaped over a lifetime. Because he learned the *trup* so well, he has also recited many other Haftorahs in *shuls* on two different continents. The elder Fondas live in Australia six months out of the year and in Israel the other half. For many years Victor maintained memberships in four *shuls*—two in each country.

No one was surprised when Victor decided to celebrate his second Bar Mitzvah at the age of 83. In days of old, the lifespan was much shorter, so if a man lived to his 70th year, it was as if he were born again. Therefore, some men chose to celebrate the age of 83 (70 + 13) with a second Bar Mitzvah. Seventy years earlier, in a small *shul* in a brand-new country filled with strange faces, Victor Fonda had recited his Haftorah for the very first time. The setting for his second Bar Mitzvah was the

Kew Shul, where he had been a member for over fifty years, and this time he faced three generations of the Fonda family, along with a room full of good friends—rather than strangers. The guests were treated to a *Kiddush* that he sponsored himself, rather than to his mother's cooking in the kitchen of their tiny cottage. The second Bar Mitzvah has brought the family full circle. As a new immigrant—regardless of time, place, or people in attendance—Victor Fonda became a Bar Mitzvah as tradition dictates. In his newly adopted country, he passed on the tradition of our heritage to his son and grandson and, as if that was not enough, chose to celebrate this rite one more time. It's as if a tiny invisible chord connects one generation to the next, with a knot squarely placed on the time of the Bar Mitzvah. In *parasha L'ekh L'ekha*, God told Abraham to "Go to a new land" and "I will make you a great nation." As Jews have spread out around the globe, this promise has come true, one family at a time.

46

MAN TO MAN

Eli Schewel—September 4, 1997

Age 13—becoming a Bar Mitzvah—is a terrible/wonderful time. It's a time when the man/child pushes away from his family and fights to hold on. He looks for independence, but doesn't want to lose his foothold in the family. The beginnings of peach fuzz grow on baby-soft skin. It's a conflicted, confusing time, with new worlds opening up and reluctance to let go of the old. The Bar Mitzvah is a beautiful, time-honored, life-affirming tradition that eases the transition from the first phase of life into the next. It's a very public affirmation that by virtue of biology or chronology, a young man is starting to become responsible for his own actions. In a confusing time of peer pressure, with the popular culture of television and movies dictating behavior, Eli Schewel chose instead to explore his manhood—all aspects of it—in a safe, positive environment with men supporting men as they cultivate their humanity. He can take his place in the Jewish community, as well as in the community-at-large, knowing that "becoming a man" means his options are limitless and he can be anything he wants to be.

Growing up in a loving, stable home, but without a father, Eli Schewel became involved in a rather unique endeavor as part of his *tzedakah* project for his Bar Mitzvah. He auditioned for and was chosen to be in a dramatic production put on by the theater company entitled TOVA. TOVA, run by artistic director Paula Sepinuk, is a "Theater of Witnesses." Themes of prior productions include women in recovery, teenagers, immigrants from Southeast Asia, and pregnant teens. The focus of this production was going to be male gender socialization, and Eli was anxious to participate. The process starts with interviews, moves into workshops, and then culminates with a production. Members of the cast talk about their own experiences, with the premise that you are an expert in your own story. The director listens, probes, watches, and finally scripts a play. Each script has to be met with the approval of the cast.

The particular production that Eli was involved in was called *Man To Man*. The theme of the play focuses on what it means to become a man. It chronicles the confusion, the mixed messages, and the pressures to "act like a man," "take it like a man," and "do the right thing." The cast, all male, ranged in age from 12 to 65 and was made up of diverse ethnic groups and backgrounds. In one scene, Eli and another young man discuss how difficult it is to live up to expectations and act politically correct even in middle school. Other scenerios include domestic violence, sports, the military, and complex father–son relationships. The experience of the play gave all of the cast members a chance to explore their feelings, air them, and then perform them in a well-choreographed, thought-provoking production. In the process of the production, the cast members bonded. It was a consciousness-raising experience for both the performers and the audience. What better way to prepare for a Bar Mitzvah than to investigate the issues, complexities, and intricacies of becoming a man!

Eli's Bar Mitzvah took place in Mishkan Shalom, a Reconstructionist temple in the Mt. Airy section of Philadelphia. He wasn't really nervous because he had just completed several performances of the play in front of large audiences, and he knew that the congregation was filled with people who cared for him. In his *parasha, Shoftim*, it says, "Thou shall not specially recognize anyone's face, thou shall not take bribes, for bribes blind the eyes of the wise." Eli commented during his speech that "Stereotyping also blinds us. These verses tell us to see everyone with equal potential to do anything."

Raised in a home and coming from a family where *tikkun olam*, repairing of the world, is a practice, not just a concept, and there is an ongoing challenge to injustice, Eli has made his own effort to discredit stereotyping. In his lower school, mini-

courses were offered to give students a chance to learn subjects that were not part of the regular curriculum. Over the
years, many minicourses have been offered for girls only. One
example is a baseball course offered for girls only, so that they
could learn and play in an all-female environment. But boys
were never offered courses in nontraditional areas. For years
Eli was the only boy enrolled in dollmaking. So he took it upon
himself to offer "Dollmaking for Boys" as a minicourse. With
slots for only eight boys, everyone was rather surprised when
eleven boys took the course.

Mt. Airy is a well-integrated, old, established community in
northwestern Philadelphia. The neighborhood has thrived on
diversity. It's a comfortable community for Eli's mother, Susan,
who is a lesbian, and her partner, Lizzy. Eli attended Miquon,
a small private school. There, the other kids asked questions
about Eli's parents—his two mothers—but they never teased.
His biological mother, Susan, would go every year to talk to the
teachers. And she armed Eli for any conflict he might encounter concerning his untraditional parentage. He went to school
knowing that if people felt some prejudice against him, it
wasn't his problem. He has a close loving relationship with
both of his mothers (as well as with Susan's former partner,
Annie). They taught him at an early age to externalize intoler-
ance, rather than internalize it.

Continuing with his speech, after he chanted his Haftorah,
Eli told the congregation:

> Most men aren't taught to express their feelings. TOVA was
> a chance for the actors to open up, with other men around
> them for support. Many men in the play thought that
> fighting and violence seemed inherent in them. I disagree.
>
> It's not in our hormones to be violent any more than it is
> in women's hormones to be ditsy. Parents worry that their
> boy will grow up to be effeminate and weak if he asks for a
> doll. So then they buy him a toy gun and then they worry
> when he shoots somebody.
>
> If I were a father, I would let my child be him- or herself.
> I would do stuff that's fun and let him grow free without

stereotypes. There is no ideal man; it's just however that boy grows . . .

The rules of war in the Torah say that men can stay home and take care of the house as an alternative to fighting. It was supposed to be a good arrangement because the men didn't have to go out and kill or be killed. Back then, men didn't have to go to war, but if they went home, did they get called "sissy boy" and "wuss" because they didn't want to fight?

Nowadays men don't have to work, just as the Jewish men didn't have to go out and fight. Men are *allowed* to stay home and do domestic things, but then they're isolated because there isn't a culture of stay-at-home dads. Men should be able to stay at home and/or take care of the kids, and women should be able to take care of the kids and/or work.

Eli ended his *D'var Torah* by opening up a discussion with the congregation on how gender stereotyping has affected their lives. After a lively community discussion, Eli invited three of the men whom he became close to from the play to the *bimah*. In honor of the occasion, they read Maya Angelou's poem "Son to Mother."

Susan was next to offer the first of the parent's blessings:

My wish is that you continue to have a fulfilling relationship to Judaism within a nurturing Jewish community.

I hope that you continue to grow in self-awareness. If you know yourself, you will develop authentic relationships, so that you will always be surrounded by loving friends and family.

Finally, my blessing is that you accomplish all these things while strengthening your clarity of purpose, your passion, your independence, and your sense of humor—traits which I admire and enjoy so much.

Lizzie then offered her blessing: "Eli, I hope that many others will be able to share your passion and love of life, and that their lives will be as changed as mine has been by the experience."

47

ON A MOUNTAIN TOP

Edward G. Pollan—November 11, 1999

High atop a mountain overlook-
ing Jerusalem, surrounded by a
group of well-wishing strangers,
amidst the singing and clapping
of the congratulatory siman tov
and mazel tov, Edward Pollan
became a Bar Mitzvah—at the
age of 60. This journey took a
lifetime and $30.

The mountaintop is quite a
distance from the Yonkers, New
York, neighborhood where Pol-
lan and his wife of twenty-three
years, Rachel, live with their son
John, age 17. Beginning life in
the Boro Park section of Brook-
lyn and moving on to the Bronx,
he started Hebrew school, but quit well before he reached his Bar
Mitzvah. Maybe it wasn't that important: maybe this was his adoles-
cent demonstration of rebellion; maybe he just didn't want to go.
Nonetheless, his Hebrew education was cut short, leaving some
deep-rooted feelings that would surface only years later.

Age 13 came and went, with perhaps a twinge of disappointment that if maybe his parents had pushed a
little harder, he might have accomplished something.
Most of his friends were not Jewish, and just as their birthdays

233

did, each of Edward's birthdays ended with "teen" and nothing more. In spite of not becoming a Bar Mitzvah, Edward continued to accompany his father to the synagogue on the High Holy Days, even though celebrating the Jewish holidays was not part of their family life.

In the late '60s, Pollan was hired by the post office after he'd spent two years in the military, stationed mostly in France. Starting as a mail handler, he moved on to become a clerk and later a letter carrier. In order to qualify as a mechanic, he was sent to Oklahoma to study, sometimes up to six weeks at a time. This training lasted on and off for almost a year. He achieved MPE status and then topped off the last few years of his thirty years of service as an electronic technician.

Although Rachel is not Jewish, she and Edward decided that they would like their son to become a Bar Mitzvah. They enrolled him in a Hebrew school at a local reform congregation at age 9. At first, Pollan was strict about attendance at the school, but as his son grew older, things became more complicated, and John asserted his independence. In spite of Edward and Rachel becoming actively involved in the parents' committees at the temple, history repeated itself. John quit a year before his 13th birthday. He just didn't want to go anymore.

Not one to impose his feelings on anyone else, Pollan was grappling with feelings of his own. He had a gnawing feeling that he should be getting closer to God and should be going to the synagogue. He always felt a compulsion, a guilty feeling that he was doing the wrong things on the Sabbath.

At the age of 57, he took his first courageous step. Donning a yarmulke and *tallis*, he entered a conservative synagogue in Riverdale one *Shabbos* and innocuously took his seat, alone. Knowing no one and being unfamiliar with the format, he not only sat through this service, but began returning week after week. It was difficult at first; however, the more he went, the easier it became. He was not terribly outgoing, so it took a long time before he felt comfortable. Now, he has established relationships with other congregants and, after services, kibitzes with them at the *Kiddush*.

In order to follow the services, as well as to participate, Edward has taken three sets of Hebrew lessons at the synagogue. His reading is halting and slow, but filled with intense feeling. Because he recently retired from the post office, he will enroll in Lehman College this year to increase his Hebrew vocabulary.

This weekly attendance at the synagogue has changed his life; however, he always harbored a strong emotional tie to Israel. For years, he has purchased Israel bonds to demonstrate his feelings of support for the country. Four years ago, he traveled with John to Israel for the first time.

In November of 1999, Pollan had a chance to join a tour to Israel. Both his wife and son had conflicts, so he decided to once again venture out alone. A few days into the itinerary, the tour director asked if anyone wanted to become a Bar or Bat Mitzvah, because they were planning a group ceremony for anyone who was interested. Edward hesitated with his response. At first, other tour members told him that this ceremony was not a "real" Bar Mitzvah. However, when he was assured that the ritual was indeed legitimate, he responded affirmatively and was given the blessing to study.

One hundred people assembled on top of the hill, and in groups of four they came forward and recited the *brachah* for before and after the Torah reading and the 48th Psalm. There was cheering, singing, and smiling as each group became B'nai Mitzvah. To complete the festivities, each participant was awarded a Bar or Bat Mitzvah certificate.

Upon his arrival back in the states, Pollan shared this story with only family members. This is a private matter, bringing one man closer to his religion and filling him with a wonderful feeling of accomplishment and an obligation completed that had been neglected so long ago.

48

A BAR MITZVAH AMONG STRANGERS

Edward Baker—September, 1942

For most boys, their Bar Mitzvah represents a new beginning— stepping into adulthood, with one toe casually testing the water. For Ed Baker, his Bar Mitzvah marked a clear ending—the turning of a page, the final chapter, and the closing of the book. There was a severing of already fragile ties that left him spinning off into orbit, alone.

Self-portrait by Edward Baker

Growing up, women paradoxically represented the strongest and weakest characters in his life. His grandmother—a dour, joyless, lackluster woman— ruled the roost, a railroad flat on 110th Street in Harlem. His mother—sweet and fun loving—didn't have the spine to stand up to her overbearing mother. She married an Italian fellow and brought him home with trepidation to meet her mother. Without taking the time to get to know him, the grandmother heard the foreign-sounding last name and chased him away.

But not before this brief union produced a little boy, Edward. With limited resources, because her second husband earned a paltry living from his horse and buggy junk business, Frieda, the matriarch, decided that her young grandson should be placed in the Hebrew Orphan Asylum. Not wanting the boy, but refusing to give him up completely, she had him placed in a succession of foster homes. Just when he became comfortable in one place, the rug was yanked out from under him, and he was moved to a new foster placement—twelve in all. His mother took on more of a big sister role. She visited him occasionally on Sundays. They went to the movies or on walks together, but the visits were infrequent and sporadic. Edward could never understand why he was living in foster care, when his grandmother had found a place in her home for his first cousin.

Edward moved from place to place and found himself in a Jewish neighborhood in the Grand Concourse section of the Bronx. This foster family, which had its own son, treated him like a member of the family. He played handball with his foster father and for the first time actually felt like part of the family. Always tongue-tied around girls, he had actually found the confidence to talk to some of the young ladies in the neighborhood and at school. He was around 12 years old when his grandmother made a rare appearance at his foster home. She told him that he was almost 13, and it was time to prepare to become a Bar Mitzvah. With this edict, she departed, leaving the details of Hebrew school and a teacher up to the foster family. The family made all of the arrangements, and Edward started walking to Hebrew school a few days each week after his public school classes were over. On the appointed day, the foster family directed him to the *shul* on Girard Avenue. He walked into a room full of strangers. Oh, yes, his grandmother was there, and he has vague memories of his mother, but the rest of the sanctuary was filled by a sea of faces he later learned were all part of his extended family. He had a family? Not for long. The ceremony was a blur, and afterward everyone disappeared.

His mother continued her visits, but his grandmother never came to see him again. It was as if she had done her duty, saw him become a Bar Mitzvah, and now her obligation was over. Perhaps the hurt of this short-lived joy at discovering a family, only to lose it on the very same morning, led him to talk back to his foster mother. He said something he can't remember to her, and she said, "You don't mean to compare yourself to my son!" He shot back in an uncharacteristic rage, "Yeah, well, if my mother were here, she'd say the same thing about me!" With that, his foster mother slapped him across the face.

Angry, humiliated, but most of all hurt, he called his social worker and was soon moved to yet another placement. He never had another home, never another family, and never the willingness to let himself connect to other people. He graduated from high school and went from one job to another. He got tired of running and found a job that didn't require much responsibility and wasn't too personal in the maintenance department at the *New York Times*. At the age of 45, a bell went off in his head, and he thought, There has to be more than this: work, home, home, work. The feeling "Is that all there is?" rang in his head. When he was a high school student, one of his teachers had seen some artistic potential in him and recommended him for the Industrial Arts Vocational School. Two other boys from his high school were supposed to go, and they arranged to meet each other there the following Monday morning. When the other boys didn't show, Edward was unprepared for this new venture alone, so he turned around and went right back to his old school. Remembering that untapped ability, Edward signed himself up for the New York Art Student's League. In his fourth decade of life, he had finally found some fulfillment. He would leave his manual laborer job and rush over to the Art League, where he could immerse himself in the smells, colors, and textures of another world.

In 1988, the *New York Times* hosted an Arts and Crafts Show. Edward paid the $5 entrance fee. He painted an 8″ x 6″ self-portrait by looking in the mirror and trying to capture on canvas what he saw. Upon seeing the final product, he exclaimed to himself, "My God, I can't put this in the show! I'm not entering." He wasn't sure whether it was his artwork or the subject that wasn't worth much. The woman in charge of accepting entries somehow convinced him that his painting

was indeed worth submitting. It took just a little encouragement to enable Edward to release his portrait for the show. He
found out that the man in charge of arranging the entries chose
to hang his picture in a prime position in front of a spotlight.

Once he'd dropped off the picture, he didn't want to go back.
He continued his business and found himself on the ninth floor
of the *New York Times* building. One of the employees spotted
him and yelled, "You won! Your picture is the best of the show!"
There must have been hundreds of pictures, but the little
self-portrait captured the top prize. That was really something.
He'd worked really hard and became so frustrated at times that
he almost stepped on it. As a mature man, now he looks back
and thinks that if he had had a normal life, he could have been
a better judge of what was good and what was not. He realized
that he always followed the same pattern, dating back to his
days in the foster homes. Any time a relationship got too close,
he moved to a new foster home. As he got older, any time
anyone got too close, he just moved on. He never married. He
never stayed long enough in one place. He slipped out of
childhood into no-man's land. Ed is now retired and spends a
good bit of his days and nights at the Arts League—the one
place where he is no longer nobody's child. It became the one
constant in the last thirty years of his life and the one place
that enabled him to find a little recognition. He won first prize
for a tiny self-portrait that let the artist see for the first time
that his subject was really worth a great deal.

49

A FATHER'S REFLECTIONS

Jonathan Kessel—October 9, 1999
(by Martin Kessel)

Jonathan is a junior at Model Secondary School for the Deaf (MSSO) in Washington, DC. He is the class president and a member of the varsity football and wrestling teams.

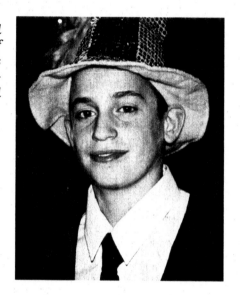

Dear Family and Friends,

Now that Jonathan's Bar Mitzvah has passed, we have some time to reflect and enjoy the afterglow. We were lucky that in spite of the great distances, many of our far-flung families and friends were able to attend. But for those close to us who were unable to attend, we hope our reminiscences will bring a touch of Jonathan's celebration into your homes.

Saturday morning we gathered at the Tifereth Israel Congregation (TI) in northwest Washington for the *Shabbat* service and the Bar Mitzvah. TI is a Conservative congregation, leaning toward orthodoxy. What makes TI unique is its commitment to full participation by women in all aspects of the religious service. Typically, close to 100 members attend the regular *Shabbat* morning service. Since this service would be either signed by Jonathan or interpreted, we extended an invitation to the Washington area Jewish deaf community to join us for the service and the *Kiddush* (lunch) afterward. All together with our guests, attendance swelled to well over 300 people.

The *Shacharit* (morning service) was led by Rhonda Weiss, a member of the congregation who is blind. Rhonda has a beautiful and forceful voice and reads from a special Braille prayerbook, and her chanting was especially moving in the context of this special *Shabbat.*

With that background, we would like to describe how Jonathan's signing enhanced the service. Like all Bar Mitzvah boys, Jonathan began his part in the service after *Shacharit* by carrying the Torah from the Ark and leading a procession around the synagogue back to the *bimah* (pulpit). Instead of chanting his Torah portion, Jonathan signed a summary of each Torah reading, while a woman from our congregation chanted. Jonathan stood erect, and everyone could see by the rhythm and tempo of his signing that he understood the passage.

Next, Jonathan signed the blessing before and after the *Maftir* (the last part of the Torah reading for that morning). The rolling close of the Torah scroll signaled the start of Jonathan's Haftorah (special reading from the Prophets). No interpreting was done. The congregation watched in silence as Jonathan stood before them, signing the blessing before and after the Haftorah, as well as his Haftorah, in American Sign Language (ASL). Once again with exceptional composure, poise, and an excellent command of ASL, Jonathan retold the story of Jonathan and David, their friendship, and how Jonathan protected David from his father, King Saul. Most of the congregation, whether they knew ASL or not, preferred to watch Jonathan's signing rather than follow along in the original text.

Immediately following the Haftorah, Jonathan gave a *D'Var Torah* (speech). This time Jonathan's signing was interpreted. With the simplicity and forthrighteousness of a boy becoming a man, Jonathan thanked those people closest to him and kept the congregation spellbound while he described what being Jewish and deaf has meant to him. There was not a dry eye in the sanctuary. Somehow Jonathan made everyone feel proud of deaf Jews because one of their own was so accomplished: TI because its members had given Jonathan an opportunity; and his friends and family (especially us) because Jonathan had the self-esteem, confidence, and character to contribute to this world. He left even the rabbi in awe.

Rabbi Seidel addressed Jonathan and presented him with books and certificates from the temple. Then, as is custom, the children of TI threw candy at Jonathan to remind him and us that this ritual is a celebration of life. Just before the service concluded, Marla Berkowitz and Daniela Ioannides (deaf Jewish teachers of Jonathan's) led the congregation in *Aleinu* (final prayer), signed in ASL. Again, instead of having the final prayer interpreted, Marla and Daniela encouraged the congregation to follow along in sign language. For those assembled, no clearer evidence was needed that ASL is a legitimate language to express fully the meaning of prayer. The service concluded with a blessing over the wine and bread, followed by a scrumptious *Kiddush* downstairs in the newly renovated auditorium, hosted by our family in honor of Jonathan's Bar Mitzvah.

Apparently, the food, along with the camaraderie, had people lingering just a bit too long at the temple. Several of our guests even missed the bus we had rented to take them to Gallaudet University's Kellogg Conference Center for the Bar Mitzvah reception and party. Eventually, and in spite of a crazy parking situation (it turns out Gallaudet's Homecoming was also on October 9th), the party began. We decided that first and foremost, this was Jonathan's party, so had hired an emcee who specialized in kids' dance, music, and games. Everything was adapted to accommodate deaf children. The emcee brought an extra-loud sound system, strobe and neon lightening, a mirror ball, and a smoker. The emcee worked side by side with our interpreter (Michael Hartman), a motivator, and the DJ. The emcee modified the games as well. For the scavenger hunt, the emcee gave the kids a slip of paper specifying the item they needed to get. The kids simply showed an adult the paper to see if they had it.

Jonathan received many wonderful gifts, and he was over-whelmed by people's generosity. The gifts of money have already been invested and, hopefully, will provide Jonathan with a nice base for college. The gifts of bonds have been securely tucked away for Jonathan to use in the future. Among the gifts were two works of art by notable deaf artists, one a Holocaust survivor.

And so, after a year of hard work and studying by Jonathan, along with careful planning and excellent teamwork by many dedicated people—especially Jonathan's tutor, Rabbi David Kastor, who is himself deaf—we remain with the memories of a really wonderful weekend with family and friends and with the temple service as proof of Jonathan's extraordinary abilities. The world knows now what we have always believed—that Jonathan can accomplish anything he wants.

Postscript: Not all Bar Mitzvah boys have an opportunity to experience two rites of passage in one year, but Jonathan has always been special. Jonathan was asked by Senator James M. Jefford's office if he would provide testimony in front of the Senate Health, Education, Labor, and Pensions Committee on the tenth anniversary of the Americans with Disabilities Act (ADA). Jonathan was the youngest representative to provide testimony. Prior to his testimony, Jonathan was introduced to two presidents—Bill Clinton, and I. King Jordan, the president of Gallaudet University. Once again with poise and confidence, Jonathan stood in front of our esteemed leaders and shared his thoughts on how the ADA has benefited him.

Mr. Chairman and Members of the Committee,

My name is Jonathan Kessel and I am 13 years old. This fall I will be starting high school. I would like to tell you a little bit about myself. I was born right here in Washington, D.C. I love science, social studies, arts, animals, and sports.

When I was 4, my parents signed me up for ski lessons at Loon Mountain in New Hampshire. When I was in the first and second grades, my mom and I would bicycle down to the Corcoran Museum for my art lessons. I celebrated one birthday with friends touring the FBI and another at the Air and Space Museum watching a movie on the Rain Forest. Last year, I went to NIH (National Institute of Health) with my Dad on "Take Your Child to Work Day" and dissected a calf's brain. For the past two years I have attended NASA Space Camp in Alabama. In a sense, I've done the normal things children do. What is notable is that I have had access to all these activities even though I am Deaf. I communicate by American Sign Language. So whether it was a ski lesson or a tour of the FBI, because of the ADA, I had the right to request an interpreter.

. . . I believe if I study hard enough, I may become a veterinarian, a teacher, or a coach. I am lucky to have choices. In the fall, I will attend the Model Secondary School for the Deaf. It's important to me at this point in my life to be in a school where I have no language barriers. I believe when it's time for me to make a decision, deaf professionals will be so common in the workplace that it will be "normal" for me to go to professional school.

I would like to thank the committee chairman and members of the committee for giving me this opportunity to speak.

50

MY INSPIRATION

Matthew Weiss—March 29, 1997

Matthew is now a junior at Wyoming Seminary, a private prep school about twenty miles from our home. He's been in several of the school's plays, runs on the cross country team and hopes to play lacrosse in the spring.

Photo by Jim Nicolais

My *parasha*, *Parah*, contains the mitzvos related to the red cow. Out of the 613 commandments, those dealing with the red heifer are some of the most difficult to understand. It is appropriate that my Bar Mitzvah would coincide with this *parasha*, since it is almost seven years to the day that an event happened in my life that we, too, find difficult to explain.

On March 27, 1990, eleven days after my 6th birthday, I was diagnosed with Acute Lymphocytic Leukemia. I was treated initially at Children's Hospital in Philadelphia, the

245

very same hospital where my father did his pediatric urology residency. . . . (excerpt from Matt's Bar Mitzvah sermon)

Leukemia . . . I didn't even know how to spell it, and now I had to learn how to live with it! Matthew, our oldest son, always seemed somehow fragile to both of us, although we never articulated that to each other until the date of diagnosis. Perhaps it was because he stopped breathing right before his *Bris Milah* (he choked on the wine administered by the *mohel*), or maybe because he was always pretty sedate.

He went to preschool with his buddy "putooh," a battered blue silk pillow that he kept in his cubby. Throughout the morning he would dart over to the cubby, covertly pop his thumb in his mouth, and rub his fingers over the fabric. When he came home from a hard morning of Play Doh and dress up, he was content to sit on the couch and watch *He-Man* and *Ninja Turtles* all afternoon. Of course, the "putooh" and the thumb were never far away.

Even though he was normally a "couch potato," he seemed more tired than usual. His beautiful olive complexion was starting to look more green than bronze. Shortly before his 6th birthday, I took him to the doctor with these nonspecific complaints. I was assured that he probably had some sort of virus and was sent home.

Two weeks later, he couldn't stand up in the morning. He also complained of stomach cramps. The pediatrician saw him that morning. At my husband's suggestion, I gently encouraged the doctor to run a CBC (complete blood count).

When the results of the blood test came back less than one hour later, rather than calling me, our pediatrician called Jeff, thinking that he could handle the news better than I could. When Jeff called the house, he said, "Our boy is in trouble. He has leukemia. Pack a bag for both of you. We are leaving for Philadelphia this afternoon."

I made four phone calls. My sister, she was in charge of telling the rest of the family; my baby sitter, I had a 3-year-old daughter and a 3-month-old baby at home; another car pool mom, to take over my driving; and another interpreter to take the jobs that I had scheduled for the next few days. I focused only on what I needed to do at that moment and then packed our bags. I had no idea how long we had to stay or what would happen once we arrived.

Since he was only 6, one of us was allowed to sleep in the room with him. A narrow window seat became my bed for the next two weeks. My husband set up camp in the hotel across the street. Matt's first roommate was also a little boy with leukemia. When we entered the room, he and his parents all sat on one chair and watched TV. They barely spoke to us. And I thought that I was in shock!!

A spinal tap was needed to confirm the diagnosis. I didn't understand the full extent of this procedure, but I knew "needle" and I knew "back," and my husband not only accompanied, but held Matt during this procedure. The diagnosis was confirmed and treatment was started.

We were handed a three-ring binder, the "road map," which was to be Matt's medication schedule for the next three years. My little boy learned firsthand what an IV (intravenous), IM (intramuscular), finger-stick (blood test when blood is drawn from the finger), and heparin flush all mean. And I got a crash course in pharmacology/oncology, learning about medications—methotrexate, vincristine, prednisone, adriamycin—that I could barely pronounce at first.

Of course, being eternal optimists, we found our first "silver lining" in the person of Dr. Jeffrey Silber, Matt's oncologist. He had a fine balance of relating to my husband and me, while attending to his 6-year-old patient. He promised Matthew from the first day that there would be "no surprises," and he always dealt with my son honestly and openly.

After the first few days in the hospital, we decided that I would stay in the hospital with Matthew, and Jeff would return back to Scranton. We had two children at home, and he had his own patients who depended on him.

On day seven, the spinal tap was repeated to check for the reappearance of any leukemia cells. I am not a squeamish woman. I held, carried, coached, and comforted Matt through all of his treatment, but I dreaded this procedure. Because I was now the sole parent, I had to get him through this. For the procedure, Matt lay on the table on his side and tightened up into a ball, head meeting knees, so that his lower back was exposed and taut. I had to half cuddle, half lay on him to keep him immobile. A small needle with numbing medication is administered. This burns a little bit. Once the area has become numb, a large needle is inserted between the vertebrae into the spinal cord, fluid is drawn out, and it is tested for cancer cells.

My sedate, thumb-sucking couch potato was so brave! He went through sticks, pinches, and prods and did everything that was asked of him without resistance. With "no surprises" and the ability to make choices, Matt became an active participant in his own treatment.

As treatment was underway, the hospital became a waiting game. At the crack of dawn, the phlebotomist arrived, drew blood, and we waited for Matt's counts. Because the chemotherapy often kills not only the cancer but also the healthy cells, we were now waiting for Matthew's counts to rise, meaning that he had at least the beginning of a functioning immune system.

Since this process was very slow, the doctor informed us that we would be spending at least several more days in the hospital. This meant that we would spend the beginning of Passover, both seders, in Children's Hospital. Mrs. Louise Leibman, a patient of my husband's who lives in Philadelphia, prepared all of the holiday food for us. Passover is a hectic and busy time for people who need to get ready for their family. I was overcome with gratitude that this gracious, wonderful woman took the time to help make a holiday for my son and me. Since we did not have a *Haggadah*, the traditional book that tells the story of Passover, Matt and I did the best we could to improvise. If we did not remember the exact blessings, we added or substituted our own. I knew that God would understand that we were both grateful and very thankful.

After two weeks of in-patient treatment, Matt was given clearance to go home. We packed up a carload of stuffed animals, toys, books, medications, and instructions, and we were on our way. Although it was almost midnight when we arrived home, we were most heartened to see a huge sign posted on the door, "Welcome Home Matt."

This two-week introduction began a "journey" (remember the road map) that would last three years. Depending upon the course of treatment, we would schlep into Philadelphia (a two-hour trip) weekly, bi-monthly, or monthly. There was always oral medication to be given at home. Matt lost his hair twice. His perfectly straight thick brown hair grew back in curly and coarse! However, after I finally conceded to the first haircut when his hair grew back in (at about ten months), the curls came off, and his hair grew in straight again.

He was hospitalized three more times during those three years. Chemotherapy is a potent killer, and, unfortunately, it often kills off the body's own immune system, leaving the patient vulnerable to a myriad of infections. We were warned about the dangers of chicken pox; however, since Matt lived in a house with two siblings, it was inevitable that he would get it. Treatment for leukemia patients with chicken pox was IV medication, so he was treated in-patient for that.

As we neared the end of the three-year treatment period, I kept hearing from well-meaning friends and family that they were sure I anxiously awaited the end of treatment. On the contrary, I was scared to death! As long as Matt was receiving some kind of chemotherapy, I knew that we had "little soldiers" in there fighting the bad guys. Were any hidden cells left to grow and spread? Would Matt's body rally on its own and protect him? The scariest part of this disease is that if we don't know where it came from in the beginning, how do we know it won't come back?

I guess this is where faith and support come in. Jeff and I had always had a very good relationship. However, since we went "to hell and back," we were stronger from having shared the ride.

So, Matthew's Bar Mitzvah was approaching. This occasion would have been very special, anyway, since he was our firstborn son and the first male grandchild on my side of the family. Now, however, this Bar Mitzvah was more than a religious rite of passage, it became a celebration of life. Yes, we wanted a big party! We had a lot to celebrate. But I really wanted to stay focused on the spiritual and religious aspects of the ceremony, as opposed to focusing on the caterer, invitations, disc jockey, and clothing.

While Matt worked diligently on his lessons, I had several of my own projects going. I decided to weave Matt's *tallis* myself. Under the tutelage of Ann Cahoon, I wove our family into this *tallis*. Matt picked out the colors, and the navy and turquoise stripes were not just decorative, but represented members of our family. My father, who died when I was 14, was woven in as fine silver threads through the back of the *tallis*. Matthew, who carries his grandfather's Hebrew name, mentioned that the spirit of his grandfather has always been "behind" him.

As the saying goes, "When life gives you lemons . . . make lemonade." One by-product of being home-bound and watching lots of TV and videos was that Matt developed a love for acting and the stage. He has since joined several children's theater companies and has acted in school and community plays. This gave him a great advantage during his Bar Mitzvah, for he chanted his Haftorah and davened *Mussaf* loudly and clearly. During his speech, the audience sat in rapt attention as Matthew delivered his words with a confidence belying his years.

During that speech, he thanked Dr. Silber for treating him with dignity and kindness and with "no surprises." He thanked Rabbi Dovid Rosenberg for all of his support and encouragement, not only in the classroom, but outside as well. He also thanked Mrs. Rosenberg for feeding him during all of the time they learned together. He thanked his sister Allie for being his biggest fan, his younger brother Ben for keeping the "monsters" away at night, his Dad for being the kind of man that he aspires to be, and his Mom for teaching him that if you have a sense of humor, you can get through anything.

Since I am a sign language interpreter and work part time at the Scranton State School for the Deaf, several of my deaf friends and co-workers attended. Because it was an Orthodox *shul*, I needed to find a male interpreter capable of following along and interpreting from Hebrew into ASL. I found Michael Hartman, a NASA employee from Washington, D.C., who interpreted the entire service. He did a beautiful job! This was the first time that most of the community had ever seen an interpreted service.

Seated in the synagogue, surrounded by friends and family, I felt overwhelmed as I watched my beautiful, healthy son lead the services. It was hard to believe that the tall, handsome young man with the loud confident voice couldn't stand by himself a few short years ago. My son became a man, and I became further enchanted with God's blessings and the miracles of life.

GLOSSARY

Aliyah—Literally means "going up" and is used when one goes up to the *bimah* in the synagogue to honor the Torah.

Aliyot—Plural of *Aliyah.*

Am Yisrael Chai—"The Jewish people live."

Bracha, brachot—Blessing.

Bashert—Meant or fated to happen.

Bimah—Platform either in the front or the center of the synagogue from which the Torah is read.

Bris Milah, Bris Milot—Ritual circumcision.

Bubbe—Grandmother.

Chazan—The person in the synagogue responsible for singing and chanting much of the service.

Chumash—The text containing the Five Books of Moses.

Chupah—A canopy under which a couple is married.

D'var Torah—Speech about the Torah portion.

Davening—Praying.

Dayenu—Translated as "enough"; usually associated with the song during the Passover seder.

Erev Shabbas—Friday night.

Frum—Religious.

Haftorah—The complementary reading from the Prophets chanted by the Bar or Bat Mitzvah.

Haganah—The underground armed forces of pre-state Israel.

Haggadah—The book used on Passover that recounts the story of the Exodus from Egypt.

Hamentaschen—Three-cornered cookies made during the holiday of Purim.

Hashem—God.

Havdalah—The closing services of the Sabbath in which blessings are made on wine, spices, and a braided candle.

252

Kabbalah—Jewish mysticism.

Kabbalat Shabbat—The prayers said to usher in the Sabbath.

Kaddish—A doxology that is used both to mourn for the dead and to close parts of the service.

Kichel—Crispy pastry, often shaped like a bow tie and covered with sugar.

Kiddush—Refreshments served after a *Shabbat* morning service.

Kipot—Plural of *kipah. See* yarmulke.

Knish—Pastry dough that is filled with some stuffing, most traditionally potatoes.

Kol Nidre—The prayer that is recited on the eve of Yom Kippur.

Kotel—The Western Wall, the last remaining wall of the destroyed Second Temple, located in Jerusalem.

Kvell—To "swell with pride."

Kvetches—Complaining.

Latkes—Potato pancakes.

Layning—Reading from the Torah.

Maftir—Literally, the last few lines of the Torah portion that are repeated and are traditionally read for either the Bar or the Bat Mitzvah.

Mamaloshen—Translated as "mother tongue" and refers to Yiddish.

Matzoh balls—Fluffy (they are supposed to be) round balls or dumplings made of matzoh meal and whipped eggs that are served in chicken soup.

Mazel Tov—Congratulations or good luck.

Mechitzah—Some kind of partition separating the men's and women's sections of an Orthodox synagogue.

Megillah of Esther—The scroll that holds the story of Queen Esther.

Mensch—A kind and gentle person who knows the "right thing to do."

Mikveh—A ritual bath.

Mincha—Afternoon prayers.

Mishpacha—Family.

Mitzvot—The plural of mitzvah, usually translated as a good deed or a commandment.

Nachis—Pride.

Parasha—A portion or chapter in the Torah.

Schnapps—Liquor.

Shacharit—Morning services.

Shalom Aleichem—Literally translated as "peace be with you"; used as a greeting and is the prayer sung upon returning home from *shul* on Friday evening.

Shechina—God's Holy Spirit.

Shema—The central prayer of Judaism, proclaiming our monotheistic beliefs.

Shlepping—To carry or drag.

Shofar—A ram's horn that is blown to usher in the new year.

Shteble—Small ghetto *shul.*

Shul—Synagogue.

Siddur—Prayer book.

Simcha—Joyous occasion.

Tallis—A four-cornered prayer shawl with fringes.

Talmud—The compilation of Jewish law containing the six divisions of the *Mishnah* (oral law) and the *Gemarah.*

Talmudic scholar—A person who is an expert on the content of the Talmud.

Tefillin—phylacteries; Two small boxes that contain a prayer inside written on parchment. One is affixed with leather straps to the head and one on the upper arm. They are worn during weekday morning davening.

Tikkun Olam—Repair the world.

Tisha B'Av—The ninth day of the Hebrew month of Av. It is a day of mourning, for the Holy Temple was destroyed on this day.

Torah—The Five Books of Moses, hand-lettered on parchment.

Trup—Traditional tune for chanting the Torah and the Haftorah.

?dekah—Charity.

sit—The fringes on the four corners of a garment worn by igious men.

—United Synagogue Youth, a national youth organization.

—Committee permission.

y—A prayer that is sung at weddings.

lke or Kipah—Skullcap.

Yasher Koach—Literally translated as "May your strength be firm"; used as an expression of congratulations for fulfilling a religious duty.

Yeshiva—A school with a dual curriculum, where both secular and religious subjects are taught.

Yeshiva Bocher—A boy who attends a yeshiva.

Zeide—Grandfather.

Author's note: The definitions in the previous glossary are my everyday explanations. I make no claim to scholarly interpretations. They are presented here only to clarify the meaning in the story. The reader will notice that the spelling of several words like *Shabbat/Shabbos* and mitzvot/mitzvos varies from story to story. The reason for this seeming inconsistency lies in the orientation of the school or synagogue. Orthodox *shuls* tend to use the Ashkenazi (Eastern European origin) pronunciation that leaves the words pronounced with an "s" (*Shabbos*) sound at the end. In *shuls* that pronounce the Hebrew with the more modern or Sephardic (of Mediterranean origin) endings, you will note the "t" (*Shabbat*) sound. While every effort has been made to keep the Hebrew words and spellings consistent throughout the book, some variations are kept out of respect to the user and to remain faithful to their story.

Arnine Cumsky Weiss is a nationally certified sign language interpreter. As the subject of a documentary entitled "Between Two Worlds" that aired on PBS, she became fascinated with video production. After an internship at a local CBS affiliate, she wrote and produced "Across America," a short documentary about two deaf college students who biked across the country. "Across America" aired on PBS. Weiss also wrote and produced several fundraising, promotional, and informational videos. She is married to Dr. Jeffrey Weiss; they live in Scranton, Pennsylvania with their three children, Matt, Allie, and Ben.